GARDENING
MADE EASY

Betty Barr Mackey

PUBLICATIONS INTERNATIONAL, LTD.

Betty Barr Mackey is a garden writer, lecturer, and publisher. She is coauthor of *The Gardener's Home Companion, Cutting Gardens,* and *Carefree Plants* and has written for major garden magazines. Her publishing company, B. B. Mackey Books, covers specialized horticultural subjects. With her publication for rock gardeners, *Creating and Planting Garden Troughs,* she won the Book of the Year 2000 award from the American Horticultural Society. She is a member of the North American Rock Garden Society and the Garden Writers Association.

Illustrators: Taylor Bruce, Joyce Shelton, Jody Wheeler
Contributing writers: Susan McClure, M.S.,
and Wayne Ambler, M.S.

Louis Weber, CEO
Publications International, Ltd.
7373 North Cicero Avenue
Lincolnwood, Illinois 60712

Permission is never granted for commercial purposes.

Manufactured in China.

8 7 6 5 4 3 2 1

ISBN: 0-7853-8365-4

Library of Congress Control Number: 2003100966

Photo Credits

Crandall & Crandall Photography: 70, 121 (bottom left), 156 (top right), 171 (bottom); McIntire: 176; **Heather Angel Photography:** Contents, 8, 12, 17, 18, 42, 44, 48, 55, 71, 76–77, 80, 81, 84, 85, 86, 102, 103 (top), 124 (top right), 128–129, 135, 142, 143, 144 (bottom), 157 (top left), 158 (bottom right), 162–163, 174, 178 (bottom right), 182, 187 (bottom right); **Betty Barr Mackey:** 20, 35; **Jerry Pavia:** 13, 15, 23, 41, 64, 79, 96, 97, 100–101, 103 (bottom), 104, 106, 109, 113 (top left, top right & bottom right), 114, 115 (top left, top right & bottom left), 116 (top left, top right & bottom left), 117, 118, 119, 120, 121 (top left, top right & bottom right), 122 (top right, bottom left & bottom right), 123, 124 (bottom left & bottom right), 125 (top right, bottom left & bottom right), 138, 139, 141 (top), 144 (top), 145, 147, 148, 149, 150, 151 (top left, top right & bottom left), 152, 153, 154, 155 (top left & bottom), 156 (top left & bottom), 157 (top right, bottom left & bottom right), 158 (top left, top right & bottom left), 159, 160, 161 (top), 164, 165 (top), 168, 169 (top), 172 (top), 173, 178 (top left & top right), 179 (top left), 183 (top left, bottom left & bottom right), 184, 185, 186 (top left & bottom right), 187 (top left, top right & bottom left); **Positive Images:** Liz Ball: 69, 180 (bottom right); Jodi Bertrand: 16 (top), 116 (bottom right), 134; Patricia J. Bruno: 21, 29, 40, 49, 66, 107, 111, 166; Gay Bumgarner: 22, 59 (bottom), 68, 88, 92, 94, 169 (bottom), 177 (bottom right), 181 (top right); Karen Bussolini: 24–25, 172 (center); Les Campbell: 165 (bottom); Phil Ellin: 172 (bottom); Margaret Hensel: 89; Jerry Howard: 16 (bottom), 19, 59 (top), 82, 105, 131, 140, 141 (bottom), 167, 177 (bottom left), 179 (top right & bottom left), 180 (top right), 181 (bottom left & bottom right); Jim Kahnweiler: 151 (bottom right); Lee Lockwood: 183 (top right); Martin Miller: 171 (top); Ben Phillips: 60, 113 (bottom left), 115 (bottom right), 122 (top left), 124 (top left), 125 (top left), 155 (top right), 161 (bottom), 179 (bottom right), 186 (top right & bottom left); Ann Reilly: 177 (top right), 181 (top left); Pam Spaulding: 130, 175, 177 (top left), 178 (bottom left), 180 (top left); Albert Squillace: 46–47, 180 (bottom left); **Richard Shiell:** 5, 6–7, 27, 170.

Contents

Creating a Garden

Have you always dreamed about starting a garden of your own but were never quite sure where to begin? Perhaps the mere mention of soil tests or sun exposure made gardening seem too complicated? Well, congratulations! You are now holding the key not only to beginning a garden but also to minimizing your efforts and maximizing your results. After perusing our simple advice and explanations, you'll wonder why you didn't start gardening years ago!

This book begins by exploring your goals for your space. Would you like to start small, maybe with patio containers or flowerbeds filled with your favorite posies? Is a vegetable garden more to your liking? Or, are you ready to start a wide-ranging project, such as landscaping a large yard? Happily, whatever your objective, you'll find all you need to get started right here. Our helpful illustrations and clear step-by-step instruc-

tions will help you get off on the right foot, ensuring great results quickly and easily.

Once you've defined your goals, you can begin creating your custom outdoor living space. Here, you become an artist survey-ing a blank canvas. Just think of the possibilities! With a seemingly limitless choice of annuals, perennials, and woody plants, you can tailor your design to fit your individual needs. You'll learn that focusing just a little extra attention on such fundamentals as soil, climate, light exposure, and water can make a major difference in your garden.

We'll make that part easy with time-saving tips and techniques for such tasks as watering, weeding, fertilizing, and pruning.

As you familiarize yourself with the amazing world of plants, you'll find our handy directories an invaluable resource. We've outlined the characteristics of many plant species, each chosen for their ease of care. Individualized propagation and maintenance tips are included in these profiles, along with beautiful color photographs to help you with your selections.

Along the way, be sure to check out our high-speed gardening techniques for instant results with minimum fuss. These fun projects are a great way to improve your yard while you wait for seeds to sprout or vegetables to flourish. We've also included handy tips to help you deal with garden tasks and challenges easily and economically. And each chapter ends with frequently asked questions, so you can find quick answers to the garden issues that are on your mind.

With today's busy lifestyles, gardens big and small can provide a peaceful refuge at the end of the day. With minimal effort, you can reap the rewards of your garden—the fragrant scent of your flowers, the sun-kissed taste of your tomatoes, the quiet shade of your vine-covered gazebo—for years to come. Enjoy!

CHAPTER 1

Getting Started

Thoughts of a quiet, private space in which to relax on a warm summer evening lead you right to your own backyard. Maybe you'd like a vine-covered gazebo surrounded by lush green grass, evergreens, and colorful flowers. Or perhaps you want a bountiful vegetable garden that is as beautiful as it is functional. Whatever your garden dream, you can make it a reality with just a little planning.

To begin, consider what you have to work with, especially when it comes to your soil, water, and light. You might want to do a simple soil test to determine whether you should adjust the nutrients in the garden beds—or maybe you just need to find a better site for your flower garden. Do you live in a dry climate? You can plan your design around plants that don't need a lot of water to thrive.

Take Gardening in Stride

Every successful plan must be grounded in reality. Take time to analyze your growing conditions: sun, shade, soil type, climate, and moisture. No plant, no matter how expensive, will look good if it is suffering. Growing conditions can be altered but only to a certain extent. The ideal plan is a balance between the plants you want and those the conditions can support.

To prevent wasted effort, think about your goals first. Do you want to improve the front entrance? Repair the lawn? Make an outdoor seating area? Grow herbs or perennials? Add some shade trees? This is not all going to happen in one day. Approach the tasks in the right order. Plants thrive in healthy soil, not compacted clay or plain sand, so soil may need significant improvement. Trees take precedence over other plants because they take the longest to reach full size. If you want to have your lot terraced, have the construction completed first so that your garden doesn't get squashed by equipment. If you can't afford the terrace yet, grow grass in its place, surround it with a flowerbed of annuals,

and plant starter perennials to divide later. Quick projects such as doorway planter boxes give an immediate reward but still fit into the long-term plan.

A GARDEN FOR EVERY PURPOSE

Different gardens suit different needs, so be sure to consider the functions of your space before you begin. Do you want to create a safe play place for your children, perhaps with room for a swingset or sandbox? Do you have household pets that also need a share of the yard space? If you travel frequently, you'll need easy-care features and plants and possibly automated watering. Perhaps you want to reserve an area for outdoor entertaining with plenty of tables and chairs and a barbeque grill. Don't forget to take the style of your property into consideration as you plan. A large, formal house calls for compatible landscaping, but a cute little cottage from the '30s can get away with whimsical accents.

Also consider the amount of maintenance you would like to perform. A water garden might seem like fun, but will the upkeep be a nuisance? Do you enjoy harvesting cherries, or will you be disturbed by dropping fruit and wasps? An organic vegetable garden can be a priority to one person and an annoyance to another—let's hope you're not married to each other!

A planter is a simple way to add an instant burst of color to your yard.

Growing Conditions

Plants have evolved all over the world, adapting over the course of time to local conditions, whether temperate or tropical, wet or dry, loamy or rocky, sunny or shady. Plants that failed to find a niche became extinct and vanished. These days, we bring plants from diverse climates and communities into our gardens. Even when we try to design with native plants, we know that they, too, have diversity in their history. Their seeds may well have been brought to the region hundreds of years ago by animals, water, wind, and native people. Each plant species has a range of conditions under which it will thrive, other conditions under which it will merely survive, and unique limitations that will cause its death in hostile conditions.

TEMPERATURE

Heat and cold influence plant survival. Understanding temperature in your garden will help you find the varieties of plants that can thrive for you, especially those plants that normally live for more than a year. Conditions in your garden are influenced by your region's climate, including frost dates, and your garden's unique exposure. Plants can be grown outside their natural climate if you provide warmth to tropical plants in winter (for example, growing a lemon tree in a greenhouse in Massachusetts) or cold to plants from temperate climates in winter (for instance, treating tulip bulbs with weeks of refrigeration before planting them in Georgia). Consider both heat tolerance and cold tolerance before your select your plantings.

HIGH-SPEED GARDENING: ENTRANCEWAY EVERGREEN

Spruce up your entranceway with a potted evergreen. It will look great all year—without major digging. You can try this project at any time of year on a paved or unpaved surface.

Decide how large and tall a feature you want to add, and choose a container that complements your home. Purchase a dwarf conifer or evergreen plant of the appropriate shape and size (its nursery pot should be about half the size of your chosen container). Be sure to base your selection on the type of light in your spot (a good garden center can help you).

Set the container in its new home, and add a layer of potting soil to it. You should add enough so that the soil line of the potted plant ultimately falls about an inch below the container's rim. Take the evergreen out of its pot (fan out the roots if they are bunched up) and set it on top of the soil layer, making sure there are no big air pockets below it. Surround the evergreen with soil partway up. Add groundcover plants (such as ajuga or liriope) near the surface if you like; space them evenly around the shrub. Firm everything in and water. Correct the soil level with more potting soil if necessary, add mulch, and water gently one more time. Keep the soil steadily moist but not soggy, and fertilize from time to time according to package directions.

USDA Plant Hardiness Zone Map

The United States Department of Agriculture Plant Hardiness Zone Map divides North America into 11 zones based on average minimum winter temperatures, with Zone 1 being the coldest and Zone 11 the warmest. Each zone is further divided into sections that represent five-degree differences within each ten-degree zone.

This map should only be used as a general guideline, since the lines of separation between zones are not as clear-cut as they appear. Plants recommended for one zone might do well in the

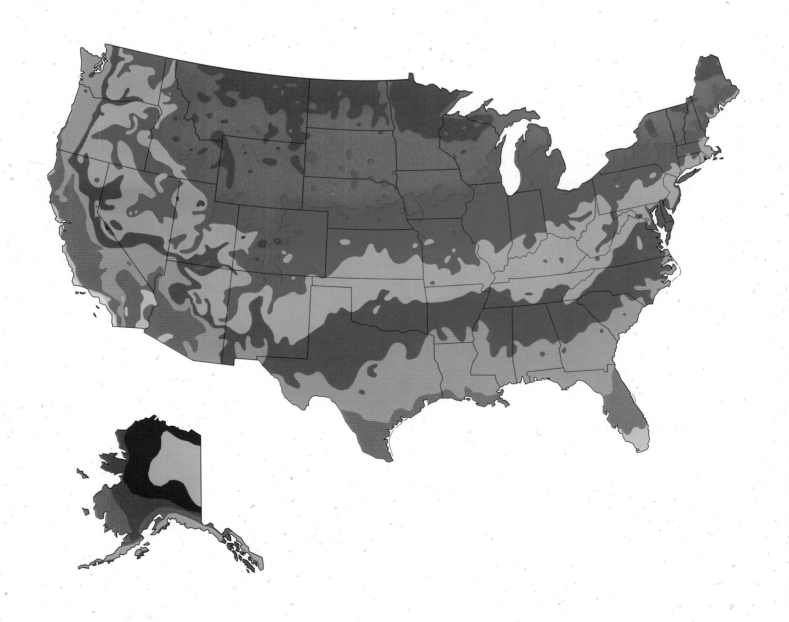

southern part of the adjoining colder zone, as well as in the neighboring warmer zone. Factors such as altitude, exposure to wind, proximity to a large body of water, and amount of available sunlight also contribute to a plant's winter hardiness. Because snow cover insulates plants, winters with little or no snow tend to be more damaging to marginally hardy varieties. Also note that the indicated temperatures are average minimums—some winters will be colder and others warmer.

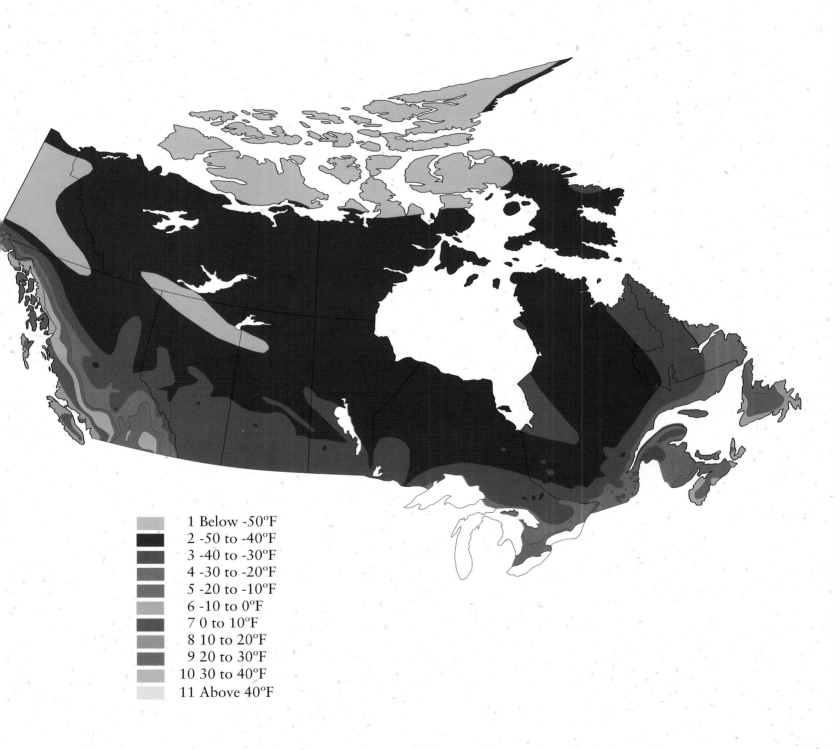

1 Below -50°F
2 -50 to -40°F
3 -40 to -30°F
4 -30 to -20°F
5 -20 to -10°F
6 -10 to 0°F
7 0 to 10°F
8 10 to 20°F
9 20 to 30°F
10 30 to 40°F
11 Above 40°F

Seasons

Some regions, such as the Midwest, are hot in summer but icy cold in winter; some are either hot or cold all the time; and others are mild or moderate most of the year. In some regions, summers are very dry but winters are wet. Others are changeable from year to year. Even though we cannot do much about local weather, we can observe its patterns and choose plants that are naturally suited.

Microclimate

Within every garden, you can find areas with different kinds of exposure to the elements. These are called *microclimates*. Even a small deck will usually have several microclimates. The part closest to the house may get more reflected light if it faces west or more shade if it faces north compared to other parts of the same deck. In larger areas, differences are even more pronounced.

Within these special niches, some plants may bloom earlier or longer into the season or be more likely to freeze or overheat. South-facing slopes or sides of buildings tend to have a longer growing season than nearby areas. Spring flowers there may bloom a week or two earlier than those in a cooler part of the garden. Although a south-facing area may be warm on

In autumn, the leaves of Japanese maples shift from summer's green or bronze shades to a riot of red and gold.

In winter, clustered red berries provide food for the birds and a bit of eye candy for us humans.

sunny winter days, the rapid drop in temperature from a bright winter day to a cold night may be too extreme for some plants. The cooler, shadier, north-facing exposure is better for marginally hardy plants and those that are prone to drying out in winter.

Wind

How windy is your garden? Strong winds can snap off branches and cause plants to dry out faster than they can take up water to replace its loss. When selecting plants for windy areas, try varieties that originated in windy climates because they have developed resistance through strength and flexibility. Leathery, stringy, or waxy leaves are another adaptation. Protection from wind may be needed for other garden plants. Windbreaks, walls, buildings, and berms (raised mounds of earth) help alter wind patterns in your garden.

PLANT A WINDBREAK

Reduce the volume of strong winds by using a layered assortment of plants as a windbreak. Wind can knock down and dry out plants and generally make it harder to get the garden to grow well. Layered plants—taller trees with shade-tolerant shrubs planted beneath them—create an irregular barrier that gently slows wind. Solid fences, in contrast, allow wind to slip up and over and swirl back in on the other side.

🌿 *A flower border in a sunny spot provides welcome color. In this early summer moment, perennials such as catmint, peonies, bee balm, and delphinium are at their peak.*

SUN, SHADE, AND DAY LENGTH

Sunshine powers the process of photosynthesis, which allows plants to make their own food using air and water. As they grow, plants provide food for grazing animals, who in turn provide sustenance for higher levels of the food chain. Sun provides the start for the whole food pyramid, so it's vital to give it the respect it deserves in the garden. Watch how shadows and sunlight hit the ground to determine how much shade exists during the growing season under deciduous trees (those that drop their leaves in fall). This test will determine which shade-loving plants will thrive there.

Consider differences in sun intensity when planting on the east and west side of shade-casting trees or buildings. Even if east- and west-facing sites receive equal hours of sun, they will not produce identical results. Gardens with an eastern exposure are illuminated with cool morning sun, then shaded in the afternoon. They are ideal locations for minimizing heat stress in southern climates or for plants such as rhododendrons that can burn in hot sun. Gardens with a western exposure are shaded in the morning and drenched in hot sun in the afternoon. Sunburn, bleaching, and sometimes death of delicate leaves can result, especially in warm climates and when growing sensitive young or shade-loving plants. Afternoon sun can also cause brightly colored flowers to fade. The west side of a building is the ideal place for sun-loving plants.

Limb up trees or remove smaller, scraggly, or unwanted saplings and brush to brighten a densely shaded spot. Prune the lowest rung of branches off young trees to raise the level of the canopy in the future. Tall, mature shade trees can have their lower limbs removed (a heavy job requiring a professional arborist) to produce light shade. For even more light, arborists can thin out overcrowded branches in the canopy, leaving some openings in the foliage for sun penetration.

Prune low-hanging branches on a sunny day so you can see how the light changes. This way you can watch the shade lighten. You can also keep an eye on the shadows, which will dance from one side of the tree to the other, changing with the time of day and position of the sun. Their silhouettes can be a beautiful part of the garden, especially in winter when the dark shadows stand out on the white snow.

LIGHTEN UP

Paint a dark wall white to reflect more light onto plants. Or try a mulch of white pebbles, sand, or gravel to reflect light up through the bottom of plants, a technique often used in gardens of Mediterranean herbs or silver-leaved plants that thrive on plenty of sun.

Full Sun

Many plants, especially lawn grass, flowers, roses, conifers (needle-leaved evergreens), vegetables, and fruit trees thrive in bright sun, which provides abundant energy for growth, flowering, and fruiting. Six to eight hours of direct sun a day is sufficient for most plants that need full sun. The term "full sun" doesn't actually mean plants must be in bright light every moment of the day, only most of the day. However, the six- to eight-hour minimum must be met for perennials, trees, and shrubs even during the shorter days of spring and fall.

Light Shade

Even in places where plants are in direct sun for a portion of the day, you also have light shade. This can be found in a garden under mature trees with long barren trunks. The sun shines in under the high leaf canopy. Light-shade conditions also exist on the east or west side of a wall or building. Here you can grow many shade-loving plants as well as shade-tolerant plants, which are sun lovers capable of growing moderately well in light shade.

Partial Shade

Filtered light, or partial shade, can be found under trees that allow sunlight to penetrate through the canopy and dapple the ground throughout the day. A garden grown beneath a lightly branched honey locust tree would fall into this category. More kinds of plants are capable of growing under these conditions than in deep shade.

Deep Shade

Full or deep shade is found under thickly branched trees or evergreens. A garden that's located here will receive little or no direct sun and remain gloomily lit. Only a limited number of plants are suitable for this situation, so choose carefully (flowers and ferns with evergreen leaves).

 With full sun in the morning and dappled sun and shade the rest of the day, many showy perennials, such as the pink peonies shown here, will be a success.

Day Length

We've all heard of the midnight sun, but we may not be aware of how our geographic position affects day length. At the equator, the length of the day stays the same through the year, but the closer you are to the North (or South) Pole, the more the light shifts with the season. In practical terms, plants get more hours of sunlight during the summer in Boston than they do in Miami, but the reverse is true in the winter. Plants react to more hours of light per day with fast growth, which is why you'll find giant vegetable contests in northern areas such as Anchorage, Alaska. Changes in day length affect plants' growth cycles.

BETTER BLOOMS

Try exposing flowering shade plants to a half day of morning sun to encourage better blooming. Extra light can also keep the plants more tidy, compact, and self-supporting.

PLANTS FOR SHADY CONDITIONS

Full Shade
- Ferns, ivy, pachysandra, periwinkle

Partial Shade
- Annuals: browallia, impatiens
- Shade-loving perennials: astilbes, bergenia, bleeding heart, hostas, mint, sweet woodruff
- Shrubs: azaleas, rhododendrons
- Spring wildflowers: bellworts, bloodroot, Solomon's seal, trout lilies

Light Shade
- Annuals: ageratum, begonias, coleus, sweet alyssum
- Herbs: basil, bee balm, parsley
- Perennials: anemones, coral bells, daylilies, hardy geraniums, hostas, lobelia
- Vegetables: arugula, lettuce, spinach

WATER

At least 90 percent of every plant is water. No plant can live without some moisture, and certain plants use it in amazing ways. Orchids and bromeliads that live on tropical trees absorb rainwater through their foliage. Succulent plants and cacti store reservoirs of water in their swollen stem tissues so they can go for a month or more without rain. Prairie flowers such as butterfly weed store water in their fleshy taproots. And daffodils store water in their bulbs.

Without water, plants wilt and die. But too much water can be as bad for plants as not enough. If land plants are submerged in water for too long—even if just their roots are submerged—they may rot or drown from lack of oxygen.

Balancing plants' water needs is like having a healthful diet. Everything should be consumed in moderation. Provide your plants with enough water for good health, but don't flood them with it. Most plants prefer steady moisture in the soil, especially in spring, so they can grow without interruption.

Impatiens wilt when the soil starts to dry out. In a planter by itself, it can have all the water it needs.

Regional Rainfall Patterns

It is rare for nature to provide exactly the right amount of water, not too much nor too little, for garden plants. You'll probably have to water your plants during dry spells to keep them looking their best. You can also observe your region's normal rainfall patterns and choose plants that are appropriate. For instance, bulbs like tulips and daffodils come from regions with wet winters but dry summers. North American wildflowers such as Virginia bluebell tend to bloom early, during moist weather at a time when tree leaves are just emerging, and then go dormant, sitting out summer in dry shade. For this reason they are referred to as *ephemerals.* Subtropic areas, such as parts of Florida, have frequent storms in the summer rainy season, bringing floods of rain. During interruptions of the usual pattern, fast-growing plants may need extra water.

To monitor rainfall patterns, set a rain gauge in an open area of the garden. You can purchase one at a garden center or use a topless

PLANTS FOR SUNNY CONDITIONS

- Annuals: dahlias, gazania, gerbera, marigolds, portulaca, zinnias
- Conifers: firs, pines, spruces
- Evergreens: arborvitae, boxwood, false cypress, junipers, yews
- Herbs: basil, lavender, rosemary, sage, thyme
- Perennials: blanketflowers, chrysanthemums, coneflowers, coreopsis, pinks, Shasta daisies, yarrow
- Shrubs: barberries, lilacs, potentilla, roses, spirea
- Trees: apples, crabapples, elms, hawthorns, magnolias, maples, oaks, peaches, pears, plums

coffee can. After each rainfall, check the depth of the rain inside. A commercial rain gauge is calibrated and easy to read. To read rain levels in a coffee can, insert a ruler and note how high the water has risen. Then keep this information in mind as you choose your plantings.

The shade in your yard will help you determine which plants can grow there.

Watering

As a general rule, most plants and lawn grasses need an inch of water a week. The idea is to keep the soil lightly moist and to prevent it from drying out completely, which can be damaging to most plants. However, plants don't always follow the rules, so here are exceptions to this guideline:

❀ Hot weather, dry sandy soil, or crowded intensive plantings or containers may require more than an inch of water a week.

 A steady supply of water is as essential for a healthy, growing plant as sunlight and soil.

❀ When the weather is cool, the plants are widely spaced, or the soil is heavy and holds moisture well, less water may be required.

❀ Young or new plantings require more moisture at the soil surface to help their budding roots get started. Water lightly and more frequently to accommodate their needs.

❀ Mature plantings with large root systems can be watered heavily and less often than younger plants. The moisture soaks deep into the soil and encourages the roots to thrive.

Some plants need more water than others, so choose plants with similar needs and plant them together. This way, you are not planting water-hogging impatiens next to dryland plants and trying to keep them both happy at the same time. Keep the water lovers in the wetter exposures of your garden or near your garden hose. Drought-tolerant plants can be grouped in areas farther from your sources of water. Moisture-loving plants include Louisiana and Japanese irises, foamflowers, marsh marigolds, Solomon's seal, sweet flag, horsetails, swamp hibiscus, cardinal flower, hostas, mosses, and ferns.

Avoid watering disease-susceptible plants at night. If water sits on plant foliage for hours, it can encourage fungal diseases to attack leaves, buds, flowers, and fruit. Plants susceptible to leaf spots, fruit rots, and flower blights are best watered in the morning, when the warming sun will quickly dry the leaves and discourage fungus development.

Soaker Hoses

Soaker hoses are are made of water-permeable fabrics, perforated recycled rubber, or other porous materials. When attached to a spigot with the water turned on low or medium, moisture droplets weep out along the length of the hose. Soaker hoses are more efficient than overhead sprinklers because they provide water directly to plant roots. Very little water evaporates and none sprays on plant foliage, which helps discourage diseases. But it may take an hour or more to thoroughly moisten the part of the garden that is in reach of the hose.

Soaker hoses require a little special attention if you want them to work properly. Here are some hints:

- Run soaker hoses straight through the garden. If set to turn or curve too sharply, they will kink and won't fill with water.

- Expect more water to be released from the end closest to the hose and less to be released from the far end.

- If the hose is moistening only one side of a plant root system, move the hose to water the dry side before you consider the job done.

- To determine if the soil has been watered enough, dig into the soil beside the hose. If the water has seeped 12 inches down, it's

❧ *Marsh marigold and iris need moist soil to thrive. Grouping water-loving plants together looks beautiful and natural and makes your job easier.*

time to turn off the hose. Remember how long this took for the next time around.

❀ For faster results, look for flat hoses that are peppered with small holes. Of course, there's a trade-off: These hoses provide water more quickly, but they are not as gentle on the soil.

❀ If you like soaker hose results, you can upgrade to permanent or semipermanent drip irrigation systems. Although more expensive, these systems are custom designed for varying soil types and individual plant water needs. And you won't need to move them around the garden.

Some gardeners get lucky with naturally rich, fertile soil. However, you may need to amend your soil so that it meets your plants' needs.

SOIL MATTERS

The soil in which your plants grow serves four basic purposes. It helps, through its structure, to hold the plant upright, and it supplies food, water, and air to the roots. Some soils are already capable of meeting these purposes and can be used with little amendment. Called loam soils, they contain a mixture of different-size soil particles and organic matter. Beneficial

microorganisms help break organic matter into nutrient-rich soil with good texture. If you have a garden with rich, fertile soil, you won't need to treat it.

It is possible, however, that you'll need to improve one or more of the conditions of your soil. For example, soil with a significant proportion of clay (at or above 25 percent) is made up of rock particles so tiny and close together they allow little air circulation. Clay retains more moisture, so it takes longer to dry in spring and may need less watering in summer. It can be made richer and more likely to produce lush growth with just the addition of compost and, occasionally, a little fertilizer. The compost is important. It helps break up clay so the soil won't be too thick and poorly aerated.

Sandy soil contains larger rock particles. Air is present in abundance in sandy soil, but water

RECYCLE IT!

Catch water from a downspout into a container. This unfluoridated, unchlorinated water is ideal for watering plants. It comes at an ambient temperature, not shockingly cold from the tap, which is hard on warmth-loving plants. And perhaps best of all—at least from the gardener's perspective—it's free!

runs straight through, sometimes carrying nutrients away too rapidly and drying out soon after a rain. This means that in rainy climates, the gardener may have to add everything the plants need.

Texture Checkup

There are a few ways to determine which kind of soil you're dealing with. For a quick test, simply squeeze some slightly moist soil in your hand. Clay soils form a compact lump and retain their shape. Loam soils form a ball but fall apart if poked. Sandy soils won't hold their shape at all.

You can also check the texture of your soil in a jar filled with water. Gather some soil from the garden, choosing a sample from near the surface and down to a depth of eight inches. Let it dry, pulverize it into fine granules, and mix well. Put a one-inch layer (a little over a cup) in a quart glass jar with ¼ teaspoon of powdered dishwasher detergent. (Dishwasher detergent won't foam up.) Add enough water to fill the jar two-thirds full. Shake the jar for a minute, turning it upside down as needed to get all the soil off the bottom, then put the jar on a counter where it can sit undisturbed. One minute later, mark the level of settled particles

on the jar with a crayon or wax pencil. This is sand. Set an alarm for four hours, and when it goes off, mark the next level, which is the amount of silt that has settled. Over the next day or two, the clay will slowly settle and allow you to take the final measurement. These measurements show the relative percentages of sand, silt, and clay in your soil.

Before you begin to plant, make sure you've taken such factors as light, soil, water, and climate into account.

Organic Material

In nature, topsoil is richer than subsoil. Topsoil is the dark brown layer of soil that is at the surface and is the product of years and years of breakdown of organic matter, whereas the subsoil below can be mainly clay or sand. Organic matter gives life to the soil. Every soil needs organic matter for its texture and workability, as well as a supply of nutrients necessary for healthy plant growth. It is the material that comes from leaves, animal droppings, twigs, fallen logs, weeds, and many other once-living sources. In the forest, leaves pile up, mixed with other organic matter, and decay into a dark, rich layer, which is where growing plants prefer to have their roots. Earthworms and beneficial microorganisms process the organic matter, turning it into simpler compounds that plants use to nurture themselves. Where there is little organic matter, the necessary compounds can be added with packaged fertilizers, but they do not address soil texture, and it can be difficult to add every necessary trace mineral that natural organic matter will provide. Ensure good soil quality, texture, and quantity by adding plentiful organic matter in the form of chopped leaves, animal manures, wood chips and other mulches, and compost. You'll find more complete information on how to do this in Chapter 2.

TESTING DRAINAGE

Test your soil's drainage by digging a hole, filling it with water, and watching how quickly the water disappears. All the soil tests in the world won't do a better job than this simple project. It tells you how quickly moisture moves through the soil and whether the soil is likely to be excessively dry or very soggy—neither of which is ideal.

When it hasn't rained for a week or more and the soil is dry, dig several holes that are one foot deep and two feet wide. Fill them to the top with water and keep track of how long it takes for the holes to empty. Compare your findings to the following scale:

- 1 to 12 minutes: The soil is sharply drained and likely to be dry.
- 12 to 30 minutes: The soil has ideal drainage.
- 30 minutes to 4 hours: Drainage is slow but adequate for plants that thrive in moist soil.
- Over 4 hours: Drainage is poor and needs help.

Summer brings a sunny bounty of flowers to harvest for bouquets, your reward for great gardening. This nosegay includes rudbeckias, zinnias, and asters in a rainbow of colors.

Frequently Asked Questions

Q: How can I grow flowers under my maple trees? Everything starts out nicely but dies off in the summer.
A: Grow sun-loving spring bulbs and wildflowers beneath your deciduous maples to make the most of the sun before the tree leaves emerge. Choose smaller plants and don't plant too close to the trunk, so as not to disturb shallow roots. This is a great strategy for people who have a shady yard and therefore have trouble getting flowers to grow during summer and fall. Snowdrops, crocuses, squills, Spanish bluebells, daffodils, windflowers, glory-of-the-snow, and wildflowers such as bloodroot and squirrel corn thrive in spring sun. When tree leaves emerge and the setting grows dark, many of these spring growers fall dormant and lie quietly below the ground until spring sun arrives again.

Q: My soil is sandy and my plants never look that great, but my neighbor doesn't seem to have any trouble. What can I do?
A: Your neighbor may be putting more into the soil than you do. Sandy soil tends to be fairly inert, lacking nutrients of all kinds, and can drain quickly without holding moisture for plants. Dig organic matter such as compost and peat moss into your soil in generous quantities, along with time-release fertilizer and a water-grabbing gel. Top with mulch and water regularly, and your plants should respond with vigorous growth.

Q: I can't afford all those products that help make the garden soil better. Any ideas?
A: Compost is the single best soil booster, and you probably can get it from your city or town hall service department. Made from leaves and grass clippings, the compost may be free or at least reasonably priced for local residents.

Q: My hanging baskets of annuals look great every spring when I buy them. But by midsummer they look dried up and have few blooms. How can I keep them fresh and full of flowers?
A: Follow three basic principles when growing flowering baskets—water, groom, and fertilize. The soil mass in a basket is very small. It heats up and dries out quickly, so daily watering may be needed. Fertilize the plant with a liquid balanced fertilizer every two weeks. And groom your plant often. Deadhead and pinch back leggy growth to promote heavier flowering and branching.

A chair or bench set in a quiet garden spot invites guests to sit and enjoy the beautiful view.

Q: I have two sites: one that is flat and shaded and one that is on a slope but gets sun all day long. Which is better for growing vegetables?

A: Because vegetables do not grow well without full sun, you'll probably have to go with the sloping site. You'll need to find a way to make the soil surface level, so the water and nutrients needed by the plants don't wash down the hill. Look into making raised beds outlined with rocks or blocks, or make a series of terraces like they do in mountainous regions around the world.

A salad garden planted with colorful varieties of lettuce is both practical and pretty. What a great way to maximize space!

Q: When shopping for a building lot, what characteristics should be considered to make my landscape plans easier?

A: First, consider your outdoor living areas. Do you need a large, flat area for children to play? If so, don't buy a steep lot. Perhaps you'll want a vegetable garden or other plants that require full sun; a wooded lot might not suit your needs. Make a list of your household's requirements for the property to determine if the lot can fill those needs.

Q: I need to make our backyard more private. Should I enclose the yard with a fence?

A: Unless you need to keep people or animals out or keep children and pets in, you probably don't need the entire yard enclosed. Strategically placed sections or panels of fence in combination with small trees and large shrubs, for example, make for a more aesthetically pleasing atmosphere. An enclosure will make the yard seem small. Take advantage of neighboring trees and gardens to make your yard feel larger.

Q: How can proper site and plant selection make insect management easier?

A: There are many types of landscape plants that are virtually pest free (or at least pest resistant). Find out which pests are a problem in your area, and steer clear of plants that attract such pests. Additionally, a plant that is growing out of its optimal environment—full sun as opposed to partial shade—may not be able to support the beneficial insect predators that normally keep the pests at bay.

Q: My neighbors have no problem growing a beautiful camellia, but after many failures, I've stopped planting them. Their soil seems to be the same as mine.

A: The successful camellia is probably growing in a microclimate that may not exist on your property. A protected microclimate is a good environment to try marginally hardy plant species, since it's protected from extreme daily temperature changes and winter winds. Visit your neighbors' site and try to determine the characteristics of the unique location—it's possible you have a site that's equally suitable.

Q: What does it mean to have well-drained soil?

A: Although it's necessary for your soil to have water available for your plants, too much water held for long periods of time will disturb the balance of air that is necessary for healthy root growth of most plant species. Without air in the soil, many plants will likely drown. Loam, a balance of sand, clay, and organic matter, is usually well drained. Heavily compacted clay soils are often poorly drained.

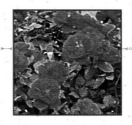

CHAPTER 2

Tools, Soil Prep, and Planting

This chapter contains the information you'll need to garden successfully. You'll discover that only simple tools are necessary, and you'll learn how to use these tools to properly prepare the soil for your new plantings. Getting your garden off to a great start early on means less work in the long run!

Once your soil is ready, you can begin to plant. We've included tips to help you select strong, healthy plants, whether you buy them from a local greenhouse, a mail-order specialist, or a roadside stand. The hints in this chapter will also help you reduce plant loss during the critical transplanting stages.

Remember: Imagination, creativity, and knowledge are the best gardening tools available. Once you understand the basics, it's easy!

Garden Tools

In any enterprise, the proper tools make the work much easier to accomplish. But you don't necessarily need a large array of tools to garden successfully, especially if you're planning a small flowerbed or container garden for your patio. For a start in an average-size garden, you'll want the basics: good gloves, a square-ended spade (useful for edging as well as spading), a spading fork, hand trowels, hoses, hoes, bow rakes and leaf rakes, pruning clippers and saws, and a sturdy wheelbarrow or large-wheeled cart. If your soil is rocky or very heavy, a small- or narrow-bladed spade (sometimes called a drain spade) will be easier to use than a standard one.

You can add to this list as your garden grows. You'll find that dealers offer special tools for special tasks, such as edging tools, bulb planters, and tiny tools for working with bonsai.

Buy the best tools you can afford. Cheap tools may fail you in the middle of a big project, just when you need them most. One way to ensure good quality is to buy tools from a reputable dealer willing to guarantee their performance. Ask the dealer to point out the features of different choices. Check with experienced gardeners about which tools they use most. For a quality test, look at the way tools are made. Compare several brands. Tools with steel blades are strong enough to last for years without bending. Stainless steel is even better, because it won't rust and needs little cleaning. Spades, shovels, and forks with hard ash handles are unlikely to splinter or break in the middle of a heavy operation. People with smaller builds can find specially designed tools with smaller blades and shorter handles, which are easier to control than larger tools. Tools with ergonomic features, such as padded handles, prevent injury and are more comfortable to use. Specialist suppliers offer tools with adjustable handle lengths. Many tools come with either long, straight handles or *D*-shaped hand holds on shorter handles.

HAND TOOLS

Once your garden soil has been prepared or is in good condition, small hand tools are right for many tasks. Look for a strongly made trowel that fits your hand well. You can use it to scrape off tiny weeds, dig holes a few inches deep for small plants or bulbs, and shape shallow rows for seeds. Simply insert the trowel into the soil and wobble it around to make a deep, slender hole for transplanting plants from flats. A hand fork (sometimes the trowel and fork are sold as a pair) is handy for working small patches of soil, setting out plants, and small cleanup jobs.

Even simpler than a trowel, a dibble stick is a gadget that is ideal for setting out a lot of plants or bulbs in soil that is already prepared. It is basically a handle attached to a glorified pointed stick. The lower part is usually aluminum or stainless steel. This slender, slightly cone-shaped implement is about ten inches long. Stick it into the soil to the depth you need, give it a few turns, and you'll have a small planting hole in record time.

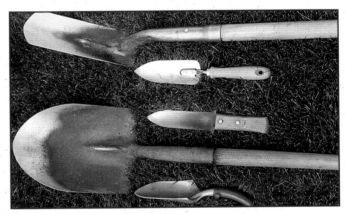

PRUNING TOOLS

For pruning, you'll want good-quality pruning shears, loppers, and a saw. Sharp blades and sturdy handles make pruning a breeze. Dull blades—rusty and sticking—make projects harder than they need to be. They can also cause wood to be crushed or torn, which is damaging to the plant. Look for hard, durable blades capable of being resharpened and a sturdy, smoothly operating nut holding the blades together. Hand-pruning shears, used for small stems under about a ½ in diameter, should also have a safety latch to keep the blades closed when not in use. Look for scissor-type blades, which make sharper, cleaner cuts than the anvil type (those with a sharp blade pressing on a flat blade). Also check out ergonomically designed pruning shears that minimize repetitive motion stress. Loppers are long-handled pruning shears with larger blades for cutting branches up to about 1½ inches in diameter. Pruning is easier if you buy shears with ratcheting action for more power with less effort. Pruning saws should have narrow blades, be easy to maneuver into tight spaces, and be toothed on one side only. Often, you can saw off a small branch with ease, which would take great force to clip.

Many garden tasks can be accomplished with just a round-point shovel (second from bottom), a drain spade (top), and trowels in various sizes.

CARING FOR TOOLS

Always set hoes, soil rakes, and other tools with horizontal teeth or blades facedown on the ground when not being used. If stepped on, the teeth or blades sink harmlessly into the soil. But if left face up, an unwary walker might step on the teeth, making the tool tip and the handle spring up into his or her face.

CHECKLIST FOR A HIGH-QUALITY SPADE

- Strong wooden or fiberglass handle
- Handle and metal portion fit well together and are not loose
- Rolled edge turned forward on top of blade to allow your foot to push there with extra pressure
- Reinforced blade shank (metal part of handle)
- Blade shank that extends along the handle for added strength
- Smooth, stainless-steel blade for easiest care and cleaning

SHARPEN CUTTING TOOLS

❧

Using a metal file, periodically sharpen the inside surface of your garden hoe and the underside surface of your spade. Sharp tools make for a much faster, more efficient job.

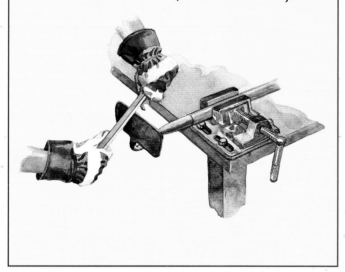

For an organized approach, make a tool holder by attaching a topless and bottomless coffee can (or similarly shaped plastic container) to a fence post and securing it with wire. You can slip in the handles of rakes, shovels, and hoes, keeping them together, upright, and out from underfoot while you work.

Keep your tools in top condition by cleaning them after each use. Have a bucket of clean sand and machine oil on hand to cure them, too. This is particularly helpful for rust-prone digging instruments such as shovels, garden forks, and hoes. After use, rinse with water and dry the blades. Then insert them in the oil/sand mixture. The sand will scour off debris, and the oil will coat the metal, retarding rust.

Always be sure to store your tools carefully in an area protected from the weather. Wooden handles shrink from weathering, resulting in a loose tool head that is impossible to use. To make it really easy on yourself, keep hand tools in a basket on the garage or pantry shelf so they are always easy to find. Then, if you see a branch in need of a quick

trim, you don't have to search all over the house and garage for a pair of pruning shears. If all your tools are kept together—and returned to their proper basket after each use—simple garden projects will stay quick.

HIGH-SPEED GARDENING: INSTALL A TOOL HANGER

❧

It's easier to put your tools away after each use if you have a good place to put them. Using screws or bolts, fasten a length of sturdy wood (a piece of 2×4 lumber will work) to the garage or utility room wall. Position big nails or hooks so that the tools can hang without overlapping each other. Label each tool position with a marker or with plastic labels so that everyone using the tools can find the right place to put them. Hanging the tools for storage will keep the blades sharp longer and cut down on clutter.

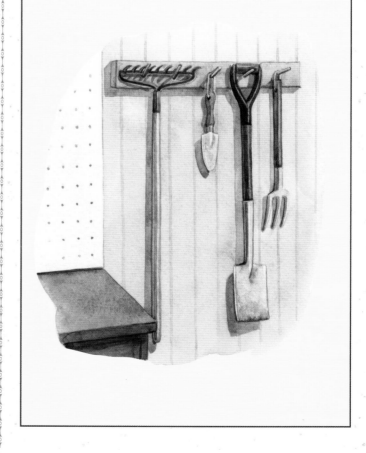

Preparing the Soil

$\mathcal{I}$f you don't have the loose, dark earth of those fabulous gardens you've seen on television and in magazines, don't despair. It can be created by improving your existing soil for fertility and good drainage. Soils can be amended with sand to make them looser and drier or with clay to make them moister and firmer. They can be given plentiful doses of organic material—old leaves, ground-up twigs, livestock manure, and old lawn clippings, plus appropriate fertilizer. Organic matter improves and nourishes any kind of soil, which, in turn, encourages better plant growth. Some soils are naturally pretty good, but others may need significant improvement if they are to support a beautiful garden.

Your soil texture checkup (see page 20) has shown the percentage of sand, silt, and clay in your soil, a good starting point for improving it. But you should also have your soil tested before you start adding fertilizers and amendments to it. This is in keeping with the old

adage, "If it ain't broke, don't fix it." Sometimes unnecessary tampering with nutrients or soil acidity can actually create more problems than benefits.

READING YOUR WEEDS

Look for the tales weeds have to tell. If a vacant garden area has few weeds taking advantage of the opening, the soil is likely to need plenty of work. If they are growing, but only sparsely, and have short, stunted stems and discolored leaves, the area may have a nutrient deficiency, and a soil test is in order. If, in newly tilled soil, weeds sprout up quickly in certain areas and more slowly in others, the weedy areas are likely to be moister and better for seed germination.

SOIL TESTS

Soil tests tell you the nutrient levels in your soil, a plant version of the nutrient guides on packaged foods. They also note pH and organic content, two factors important to overall smooth sailing from the ground up. To have your soil tested, call your local Cooperative Extension Service, often listed under federal or county government in the phone book. Ask them how to get a soil-testing kit, which contains a soil-collecting bag and instructions. Follow the directions precisely for an accurate report.

The results may come as a chart full of numbers, which can be a little intimidating at first.

Keep small maintenance tasks simple—hand tools stored in a basket are always accessible and are easy to transport.

But if you look carefully for the following, you can begin to interpret these numbers:

❀ If the percentage of organic matter is under 5 percent, the garden needs extra compost.

❀ Nutrients will be listed separately, possibly in parts per million. Sometimes they are also rated as available in high, medium, or low levels. If an element or two comes in on the low side, you'll want to add a fertilizer that replaces what's lacking.

❀ Soil pH refers to the acidity of the soil. Ratings below 7 are acidic soils. From 6 to 7 are slightly acidic, the most fertile pH range. Above 7 is alkaline or basic soil, which can become infertile above pH 8. Excessively acidic and alkaline soils can be treated to make them more moderate and productive.

Add only the nutrients your soil test says are necessary. More is not always better when it comes to plant nutrients. Don't feel compelled to add a little bit more of a fertilizer that promises great results. Too much of any one nutrient can actually produce toxic results, akin to diseases or worse. Buy only what's required and save the rest of your money for a better use, like more plants. However, you can use lots of compost, the more the better, in most cases.

pH Levels

If your soil test indicates that your soil is very acidic, consider growing acid-loving plants, or try ground limestone to raise the pH. Limestone is nature's soil sweetener, capable of neutralizing overly acidic soils. It's best to add limestone in the fall to allow time for it to begin to dissolve and do its job. The amount of limestone you use will vary depending on the specific soil conditions. Don't dump limestone on soil randomly, because you run the risk of overdosing the soil with lime. Follow guidelines on the limestone package or on your soil test. Maintaining the new and improved pH is an ongoing project. Recheck the soil's pH every year and continue to add limestone as needed.

If, on the other hand, your soil test shows that your soil is on the alkaline side, add cottonseed meal, sulfur, pine bark, compost, or pine needles. Garden sulfur is a reliable cure when added as recommended in a soil test. It acidifies the soil slowly as microbes convert the sulfur to sulfuric acid and other compounds. Soil amendments such as compost, decaying pine bark, and ground-up pine needles gradually acidify the soil while improving its texture.

SOURCES OF SPECIFIC NUTRIENTS

Many of these fertilizers are available processed and packaged. You don't have to harvest your own.

- Nitrogen: bat guano, blood meal, chicken manure, cottonseed meal, fish emulsion, kelp meal, livestock manure (composted)
- Phosphorus: bonemeal, rock phosphate, super phosphate
- Potassium: granite meal, greensand, seabird guano, shrimp shell meal, sulfate of potash, wood ashes
- Calcium: bonemeal, chelated calcium, eggshells, limestone, oyster shells, wood ashes
- Boron: borax, chelated boron, manure
- Copper: chelated copper
- Magnesium: chelated magnesium, dolomitic limestone, Epsom salts
- Sulfur: iron sulfate, sulfur, zinc sulfate
- Zinc: chelated zinc, zinc sulfate
- Iron: chelated iron, iron sulfate

COMPOST AND ORGANIC MATTER

Every type of soil can be improved with additional organic matter, and one of the best and easiest ways to get organic matter into your soil is by adding compost. In fact, compost is simply organic matter that has already broken down sufficiently for its minerals and nutrients to be accessible to plants. You can buy compost, or you can make your own.

COMPOST BLENDS

Organic material decays most quickly if blended with approximately equal parts of the following:

Nitrogen-rich soft and green material

Manure from chickens, cows, horses, rabbits, pigs, guinea pigs, and other herbivores

Fruit and vegetable peels

Grass clippings

Green leaves

Strips of turf

Alfalfa

Carbon-rich brown and hard material

Wood chips

Ground-up twigs

Sawdust

Pruning scraps

Autumn leaves

Straw

Making Compost

To begin a compost heap, dump yard scraps in a far corner of the yard. An ideal blend would be equal amounts of soft or green material (manure and fresh leaves) and brown or hard material (dead leaves and chopped twigs); see the list above. Or, if you prefer, keep the compost materials neatly contained in a wooden slat or wire-mesh bin. If you put an access door

GET MORE FROM MOWING

Use a lawn mower equipped with a bagger when you mow the grass and any fallen leaves in autumn. The mower will begin to shred up the leaves and mix them with the grass. This does twice the good of ordinary mowing: It saves you from raking, and the blended leaves and grass clippings are a dynamite combination for making compost. Empty the mower bag in an out-of-the-way place to make a compost pile. Use a garden fork to fluff the pile occasionally during winter, and you could have great compost by spring or summer.

on the bottom of the bin, you can scoop out the finished compost at the bottom while the rest is still decaying.

Add compost starter or good garden soil to a new compost pile to help jump-start the decay of organic materials. Compost starter, available in garden centers or from mail-order garden catalogs, contains decay-causing microorganisms. Some brands also contain nutrients, enzymes, hormones, and other stimulants that help decomposers work as fast as possible. Special formulations can be particularly helpful for hard-to-compost material such as wood chips and sawdust or for quick decay of brown leaves.

Good garden or woodland soil, though not as high-tech or as expensive as compost starter, contains native decomposers well able to tackle a compost pile. Sprinkle it among the yard scraps as you are building the pile. You can speed up the compost-making process by chopping up leaves and twigs before putting them on the compost pile. The smaller the pieces are, the faster they will decay. Chopping can be done easily with a chipper-shredder or a mulching mower.

Use perforated PVC pipes to aerate compost piles. An ideal compost pile will reach three to four feet high, big enough to get warm from the heat of decay. High temperatures—when a pile is warm enough to steam on a cool morning—semisterilize the developing compost, killing disease spores, hibernating pests, and weed seeds. But for decomposers to work efficiently enough to create heat, they need plenty of air—and not just at the surface of the pile. Aeration is traditionally provided by fluffing or turning the pile with a pitchfork, which can be hard work. But with a little advance planning and a perforated pipe, this can be avoided. Start a compost pile on a bed of branched sticks that will allow air to rise from below. Add a perforated pipe in the center, building layers of old leaves, grass clippings, and other garden leftovers around it. The air will flow through the pipe into the pile.

HIGH-SPEED GARDENING: THE EASY WAY TO MAKE COMPOST

Make compost the lazy way by layering leaves, lawn clippings, and kitchen waste in an out-of-the-way spot. Then simply leave it until it's ready. Nature's recyclers will take organic matter no matter how it is presented and turn it into rich, dark compost. This process just takes longer in an untended pile.

MULCH FOR SOIL IMPROVEMENT

Add a thick layer of mulch and let it rot to improve the soil of existing gardens. Minerals, released as the mulch is degraded into nutrient soup, soak down into the soil and fertilize existing plants. Humic acid, another product of decay, clumps together small particles of clay to make a lighter, fluffier soil. For best success, remember these points:

❊ Woody mulch, such as shredded bark, uses nitrogen as it decays. Apply extra nitrogen to prevent the decay process from consuming soil nitrogen that plants need for growth.

❊ Don't apply fine-textured mulches, like grass clippings, in thick layers that can mat down and smother the soil.

❊ Use mulch, which helps keep the soil moist, in well-drained areas that won't become soggy or turn into breeding grounds for plant-eating slugs and snails.

FERTILIZERS

Depending on your soil test results and what you are planting, you probably will need to add packaged fertilizers to your garden soil in addition to mulch and compost. Use packaged fertilizers according to directions. In most cases, use balanced formulations with similar numbers (5-5-5). The numbers stand for nitrogen (N), phosphorus (P), and potassium (K), in that order. Sometimes you need special formulations for special purposes. Lawn food is high in nitrogen, which is great for leaf growth, whereas "bloomer" fertilizers for flowers and fruit are proportionately lower in nitro-

gen and higher in phosphorus and potassium (5-10-10, for instance). Formulations for roses, vegetables, tomatoes, holly trees, and others have special attributes that are matched to the plants. Slow or time-release fertilizers are usually in a beadlike form and give out their nutrients little by little, through many rains or waterings. They help keep plants blooming or producing all season long. Liquid or soluble fertilizers reach the roots immediately for an instant boost but must be reapplied on a regular basis. For details on how to use fertilizers properly, read the package labels. The volume of fertilizer required may vary depending on the kind of plant being fertilized and the time of year.

Compost and bulky organic material, such as composted manure, also provide major and minor nutrients and should give you trace elements your soil needs. They improve the texture of the soil and add organisms that contribute to replenished nutrient supply, naturally. Expect to use more organic fertilizer, by volume, than synthetic chemical fertilizers because organic fertilizers contain fewer nutrients by weight, averaging from one to about six or seven percent. Contrast this with an inorganic lawn fertilizer that may contain up to 30 percent nitrogen, more than four times as much as organic fertilizer.

More is not always better when it comes to fertilizers. Lower-dose organic fertilizers are unlikely to burn plant roots or cause nutrient overdoses. Many forms release their components slowly, providing a long-term nutrient supply instead of one intense nutrient blast. Organic fertilizers may also provide a spectrum of lesser nutrients, even enzymes and hormones that can benefit growth.

Composting

Making your own compost takes several months, so many gardeners find it easier to purchase bagged compost. Either way, compost is a good additive for soils low in organic materials. Added to clay soil, compost lightens the soil and improves aeration; added to sandy soil, compost improves water-holding capacity.

Liquid Fertilizer Solution

Liquid fertilizer is an immediate source of nutrients. The concentrated form is diluted by mixing with water according to the manufacturer's directions. Use a mild solution on new transplants to help them quickly recover from the shock. Liquid fertilizer can be applied in place of granular side-dressings.

Side-Dressing

Granular fertilizers release nutrients more quickly than organic fertilizers. Sprinkling a handful of 5-10-5 around each plant (known as side-dressing) in spring and again mid-summer will give annuals a feeding boost that will keep them in top growing and flowering condition through the summer. Use slow-release fertilizers once in the spring.

FISH EMULSION FERTILIZER

Use fish emulsion fertilizer to encourage a burst of growth from new plantings, potted flowers and vegetables, or anything that is growing a little too sluggishly for your taste. High-nitrogen fish emulsion dissolves in water and is easily absorbed and put to immediate use by the plant. For best results, follow the package directions.

SOIL FOR CONTAINERS

Soil texture and fertility are very important in containers; your plants have to depend on what's in the pot for their necessary moisture and nutrients. They can't send their roots out farther, looking for more. And they can't escape rotting if they are trapped in soggy conditions. The correct soil depends on varied factors such as the type of plant and the climate and exposure of the site. Most gardeners avoid pests and diseases in their pots by using bagged products, but you can use your own compost if you really trust it. For most plants, choose a commercial mix prepared for potted plants. If it has been formulated without additional fertilizer, mix in time-release fertilizer beads according to package directions. Or mix your own potting soil with a third each of loam, peat moss or compost, and perlite, incorporating time-release fertilizer. Gel granules (for keeping soil moist)

Mixing vermiculite (gray), peat moss (brown), and perlite (white) will give you a good medium for sowing seeds or rooting plants. Add loam and it will be excellent for plants in containers.

can also be stirred in. For plants that need especially good drainage, such as narcissi, tulips, cyclamen, and others with bulbous roots, add plenty of extra perlite in the mix, and top the pots with tiny pebbles or a quarter-inch layer of perlite.

Working the Soil

There are varied digging techniques from which to choose. Some are more appropriate than others for your unique conditions, the type of garden you are making, and the amount of work you are willing to do. You can tuck plants in, just making small holes, if the soil is already excellent. If it's not, which is more likely, choose the most appropriate method of working the soil for your garden style and needs: single digging, double digging, or simply mulching. As the mulch breaks down over the course of several months or longer, the soil will be improved.

SINGLE DIGGING

Till or spade a thick layer of compost into lightly moist (never wet) soil to bring it to life before planting a new garden. Your well-tilled soil, like screened topsoil, may look great at first, but silt or clay soils are likely to get stiff, crusty, and hard after a few heavy downpours. The best way to keep soil loose and light is to add organic matter. Add a 4- to 6-inch-deep layer of compost to the soil and work it down until it's 10 to 12 inches deep. The soil will become darker, moister, and spongier—a dramatic conversion right before your eyes.

On a day when the soil is neither too wet nor too dry, measure the garden bed or area where you plan to dig, and mow down or remove grass and weeds. Mark the area with an outline of ground limestone or even spray paint. If you are working near the lawn or in a tight space, be sure to have a wheelbarrow or tarp handy for storing the soil you remove from the area.

Using a fork or spade, remove a chunk of soil a foot deep from an edge or corner, and set it in the wheelbarrow. Two or three inches behind the first hole, or farther if your soil is light and sandy, make the next slice. It will be easy because the air space from the first hole gives you some room for pushing the soil around, even if it has become compacted. Flip the second slice over and into the hole from the first cut, chopping it up. Remove and discard any large weed or grass roots. After you make a few more slices, filling and chopping, you have a place for the rototiller to bite into, if you are using one.

Lightly rototill the entire bed. Or, if you are working with hand tools, continue roughly slicing, filling, and chopping with the spade or fork until you have gone over the bed completely one time.

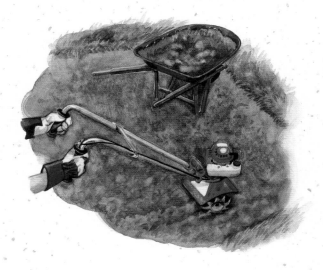

Spread soil improvers (following guidelines from your soil test) in an even layer on top of the bed. With the rototiller or by hand, dig them evenly into the soil. Rototill or dig once in one direction and again in another. Finely work the soil until the additives are evenly distributed to a depth of 12 inches, across the whole bed. Using the spade, even up the outer edges of the bed if necessary. Use a bow rake to smooth the bed, and your garden is ready to go.

DOUBLE DIGGING

These steps will help you create a deeply enriched, well-drained garden bed and will correct even serious soil deficiencies. You will need a spade, a tarp or wheelbarrow, a bow rake, and a generous supply of soil amendments as suggested by your soil test.

At a time when the soil is neither too wet nor too dry, measure the garden bed that will be double-dug. You may want to mark the edges of your bed with an outline of ground limestone or spray paint.

Beginning at one end of the garden, remove a strip of soil a spade's length deep and a spade's width wide. Make each cut with the spade adjacent to the last one, for easier digging. Put the soil you remove into a wheelbarrow or on a tarp. Use your shovel to turn the soil below it and break it up. Another option is to jab a garden fork (like a big pitchfork) into the hard lower soil and rock it around until the soil breaks up. If organic matter is needed, you should add it to the lower level at this point.

Do the same thing to the second strip of soil next to the first row. Remove rocks and large roots as you find them. Turn the surface topsoil from the second trench into the first trench, adding organic matter as desired. Then loosen and amend the exposed subsurface soil, working it well.

In an orderly fashion, continue filling each trench with the soil taken from the adjacent row and loosening the soil below, adding soil improvers throughout all levels of soil. Fill the final strip with the soil from the wheelbarrow, plus amendments. Finely work the surface of the bed with the spade or a rototiller, and trim the outer edges of the bed neatly with the spade. Use the bow rake to smooth the surface, and the new bed is ready for planting.

Planting

Once the soil is ready, you can begin to plant. We've covered only the basics here; additional details can be found in the appropriate chapters on annuals, perennials, and woody plants.

PURCHASING GREAT PLANTS

Landscape plants available in the United States and Canada are generally of high quality.

> ### HIGH-SPEED GARDENING: HANDY HERBS
>
> Herbs need a little space in the sun, not much more. You can find a rectangular container with matching liner that fits on your sunny kitchen windowsill or one of any shape that fits in a small spot near your doorway. You'll need potting soil with extra perlite for good drainage and six to eight hours of sunshine per day. Buy small starter plants of your favorite herbs, such as chive, parsley, basil, thyme, oregano, and mint, and combine them attractively in the planter. Set each plant as deeply as it was growing in its pot. Water the container, firm the planting medium, add more planting medium if necessary, and grow.
>
>

Whether you make your purchases through a local greenhouse or nursery, a mail-order specialist, a chain store, or a roadside stand, you'll usually find vigorous, insect- and disease-free plants. What's more, with rare exceptions, these offerings can be relied upon to be correctly labeled.

Because of this consistently good quality, it's possible to buy plants wherever you find the best price on the variety you want. Bedding plants and perennials are generally sold in packs and small containers. Unless you need to evaluate the color of the flowers, the presence of blooms is unimportant. In fact, annuals that are not flowering in the pack tend to establish root systems quicker than those that are in bloom, resulting in side

branching and abundant flowering. To ensure an easy transition from the greenhouse to the garden, purchase plants at nurseries or garden centers at the proper planting time. Good plants are stocky, not leggy, and have healthy green leaves. They are not root-bound (having matted roots and too big for their pots), so the roots are ready to stretch out and grow in your garden. One way to check is to see if roots are already growing out the bottoms of the market packs.

Although plants are usually grown well, they are not always treated well at supermarkets and other places that do not specialize in live plants. Try to get them shortly after delivery from the greenhouse source, or purchase only from stores that keep tabs on the needs of the plants.

SIMPLE STEPS TO A PERFECT PLANTER

Gather your ornamental container (with drainage holes), potting soil formulated for containers, and the plants you will use. Water the plants. Moisten the potting soil according to package directions, making sure it's not too wet. Partly fill the container (approximately halfway to the top) with the moistened potting soil. Tamp it down gently. Decide how you will arrange the plants in the container. You can try them out several ways, without planting them.

When the planting is finished, the level of soil in the container should be an inch below the rim, to allow space for watering and rainfall. Each plant should be planted at the same depth that it is in its nursery pot. Measure or estimate this depth. Remove each plant from its pot and set it onto or into the potting soil at the correct level. If a plant is too low, build up the potting soil below it, and if one is too high, scoop out some soil as necessary. If you also use an ornamental rock, it should be at least a third buried, not just resting on top of the soil.

When the placement of each plant is just right, fill the spaces between the plants with potting soil and tamp it in place. Every root should be packed tightly against potting soil. Smooth the top surface. If you like, add a layer of moss or a mulch of small stone or bark chips. Water again, and the container is ready to display.

Shrubs in nursery containers make an easy transition from pot to garden; their roots suffer very little damage when they are transplanted. As long as the soil is not frozen, they can be planted at any time of year.

Young annuals are tender. If these plants will sit for a few days before you have time to plant them, be sure to attend to their needs for light, warmth, and water. Keep them outside in bright light but protect them from the strong afternoon sun and from high wind. Check the soil moisture daily; bedding plants dry out quickly and require regular watering. Each time bedding plants wilt, some of their strength is lost.

Trees, shrubs, and vines that have been grown in containers may be purchased and planted any time the ground isn't frozen. Moving a plant from a container to the garden does not shock the plant as does digging it up from a nursery row. Look for plants with vigorous growth that are well rooted but not crowded in the container and have no visible signs of pests or damage.

Landscape plants that have been dug from the nursery and have had their root ball wrapped in fabric are referred to as "balled and burlapped" (B&B). Purchase B&B plants only during spring and fall—their root systems are most actively growing at those times and are able to overcome the shock of disturbance. Pick plants that appear to have been freshly dug. A loose ball of roots indicates damage—choose another specimen. Choose trees carefully. By the time they are big enough to purchase, their trunk shape and branching habit have been determined. If there is a problem, it may not be correctable.

Bare-Root Material

The term *bare root* refers to a plant that has no soil around its roots when you unpack it, though there is often a bit of moist packing. Plants sent by mail order are often packed bare-root. You can occasionally find perennials in garden centers that are packed this way. They should be dormant but ready to grow new leaves when planted.

Bare-root packing works perfectly well and is in no way harmful to the plants, as long as the roots have remained moist in transit. The plants should have well-branched roots, including the smaller feeder hairs. If you find the roots are bone-dry when you receive your shipment, there is some cause for concern. If this happens, thoroughly soak the plant roots in a container of water for about an hour. Plant them outdoors, and most will revitalize. Report any plants that do not show signs of new growth after three weeks, explaining that they arrived in dry condition. Plant supply houses are so experienced in packing bare-root plants that there is seldom a problem. When there is, it's usually because the shipment was somehow delayed in transit.

Ideally, bare-root plants should be planted immediately after arrival. If that's impossible, unpack them right away and place their roots in a container of water (do not submerge the tops). This will hold them a day or two at most. To hold them longer, plant them in a temporary garden spot in loose, moist soil

into it. Thorough preparation at planting time is a guaranteed timesaver. Make the hole large enough so you can carefully spread the roots out in all directions. You may need to place a pyramid of soil at the bottom of the hole, under the center of the plant, to have it at the right depth, with the roots spread down and around the mound. Then fill in the hole carefully, getting rid of all air pockets, which can cause the death of roots.

Potted Material

Many garden shops and nurseries offer an extensive variety of perennials planted in containers. It is possible to find a diverse array in nearby places and an even wider selection by mail order. When you shop locally, you can choose the individual plants you prefer and see their condition before you buy. Plant societies and garden clubs (the Rhododendron Society, for instance) often have plant sales where you can find unusual varieties.

Potted perennials are offered in a number of sizes, from small plants in three- to four-inch

mixed with builders' sand or perlite; be sure to plant them in their permanent spaces within a week or two. If you must delay planting longer than that, pot the plants in containers and grow them as potted plants until you are ready to plant them in the ground.

Most perennials are best transplanted in the spring or, as a second choice, in the fall. Bearded irises, oriental poppies, and peonies usually fare better if moved only in the fall.

Place bare-root plants at the same depth as in the nursery—look for the soil line on the stem as a guide. Those that arrive as dormant roots have no stems or top growth as indicators. In these cases, specific planting instructions will usually accompany your shipment.

When planting bare-root plants, don't just dig a small hole and jam the roots

🌱 *Good transplants like these should be short and stocky, not spindly or leggy, and have leaves with a healthy color. They should be planted before they become overgrown or root-bound, for fast growth in the garden.*

pots to mature plants in large metal or plastic containers. The small plants are usually only a few months old. In most instances, these will not produce blooms the first season. Those in large containers (often a gallon or more) may be in bloom at the time of purchase and can be expected to quickly become established in their new sites. Smaller plants usually cost less than larger ones; when small plants are priced high, it's because they are rare or exceedingly slow or difficult to propagate.

Container plants should be planted outdoors as soon as possible after purchase. The longer they're kept in containers, the more likely they are to become pot-bound and dry out. If you must hold plants for a long time prior to planting, place them where they'll be under light shade and be sure to water them.

When you are ready to plant your potted perennials, thoroughly moisten the soil before knocking them out of the pot. You can do this by plunging the container into a pail of water (to above the pot's rim) for a few minutes. Remove the container, and cut off any roots sticking out of the pot bottom. Tap the pot on the sides, and then slide the plant out into your hand. If it is stuck, cut the pot open (assuming it is plastic) and peel it off, to avoid damaging to the roots.

Loosen and remove excess soil from around the roots. Most soilless potting mixes will fall away on their own. If the mix adheres to the roots, take away only what comes off easily or you could damage the feeder root hairs. Soilless mixes dry out faster than garden soil, so eliminate what you can without disturbing the root ball.

Always place the plant in the ground at the same depth as it was in the nursery pot. Pack the soil well around the root ball, eliminating air pockets. At the surface, provide a soil dam to hold water near the root area by making a mound of soil in a ring around the plant.

Mail Order

When you unpack a box of plants that have arrived by mail, handle them gently. You'll find they are packed tightly together; this is done to prevent shifting in transit. Check the plants' condition. Are they dormant or growing? Are the roots wet or dry? Are there any rotten spots on the foliage? Are the stems broken? It is amazing what a good job the packers do, but sometimes problems are evident. If so, contact the supplier for a refund or replacement plant.

Even in the best of conditions, plants that have gone through the mail need a period of adjustment. Because the plants have not had a normal amount of light for a few days, they'll need partial shading at first. You can gradually increase the light over a few days. Plant and water them as soon as possible, and make sure they get extra care to harden them off (see below).

TRANSPLANTING

Whether your new plant is coming from your own seedlings or the garden center, care is needed when it's time to plant it in the garden. Transplant in the evening or on a cloudy day to keep the sun from causing too much water loss in the plants and burning tender roots or leaves. Otherwise, provide shade for three to four days while the plant adjusts by setting an overturned box or newspaper cone over each plant. Mulch the plant, and water it well for its first growing season.

Hardening Off

"Harden off" seedlings and cuttings before they go out into the garden. When growing in the protection of a windowsill, light garden, or greenhouse, young plants are tender and can be easily damaged by strong winds or sun. Toughen them up (a process called "hardening off") to make the transition from indoors to outdoors successful.

❀ Days 1 and 2: Put well-watered young plants outdoors in a shady location for several hours, then bring them back indoors.

❀ Days 3 and 4: Increase the length of time seedlings stay outdoors in the shade.

❀ Days 5 to 7: When well adjusted to shade, gradually move sun-loving plants into brighter light, starting with an hour of sun the first day.

❀ Days 8 and beyond: When seedlings can stay out all day without burning or wilting, they are ready for transplanting.

SOURCES OF ORGANIC MATTER

Use these in your compost pile or dig them into garden beds:
- Agricultural remains such as peanut hulls or ground corncobs
- Bark chunks
- Grass clippings
- Kitchen vegetable scraps
- Livestock manure
- Mushroom compost
- Peat moss
- Salt hay
- Seedless weeds
- Shredded bark
- Shredded leaves
- Straw

Frequently Asked Questions

Q: I'm a weekend gardener, and I'm not sure I want to expend the energy it takes to double-dig my new perennial bed. What are the advantages?
A: Double-digging provides richer, fluffier soil for the deep roots that many perennial plants develop. Remember, perennials are long-lived plants, and the time and effort you use to develop their growing environment is well spent. Imagine your disappointment if your investment in perennials was lost because the soil a foot under the surface was too compact for the roots to develop properly.

Q: Which type of pruning shears is best?
A: There are basically two types of pruning shears: anvil and scissors. A good-quality pair of shears should last many years. An advantage the scissors type has over the anvil is that it won't crush the stem while cutting. Good shears can be taken apart for sharpening, and replacement parts can easily be obtained for high-quality models. Long-handled lopping shears are helpful when thinning shrubs and cutting larger stock than hand pruners can cut.

Q: Whenever I make a new place to plant something, I have trouble getting the soil back where it belongs and out of the lawn. What should I do?
A: Put soil on a tarp instead of on the grass when digging a hole for planting. You can easily drag away any excess soil, and you won't have to rake up little clods trapped in the turf. Don't waste that soil. You can use it to fill a raised bed for herbs or vegetables.

Q: There's an old tree stump in the area I want for my perennial border. How can I get rid of it?
A: It takes a professional to remove a large tree stump, and it's costly. An alternative is to make it into a planter. In nature, old stumps slowly begin to decay and provide fertile places for ferns and other interesting small plants to grow. You could plant flora native to your area or fill the opening with brightly colored annual flowers and vines.

Follow nature's lead, and you will get several benefits: You won't have to pay to have the stump ground out; you can grow plants that need good drainage or special soil mixes right in the trunk; and you can create an interesting, sculpturelike structure.

Chip some wood out of the top of the stump to create rooting space. Fill with a soil mix that's appropriate for the plants you intend to grow.

After planting, water as necessary to keep the soil moist. If the stump is too solid to chip away, you can use it as a pedestal for a container filled with trailing or flowering plants.

Q: What is organic gardening, and does it really work?
A: Organic gardening is popular today, and for good reason: It works wonderfully! Organic gardeners shun the use of synthetic chemicals to keep their yards free from potential hazards. But the real success of organic gardens lies in the methods used to keep plants growing vigorously, without a heavy reliance on sprays. Organic gardening cuts right to the heart of the matter: soil.

Soil is the life force of the garden. When enriched with organic matter, the soil becomes moist, fertile, and airy—ideal for healthy plants. It also nourishes a rich population of beneficial organisms such as earthworms and nutrient-releasing bacteria. And it harbors root-extending fungi that help make growing conditions optimal.

Organic gardeners also stress problem prevention in the garden. Putting plants in the right amount of sun, along with suitable soil, proper spacing, and ideal planting and watering, allows most plants to thrive with minimal upsets.

Q: What is the best method of fertilizing a perennial border of many different types of plants?
A: If the soil has been properly prepared with organic matter and the bed is mulched, only an annual application of complete fertilizer is needed, in most cases. In regions with a very long growing season or a lot of rainy weather, you may need periodic applications of fertilizer. In early spring, when the plants begin actively growing, sprinkle all-purpose fertilizer on the soil, following package directions. Apply it by hand to avoid fertilizer landing on and burning the leaves. In addition, top-dress the bed with compost, especially in fall, to rebuild the soil for next year's growth.

Q: Can a live Christmas tree be planted after the holidays?
A: Yes. Prepare the hole well before the ground freezes. Amend the loose soil as you dig so it will be ready for planting, and store the soil where it will not freeze. Choose a tree with a tight, solid root ball, and wrap the ball in plastic to keep it moist while it is in the house. Keep it indoors in a cool room for no more than a week. Plant the tree as soon as possible, then water it well and mulch it.

Q: Is it possible to transplant trees from the woods to the yard?
A: Although it is possible, the success rate is low. Forest tree roots are quite entangled with other trees. They may have either wide-spreading roots or a deep taproot, depending on the species. For the best chance of success, choose only a small specimen, a few feet high at most, and dig and replant in early spring just before new growth will begin. But remember, the tree is already acclimated to the woodland exposure. The shock of being transplanted and the loss of roots conspire to make its survival difficult. Nursery-grown trees have been container grown or root pruned to encourage the development of a small but concentrated root system, which makes them much easier to transplant.

Q: Should I always stake newly planted trees?
A: It is usually best to leave the young tree unstaked, but if the crown of the tree is relatively large compared to the size of the root ball, staking may be needed to prevent the tree from tilting as it settles. Be sure the root ball sits on a firm soil base. Tie the trunk to the stakes with soft or flat plastic string or with wire covered in an old garden hose. This will protect the tender bark from being wounded by the ties. Remove stakes and ties as soon as the tree roots become established.

CHAPTER 3

Garden Care

Once your garden is on its way, you'll really enjoy caring for it and observing its unique development. With a bit of tender loving care, regular maintenance, and more plants, your garden will reward your efforts.

Weed control is important, and it is much easier to achieve if you bid them good riddance from the first sighting. Neatness counts, and nipping and pruning will help keep things in shape. Pests can range from runaway aphids to runaway deer (or moose in some regions), so be prepared.

Sometimes it's hard to categorize garden tasks because they have a natural way of merging. But don't let yourself become overwhelmed by your to-do list. Your garden is a work in progress; your plants require your ongoing participation in their lively growth, development, health, and beauty. As you work in your garden, take the time to savor the seasons and develop a deeper connection with the earth.

Daily Patrol

Most gardeners mix business with pleasure. They ramble around their yard regularly, stopping to admire a healthy plant here, snapping off a few dead flower heads there, then pulling out some weeds in another area. Get in the habit of checking your garden in this way each day. Take the time to appreciate the good points of your garden and also to notice and put a stop to problems when they begin. Keep notes on what you see and what needs to be done. Take a bucket and pocket-size clippers with you, either for harvesting cut flowers or nipping away dead leaves or stems, whichever is your style. Look for new growth and new flowers in addition to checking for pests and problems.

Keeping a watchful eye, you can pull weeds before they drop their seeds, get rid of the first few beetles and prevent their population explosion, and look for places where slug damage has begun. You'll notice flowers that need staking before they land with their faces in the mud. You'll notice the yellowish tinge to the leaves of your favorite plant in time to renew the fertilizer. Perhaps it's especially true with gardening: An ounce of prevention is worth a pound of cure.

 This mixed border of annuals, perennials, and shrubs is a joy to experience. During your daily patrol, note its seasonal changes and deal with small problems before they get out of control.

GARDEN RECORDS

If you find it difficult to stay on top of gardening tasks, a garden journal may be the perfect solution. Keep records on such information as what is happening in your garden, what plants and equipment you have acquired, and garden chores. You can store your notes in a blank notebook, a structured garden journal, a planning calendar, or a handheld digital organizer or computer. Another option is to create your own personalized garden journal complete with prompts that are specific to your garden. Print or photocopy multiple pages with whatever headers you choose, and store them in a three-ring binder. Then, all you'll need to do is fill in the blanks.

WALKWAYS

Before you can maintain anything, you have to get there. A path in the middle of a wide garden gives you access without having to walk through the soil. A narrow path can run along the front of a garden, serving as an edging, making the garden look neat and keeping the grass out.

Some prompts you might include are:

- ❀ The date
- ❀ Weather this week (or today)
- ❀ To-do checklist
- ❀ General observations
- ❀ Equipment purchases
- ❀ Plant acquisitions (common name, botanical name, cultivar name, source, etc.)
- ❀ What was planted today
- ❀ Plant performance
- ❀ Garden problems
- ❀ Plants in bloom
- ❀ Harvests
- ❀ Tasks done
- ❀ Ideas for improvement
- ❀ Wish list
- ❀ Wildlife sightings
- ❀ Garden visitors
- ❀ Gardens visited

You'll also need a place to store tags and records of your plant acquisitions. If you take pictures of your garden, keep them with your notes. Over time, your garden journal will prove to be an invaluable planning tool. For example, if you're browsing through seed catalogs during the winter season and need to know what blooms at the same time as peonies so you can group them together, the answer will be in your notes. If someone asks you which of your tomatoes tastes so wonderful, but you can't quite remember what you planted, you can simply refer back to your records. Each season's successes and disappointments will be on hand so you can make informed decisions when planning new plantings.

Your notes can also remind you when to plant seeds or take cuttings. For example, seeds such as tomatoes and peppers need to be planted six to eight weeks before the last spring frost, but squash and cucumbers need to be planted only three weeks before the last spring frost. It can be hard to remember everything unless it's written down. Keep good propagation records to track how successful each operation has been and how the young plants are proceeding through the seasons. These records will guide you about when to

❀ *Take a basket or bucket along on your daily patrol, so you can deadhead flowers and trim the garden as you go.*

plant, divide, start seeds, or collect seeds for future years. Avid plant propagators may appreciate records like these:

❀ How long seedlings grew indoors before being transplanted outdoors and whether that timing allowed enough, too little, or too much time for a great performance outdoors.

❀ When you planted seedlings outdoors and how well they responded to the weather conditions at that time.

❀ When the first shoots of perennial flowers and herbs emerged in spring and were ready to divide.

❀ When you took stem cuttings from roses, lilacs, geraniums, impatiens, chrysanthemums, dahlias, and other plants. Rooting success often depends on the season in which the cuttings were taken.

❀ When seedpods matured and were ready to harvest for next year's crop.

Fertilizing and Feeding

Fertilizing your garden after it has been prepared is part of its continuing care. Commercial fertilizers are applied in dry granular form or are mixed with water prior to application, according to the type and the instructions on the package. Dry fertilizers are broadcast over the soil surface and dug in, and liquid ones are applied with a sprayer connected to a garden hose or with a watering can. Regular granular forms such as 5-10-10 only last in the soil for about four weeks. Slow-release pellet fertilizers last longer, dissolving into the soil over an extended period of time, releasing essential nutrients throughout the growing season. Although they may cost more, a single application in spring lasts for months. Fertilizer brands and types vary in their proportion of main ingredients as well as in trace elements and microingredients.

Manures, rock powders, and organic supplements are used as fertilizer. They are bulkier than chemical fertilizers, in most cases, and

deliver long-lasting results. Some supplements to investigate include cottonseed meal, peanut

HIGH-SPEED GARDENING: FERTILIZE WITH COMPOST TEA

Make your own mild liquid fertilizer to give established plants a quick boost. Add finished compost from any source to a bucket, filling it a third of the way. Fill the bucket with water and give it a couple of stirs with a trowel or stick. You should have mud. Let it settle for a moment, then use this nutrient-laden water on the soil around your plants. With large shrubs you can pour it directly from the bucket. Strain it and pour it from a watering can with a water-breaker if you use it on small plants. The compost residue left in the bucket can be used as mulch or top dressing anywhere in the garden.

hulls, dried and bagged cow manure, greensand, ground limestone, granite dust, and many more, some of which are regional. Our nation's zoos have even begun selling "Zoo Doo." If supplements like these are not packed in bags or boxes with labels, the dealer can usually tell you which nutrients they supply.

Applications of liquid fertilizers deliver immediate results because the nutrients are directly available to the plants. The liquids can be organic, such as fish emulsion, or not. When fertilizing transplants, make a weak solution and apply it after the plants have been set into the soil. Half the usual strength is often recommended. Thereafter, several side-dressings of granular plant food sprinkled around each plant at two-week intervals should carry annuals through the rest of the growing season.

For best absorption, fertilize when the soil is moist. Apply fertilizer on the soil rather than on the plants' leaves. The plants, your hands, and the fertilizer itself, if granular, should be dry. Always wash your hands after handling fertilizer.

Although the concentration of nutrients in compost and organic mulch is low compared to granular fertilizer, it releases its nutrients in a gradual way and improves the vitality and workability of the soil.

Mulching and Top-Dressing

Cover garden beds with a layer of mulch to keep weeds down and reduce the need for water. Annual weed seeds are less likely to sprout when the soil is covered with enough mulch to keep the soil surface in the dark. When it comes to water, even a thin layer of mulch—nature's moisturizer—will reduce evaporation from the soil surface. Thicker mulches can reduce water use by as much as 50 percent. Organic mulches break down slowly and add nutrients to the soil, so mulch should be renewed from time to time.

Apply mulch over the entire root area of the plant. Although a depth of only a few inches of mulch is sufficient, it is best to use it in a broad area. Mulches vary in their appearance, makeup, and texture, which will influence how you use them. Here are some examples:

❀ Appearance: For a soothing, natural-looking garden, use dark-colored organic mulches made of bark or compost. For a brilliant-looking garden, consider a mulch of bright gravel. In utilitarian gardens such as a vegetable garden, plastic sheeting or straw make an excellent mulch.

❀ Soil improvement: This calls for the use of organic mulches that break down to add organic matter to the soil.

❀ Texture: For maximum effectiveness with only a thin layer, look for fine-textured mulches such as twice-shredded bark, compost, or cocoa hulls. For an airy mulch, try thicker layers of coarse-textured mulches such as straw or bark chunks.

Watering

You've watered well at planting time, but the need for water goes on and sometimes exceeds the supply. If plants receive the water they need, whether from nature or irrigation, they will respond with vigorous growth. How do you judge when to water and how much water to give? Much depends on weather and soil conditions. You can test by poking your finger into the soil (the surface can look deceptively wet or dry) and feeling how moist or dry it is. Or peel back some mulch and feel the soil beneath it. Leaves begin to wilt after drought damage has begun—prevent this if you can.

It is important to water plants on a regular basis but also to keep from wasting water with excessive usage. We have all seen timed systems watering a lawn during a rain. Different plants have different water needs. A vegetable garden drinks a lot to keep growing fast, but trees and shrubs have deeper roots and can usually reach adequate water supplies on their own, except when newly planted or during times of drought. Water new plants the first season after planting if nature doesn't supply enough rain. The young root systems need a little extra care to become established in the new location. Estab-

HOSE CARTS

Wheel hose carts around the yard instead of dragging armloads of hoses and causing wear and tear on your back. Hose carts consist of a reel with a crank that you can use to neatly coil the hose, eliminating tangles, knots, and kinks. This reel is set on a two- or four-wheeled base with a handle for easy pulling. Look for large-wheeled types if you're rolling the cart over the lawn or rough ground. Smaller wheels are fine on a paved path or patio.

lished perennials can get by with less water, but annuals require more frequent watering because their root systems do not extend as far down into the soil.

There are times when gray water can be used on plants to reduce water use. Gray water is the leftover tap water from activities such as rinsing vegetables at the kitchen sink. However, avoid using water contaminated with water-softening salts, harsh detergents, fats, oils, or other extras. Gray water has been used successfully in arid regions and is well worth using anywhere. It helps prevent stress on wells during drought and lowers utility bills for people with municipal water. Capture gray water in a basin or other container stored close to the sink, where it will be handy to pull out and use. Transfer the gray water to a watering can before watering potted plants or new plantings. A little moisture in a time of need will make a big difference.

GRAY WATER

Capture the cool, clean water that otherwise runs down the drain when you are waiting for warm water to come from the tap, and use it to water plants. Keep an empty watering can or milk jug near the sink for this purpose.

Use a water breaker on the end of your hose to change heavy water flow into a gentle sprinkle. This helps prevent soil compaction and spreads the water more evenly across planting areas. Put an adjustable spray nozzle on the end of the hose, watering only with the setting that produces fine droplets in a gentle spray and wide arc. Save the strong blasts for washing the car. Or, look for spray heads developed specifically for garden use. Some are set on angled bases, making it easy to reach in between plants. Others are on long poles for watering hanging baskets. Water breakers should be put on watering cans, too, especially when watering young plants such as seedlings, which can be broken or uprooted with a strong drenching.

WATER-SAVING TIPS

Redirect runoff from downspouts into flowerbeds or lawn areas to give plants extra water every time it rains. Flexible tubing can be connected to the end of the downspout and directed into nearby plantings around the foundation of the house or to flower or vegetable gardens. For maximum benefits, shape beds like a shallow bowl to collect the water and give it time to soak in. Or, as an alternative, the garden could be made fairly level with moisture-gathering saucers made around newly planted trees or shrubs or plants with high moisture needs.

In dry climates, the tubing can be covered with soil or mulch and kept connected all the time. In climates with periods of overly wet weather, the tubing should be disconnected during soggy seasons to prevent oversaturation of the soil, which causes plants to rot.

PLANTS TO WATER IN THE MORNING

Apples
Beans
Begonias
Blackberries
Cherries
Chrysanthemums
Cucumbers
Dahlias
Geraniums
Grapes
Melons
Peaches
Pears
Peonies
Plums
Raspberries
Roses
Strawberries
Tomatoes

Place hose guides at the edges of garden beds to keep the hose from crushing nearby plants when you pull it taut. Hose guides, such as a wooden stake pounded into the ground at an outward angle, prevent the hose from sliding into the garden and squashing plants. Decorative hose guides can be found at some garden centers, mail-order garden suppliers, or craft shows. You could also improvise by using things like garden statues or birdbaths.

Growth and Overgrowth

A garden is a busy place, with many things to see at once, so it's astonishing how one small dead plant will stand out in a healthy flower border. Keeping order involves getting rid of messy tidbits such as flowers gone to seed and yellowed leaves, preventing or removing weeds, training or staking tall or climbing plants, and nipping and cutting for overall plant shape, tidiness, and health.

PINCHING BACK

Pinch annuals like coleus, browallia, and petunias to keep them full. These plants can get tall and gangly as they grow. Removing the top inch or two of stem will correct this. More is at work here than shortening the stem. Removing the terminal bud (at the stem tip) forces side branches to grow, making the plant fuller.

PINCHING SCHEDULE

When pinching for bushiness, scheduling is important. You want to start early enough to make an impact. And you need to stop in July so flower buds can develop before cold weather strikes. Start with this pinching schedule but feel free to modify it as you gain experience:

- Pinch shoot tips when the stems are four to six inches high.
- Pinch again three weeks later.
- Pinch again in late June.
- In regions with a long growing season, such as Zones 7 and 8, pinch again in mid-July.

Also pinch perennial asters and mums. Remove the stem tip with a pinch of your fingernails or with pruning shears to keep the plants compact and bushy. Flowering plants purchased in a pot have been specially treated to make the plants bushy and full. If left untouched the following year, they will grow tall, scraggly stems that are more likely to need staking.

If you want fewer but larger flowers on your peonies, pinch off two of the three flower buds in a cluster on a single stem, well before they are ready to open. The plant's energy will be routed to the remaining bud. Blossoms of peaches, apples, and roses can be thinned, too.

Shear reblooming perennials such as catmint and 'Moonglow' coreopsis to promote a second flush of flowers. Getting rid of the old flowers and seedpods encourages new growth, new buds, and new flowers.

WEEDING

The best cure for weeds is prevention. Plant weedy spots with thick-growing ground cover to minimize weed growth. Ground cover works well on banks, in sun or shade, under fencing where it's hard to keep weeds down, beside outbuildings, and even under trees where it's too shady for grass to grow. It's important to start the ground-cover bed in weed-free soil, however, so the ground cover can take over without competition. Turn the soil with a rototiller or spade, let the weeds sprout, and then turn it again. Repeat this until the weeds are almost gone.

Choose a ground cover that will spread vigorously and grow thickly enough to crowd out any weeds that try to get in. In shady areas, try ivy, pachysandra, barrenwort, wild ginger, or periwinkle. In sun, try creeping junipers, daylilies, ground-cover roses, or other plants that are suited for your climate.

For good results fast, buy plenty of plants and space them relatively close together. If this is too expensive, spread plants farther apart, and mulch the open areas to discourage weeds. Plan to keep a close eye on the new garden for the first year and pull up or hoe down any weeds that appear. Water and fertilize as needed to get the ground-cover plants growing and spreading quickly. Once they've covered the soil solidly, there won't be any space for weeds.

Unfortunately, no matter how diligent you are, weeds are bound to crop up somewhere eventually. Use a sharp hoe to scrape off weeds, especially annual ones, instead of stooping and pulling them. Using a hoe is quicker and easier than hand-weeding, plus it does a superb job. If you catch weeds when they are young seedlings, a single swipe will eliminate them. If they are older, cut them down before they go to seed to prevent future generations of weeds. If

your garden is too small for a long-handled hoe, get a small hand tool with a hoe or scraper on the end.

Perennial weeds such as dandelions may have large underground roots that will resprout after hoeing. When the soil is moist, use an asparagus fork or dandelion weeder (a stick with a forked prong on the end) or the corner of the hoe blade to dig down and loosen the root. Then pull it up by hand.

PRUNING

Pruning is an aspect of gardening that many people find confusing. When to prune? What to prune? How to do it? When to call in the experts?

When to prune depends on the type of plant and the reason for pruning. As a general rule, you should prune in late winter or early spring to stimulate growth and in early summer to slow growth. However, there are exceptions. Trees, shrubs, and vines that bloom in spring are blooming on branches whose flower buds have formed the previous year. They are usually pruned immediately after they finish blooming,

Spring-blooming shrubs like this rhododendron can be pruned after they finish blooming, not before.

to prevent losing this year's flowers and to stimulate fresh new growth that will produce more flowers the next year. Those that bloom in summer are usually blooming on new wood. Prune them during the following spring.

Most hedges can be pruned in any season, as needed. It is best not to prune at the very end of summer because this can promote soft, new growth that is susceptible to winter damage. You can always eliminate dead wood or a badly straggling branch. Informal blooming hedges such as forsythia and rose-of-Sharon may be pruned after blooming.

There are two types of coniferous plants that require different types of pruning. The first are those that put out their entire year's new growth all at once, in late spring. This group includes pines, spruces, and firs. They can be pruned by removing up to two-thirds of the new growth while it is still fresh and pale green. With pines, this process is called *candling*. Do not prune the shoots all the way back to old wood because they will not produce new shoots from those sections. Evergreens that grow throughout the summer, such as yews, arborvitae, and junipers, are pruned once in early summer and again, if necessary, later in the season. They can also be pruned more heavily, down to old wood if necessary.

What to prune depends a great deal on the effect you want to create. There are major differences between the way to prune shrubs and the way to prune trees. Except under rare circumstances, ornamental trees should be left to take their natural shape and appearance, resulting in little need for pruning. They are usually pruned only to remove damaged or diseased branches or ones that cross, rub together, or form an overly acute angle with the trunk. Suckers (also called water sprouts) should also be removed. Suckers are upright, unbranched sprouts that often appear at the base of the tree or on the lower trunk. Sometimes the upper limbs of overly dense shade trees can be thinned to open them up, allowing more light to reach the garden below. In most cases, major pruning on a large tree should be left to a professional arborist, especially if there are electrical wires nearby. Large branches require a pruning saw and should be removed back to the trunk or a main branch. Do not leave a stub, or the healing process will take too long.

Pruning Shrubs

Different pruning techniques are used on shrubs, depending on the desired effect. Formal hedges, topiaries, and other closely clipped forms are sheared, which means all branches are clipped to the same length for a smooth edge. Some shrubs that bloom on new wood are also sheared back annually to the base to encourage a maximum number of branches and, thus, more flowers.

When a more natural shape is desired, shrubs are generally thinned, especially fast-growing types of deciduous shrubs such as forsythia and weigela. Older or excessively long branches and weaker secondary branches are removed down to a main branch or to the base of the plant. This allows room for younger branches to grow, producing a heavy flush of flower buds for the next bloom season. Thinning (renewal pruning) is usually the preferred method for pruning spring-flowering shrubs and is carried out as soon as the year's flowers have faded. The prunings can sometimes be used for cuttings.

When pruning, begin by removing old, weak, damaged, or crowded branches at their base. But don't indiscriminately shear off the top of the plant. The terminal buds on the branch tips release hormones that encourage root growth and maintain a slow, orderly pattern of growth. These are both desirable qualities worth preserving in your shrubs.

Consider changing an overgrown shrub into a multistemmed tree. This works nicely with flowering plums, black haw viburnums, winged euonymus, and lilacs, all of which can grow to be 12 to 15 feet tall. Begin by removing small, crowded upright stems to reveal a handful of shapely mature branches that can serve as trunks. Cut side shoots off the trunks up to about five feet off the ground, creating a tree form. Continue pruning as needed to keep the trunks clear of growth.

BRING NATURE INDOORS

Cut flowering stems from your shrubs and bring them indoors to use in big bouquets. If you have large vases that dwarf ordinary annual or perennial stems, fill them with long branches of forsythia, lilac, or viburnum. What a wonderful way to celebrate spring!

Pruning Vines

In general, vines should be treated in the same manner as shrubs. Vines grown for their foliage often produce overly exuberant growth, especially once they are established. They need to be pruned regularly and can be pruned at any time except late summer or early fall. Pruning at that time of year can result in new growth that does not have time to harden properly before winter arrives.

TRIMMING AND DEADHEADING

Plants are trying to live their lives, not just please a gardener. They flower and go to seed. The seeds are their next generation, and they receive energy from the plant. If you want your garden plants to go on growing and blooming, you need to trim off the seed heads (unless you wish to collect and grow those seeds). This makes the garden look neater and diverts energy away from seeds and into fresh roots, leaves, and flowers. Just a few straggly seed stalks or pods can make a garden look untidy. If you don't notice it at first, take a photograph and check it out. However, dead-heading can sometimes be carried too far. Seeds of rudbeckia and other meadow plants can feed our songbirds, and seed plumes of sedum and ornamental grass can become attractive garden features in winter.

With reblooming roses, you'll want to remove the spent flowers in the early summer to promote a new crop of blooms. But in late summer or fall you may choose to leave them in place to make fat orange pods (the rose hips) for winter ornament.

DEADHEAD TO INCREASE BLOOMS

Deadhead hybrid rhododendrons and mountain laurels to increase next year's bloom. Once the flowers begin to fade, use your thumb and forefinger (or small needle-nose pruning shears) to cut off the soft, immature flowering cluster. Just be careful not to damage nearby buds or shoots, which will soon be sprouting into new branches.

STAKING

To stake plants well, it helps to anticipate the growth that occurs in a season. Plants that look fine in June can be top-heavy and keeling over by July or August. Tall flowers and vegetables may not be able to support the weight of their flowers and fruit. Plants growing in less sun than they like are more in need of staking or props than others.

Stakes, cages, or wire grids keep tall plants from falling on their faces. Stakes can be made of wood, bamboo, or wire coated with plastic. You can even use tree or shrub prunings, straight or branched, as natural-looking props for your plants. This is an old British trick called *pea staking*. It helps perennials stay upright and look natural without glaring metal-lic stakes or forced shapes that result from corseting with twine. Even better, pea staking costs nothing but a little time. When the peren-nials begin to arise in spring, set the ends of sturdy branched twigs around the plant. The twigs should be about as long as the height of the perennial. As the stems grow, they will fill out to hide the twigs. You can cut off any errant woody stems that remain in sight after the perennials reach full height. When you tie plants to their stakes, be sure to use garden twine or soft string or yarn, not wire, which can easily slice through plant stems.

A classic staking system for climbing plants such as beans, peas, cherry tomatoes, and morning glories is a teepee made of four or five sturdy, bamboo, wood, or metal poles (six feet is a good length). Set the bottoms about six inches into the ground in a square or circular manner. Tie the poles together firmly at the top with garden twine. This will make a cone-shape support that can be taken down after use and used again the next year. Peas have tendrils that clasp the poles, and morning glories twine around them, but most other plants need to be trained as they grow and tied with string.

Flowers such as delphiniums, asters, dahlias, and Shasta daisies are now available in compact sizes that are self-supporting. Shorter types of daylilies are less likely to become floppy in low light than taller types. Compact types of peas and tomatoes, though not entirely self-supporting, can be allowed to grow loosely on their own, or they may need only small cages or supports such as twiggy brush.

For taller types, you can stake each plant individually, inserting the stake several weeks before the growth gets going and tying the plant loosely to the stake at intervals as it grows. The ties should loosely connect the main stem to the stake and should not bind the individual leaves or flowers. Once a plant has flopped over, it is usually too late to do much about it.

Bushy plants such as peonies can be propped up with greater ease by using grow-through or grid supports. You can buy commercial grid supports, which are handsome round or square grids neatly set on straight legs; green grids are more camouflaged amid the foliage than metallic grids. You can also make your own grid supports out of a sheet of wire mesh, cut a little wider than the plant it will support. The extra length can be bent into legs, or legs can be made from wire or coat hangers. Get the supports in place early, before the small flower buds start expanding and become too large to grow through the holes in the grids. Set the grid over a newly emerging perennial in spring. The stems grow though it, retaining their shape while staying firmly upright.

Larger garden structures such as trellises, pergolas, arches, and fences can be used as plant supports. A chain-link or wire-mesh fence can be used to support vegetables or flowers.

END-OF-SEASON CLEANUP

At the end of the growing season, it is cleanup time. You should eliminate plant debris where pests can lurk over the winter. The compost pile is a better place for brown flower stems, frozen impatiens plants, dead leaves, cornstalks, and weeds. But don't throw away things that are beautiful. Hosta leaves turn golden, just like autumn leaves, and you may as well enjoy them that way before they turn brown and you clean them up. Throw any disease-infested plant parts into the trash; do not compost them. When the garden is clean, you can mulch it for easier digging next spring. Mow down old flower stalks in late fall to clean up a flower garden with ease. Before mowing anything but grass with your mower, make sure it has a safety feature that will prevent debris from being thrown out at you. Using a suitable lawn mower can save you plenty of time compared with cutting back the flower stalks by hand. If you allow the old stems to scatter around the garden, instead of bagging them, you may find an abundance of self-sown seedlings arising in the springtime.

Plant Propagation

Starting your own plants from seeds, cuttings, divisions, and layering saves money and expands options. But be prepared to give propagation a certain amount of attention. Young plants need tender loving care to get them off to a good start.

Many plants grow well from seeds, especially annual flowers, herbs, and vegetables. You can find new, rare, or old-fashioned varieties that aren't available in local nurseries in seed catalogs. Seed sowing allows you to grow a few, dozens, or even hundreds of seedlings from a seed packet that costs a dollar or two. That's economy!

Certain special plants don't grow from seeds. They need to be cloned (vegetatively propagated). This is done by rooting sections of stems, roots, and, in a few cases, leaves. Clump-forming perennial plants can be divided into several pieces. Stems of some kinds of plants can be rooted while still attached to the mother plant. This is called *layering*. Some plants can be propagated equally well in several ways. For example, lantana can be grown from seed (flower color will vary); started from cuttings, either in soil or in water; or propogated via layering.

DIVISION OF PERENNIALS

Easily divide daylilies, hostas, astilbes, or other clump-forming perennials with a sharp shovel. Just slice off an edge of the clump in spring or late summer. Uproot it and replant elsewhere. Keep the new division watered for at least several weeks or until it has regenerated lost roots.

Divide a large perennial clump into small divisions to get many little plants fast. This is a quick and easy way to make enough plants for the big drifts of perennials such as asters, goldenrod, sneezeweed, and blazing stars before encouraging them to grow. Division renews a declining clump of perennials. As many perennials grow, new shoots emerge at the perimeter of the clump, which keeps spreading outward. The center becomes increasingly older—sometimes woody, sometimes completely barren. In spring, late summer, or fall, dig up the entire clump. Cut out the old heart and discard it. Refresh the soil with organic matter, and replant the healthy young pieces.

Perennials that can be divided easily include asters, daylilies, yarrow, phlox, lady's mantle, salvia, coreopsis, hardy geraniums, irises, mint, thyme, oregano, and winter savory. Here's how to make smaller divisions:

❀ In spring or late summer, dig up the entire perennial plant clump and wash soil off the roots with a hose.

❀ If dividing in late summer, cut back the foliage by half or more.

❀ Use your hands to break rooted sprouts into individual pieces. If roots are too hard to work apart by hand, slice them free with a knife or pruning shears. Each section should contain at least one leafy sprout and one healthy root.

❀ Replant very small divisions into pots of peat-based planting mix and tend them carefully until they get a little bigger. Larger divisions can go right back into the garden if kept moist until they become reestablished.

PLANTS FROM SEED

There are many good reasons to grow plants from seed and as many ways to do so. Each type of plant has its unique seed. It is designed to grow but will only be coaxed to sprout in an environment that seems to offer life support to the plant. It's a challenge to meet the special needs of certain types of seeds but easier with others whose requirements are more straightforward. Be sure to read seed packet instructions. You can start seeds indoors or out, during different times of year. There is more than one right way to handle most types of seeds.

Seedlings Indoors

Indoors you have more control over growing conditions and a lot of flexibility about what time of year to plant the seeds. Use specially prepared seed-starting medium, which is available from mail-order seed companies and from garden centers. Start seeds indoors under lights,

MINI-GREENHOUSES

Start seeds or cuttings in an aquarium or clear sweater box to keep humidity high. These are more permanent alternatives to makeshift options with plastic and are good for cuttings that need more overhead and rooting room than seedlings. To reuse these containers, wash them with soapy water, rinse, and sterilize with a solution of 1 part bleach to 10 parts water.

rather than in a window, for even, compact growth. Seedlings must have bright light from the moment they peer up out of the soil or they will be weak and leggy. In climates with cloudy weather or homes without south-facing windows, sun may not be reliable enough. A light garden is an ideal solution.

Set seedlings in their containers a few inches below a fluorescent shop light. You can place seedlings on a table or counter and suspend the shop light from the ceiling over them, or set up three or four tiered light stands. You can adapt ordinary shelves by attaching lights to the bottoms of the shelves and setting growing trays below each light. Put the lights on a timer set to turn on 14 hours a day and then off again (one less job for you). You can't beat the results!

Make a mini-greenhouse under lights with a clear plastic garment bag. This traps humidity near seedlings, helping to protect them from wilting. To cover nursery flats full of seedlings, bend two wire coat hangers into arches and prop them in the corners of the flat, one at each end. Work the plastic over the top of the hangers, and tuck the loose ends in below the flat. It's even easier to make a greenhouse cover for individual pots. Slide two sticks into opposite sides of the pot. Then top with the plastic and fold it under the pot.

If starting seeds in a window, take extra care to maximize light. Use a south-facing window that will receive sun all day. It should not be blocked by a protruding roof overhang or an evergreen tree or shrub. (If you don't have a south-facing window, you should consider using plant lights.) Hang foil reflectors behind the flat to keep seedlings from leaning toward the sun. If the seedlings are sitting on a windowsill, make a tent of foil behind them, with the shiny side facing the seedlings. This will reflect sunlight and illuminate the dark side of the seedlings. They will grow much sturdier and straighter as a result.

Don't transplant seedlings into a larger pot until they have one or two sets of true leaves. This allows seedlings to develop enough roots to be self-supporting, even if a few roots are lost in the process. It's also a time when seedling roots are fairly straight and compact, making them easy to separate from nearby plants. This is not as simple as counting the number of leaves on the stem, however, because the seedling usually has an extra set of leaves called *cotyledons*. They emerge first and store food that nourishes the sprouting seedlings. Looking closely, you can see that cotyledons are shaped differently from true leaves. Squash seedlings, for instance, have oval cotyledons, but the true leaves are broad and lobed. When transplanting, handle the seedlings by the cotyledons to prevent squashing the delicate stem.

Seedlings Outdoors

There are times to plant seeds directly in the garden. When this is successful, it is economical and very effective, for the plants grow without the disruption of being transplanted. Prepare the soil for planting (see Chapter 2) and be sure the plot is fertile and smooth. Make rows or wide swaths for the seeds, following the timing and spacing directions on the packets. Straight lines help you discriminate between your plants and the weeds. The classic way to make straight lines is with posts and strings as a guide. Hoe along the string line for the shallow row. Plant seeds at the depth indicated on the packet and cover lightly with soil. Tamp down the soil over the seeds to make sure they are contacting the soil, and water them in. Be sure to mark the rows.

Many of the guidelines for indoor planting also apply to outdoor planting, but a main difference is pest control. Tiny plants are vulnerable to everything from aphids to chipmunks, so it's a good idea to plant more than you need and thin the plants later. Once they get past babyhood and are several inches high, thin them; they need space for the fast growth they are about to make.

Using a Coldframe

If a greenhouse is not for you, perhaps you can find a place for the similar but much smaller coldframe. Make a coldframe from cinderblocks and old window frames, or purchase one ready to go. It helps keep frost and pests out, gets

---

HIGH-SPEED GARDENING: SIMPLE SEED STARTER

Plastic containers with transparent lids (such as yogurt cups and salad bar containers) are an excellent, carefree environment for starting small or difficult seeds. They provide a "bubble," like a terrarium, which keeps moisture steady without outside intervention. Wash the containers thoroughly with soapy water, sterilize them with a solution of 1 part bleach to 10 parts water, and drain. Fill them partway (half to one third full) with a freely draining, sterile seed-starting medium that is premoistened so that it is neither dry nor soggy. Plant the seeds, label the containers, provide light with a timed lighting system (direct sun would cook them), and wait for the tiny plants to emerge.

good light, and is an ideal place for starting seeds. You can start seeds in a coldframe as if they were indoors, though a little later in the season if you have cold winters and springs. Coldframes are also good for starting perennial seeds that need a cold spell to break dormancy before they germinate.

Self-Sown Plants

In nature, most plants are self-sown. Your garden can contain self-sown plants as well. When plants are in the appropriate habitat, their seeds will ripen and grow. Some of the best plants for self-sowing are poppies, foxgloves, sweet William, money plant (lunaria), and columbine. If there are too many, thin them, and transplant the extras to pots or other garden spots that suit them.

PLANTS FROM CUTTINGS AND LAYERING

If you need another chair you may have to buy one, but if you want another butterfly bush or azalea, nature will help you make one free of charge. Taking cuttings or making layers (rooted pieces still attached to the parent plant) is easier with some types of plants than others. The options widen as your skill grows. Plants from cuttings and layers (vegetative propagation) give you new plants that are genetically identical to their parents. Roots emerge from the green cambium layer just under the bark of shrubs; try to expose some of the cambium so it can connect to the rooting medium.

❧ Coleus (back) is one of the easiest plants to root from cuttings. Trim off a piece about four or five inches long, remove the lower leaves, and set it into a glass of water on a windowsill or into shaded soil that is kept very moist.

CUTTING TIP

Set a large, clear glass jar over cuttings of roses, willows, dogwoods, or other easily rooted stems put directly in the garden. The jar will maintain high humidity around the cutting and help prevent wilting. But be sure to protect the jar from the hot sun so the cuttings don't get cooked.

Cuttings from Stems

With the right kind of coaxing, you can get pieces of plant stems to sprout roots and new leaves. These are often pieces from the branch tips and vary in size, though six inches long is a basic size.

Softwood Cuttings

Softwood stem cuttings are taken in late spring or early summer for fast rooting. Early spring shoots are vigorous but soft and succulent. They may wilt before they root. But if the shoots are allowed to mature for a month or two, they firm up slightly and are ideal for rooting.

Clip stems for cuttings in the morning when they are fresh and full of water. Once the stem is severed from its root, it will not be able to soak up moisture for several weeks or until new roots develop.

Use a sharp knife or razor for a clean cut. Soak the cuttings in water to hydrate them fully.

Remove lower leaves. If any leaves are very large, cut them in half to reduce water loss through the leaves.

Insert the lower half of the cutting into a pot or flat filled with propagating soil. Put it in a shaded coldframe or area with good light but not direct sunlight. Mist it twice daily if possible, and keep the soil constantly moist. Plants also root readily in sealed plastic containers that serve as mini-greenhouses.

After several weeks (rooting time varies with species and with weather), test to see if the cutting has formed roots by tugging at it slightly. If it has made roots, it will resist. If not, tuck it back into the soil and be patient another few weeks. Allow the roots to grow until the newly rooted plant can be set in the garden. Then treat it like any new transplant.

 These clippings provide a touch of beauty to a windowsill, where they can be enjoyed until their roots are long enough for transplanting.

Hardwood Cuttings

Hardwood cuttings are taken the same way as softwood cuttings but from older wood or plant portions, often in fall for rooting over winter. Use rooting hormone on older or hard-to-root cuttings. Rooting hormone, available in powdered and liquid forms, contains chemicals (called *auxins*) that allow cut stems to begin to produce roots. It must be applied as soon as the cutting is taken and before the cutting is put into sterile planting mix. Not all stems need rooting hormone (mints and willows, for instance), but it can make slow starters much more reliable.

Test to see if a cutting has rooted by gently tugging on the stem. If it shows resistance, roots have formed. After the first sign of rooting, allow the roots to develop for several more weeks before transplanting.

Cuttings from Roots

Take root cuttings when stem cuttings are not possible. Some perennials, like Oriental poppies and horseradish, have clusters of foliage close to the ground without any stems at all. You can dig up a root and cut it into pieces that may sprout into new plants. With horseradish, you can cut off a side root in the fall and replant it for a new start in the spring. But root cuttings of most perennials need more help. Here's the method:

❁ Dig the root in early spring before shoots begin to emerge.

❁ Cut the roots into pieces an inch or two long.

HIGH-SPEED GARDENING: PLANTS THAT ROOT IN WATER

There are a few easygoing plants that will form roots in a glass of water on a windowsill. Some of these are ivy, wandering Jew, coleus, basil, and salvia. In a few weeks, when the roots are an inch long, set your new plant into the garden or a flowerpot filled with moist, rich potting medium. Keep it shaded and moist for a few more weeks, and then it is on its own.

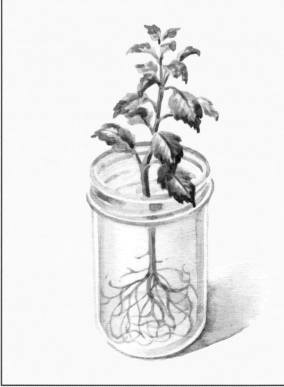

❈ Lay them horizontally in a flat of well-drained propagating mix. Cover lightly.

❈ Keep slightly moist but not wet (to prevent root rot) and watch for new sprouts to emerge.

❈ When the cuttings are growing strongly, transplant them into containers or plant them in the garden.

Layering

Use layering to propagate hard-to-root shrubs such as azaleas. Layering also works with shrubs that have low-growing or creeping branches, such as creeping rosemary. Layered stems develop roots while still connected to the mother plant, which helps nourish the rooting process. Follow these steps:

❈ In spring, select a low, flexible branch that will bend down to the ground easily.

❈ Prepare well-drained but moisture-retentive soil where the stem will touch the ground.

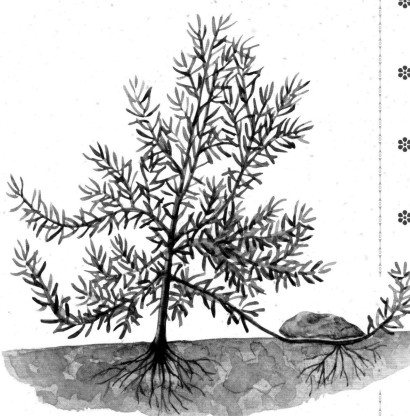

EASY PLANTS TO ROOT

- Chrysanthemum
- Coleus
- Dahlia
- Fuchsia
- Hydrangea
- Impatiens
- Ivy
- Mint
- Plumbago
- Red-twig dogwood
- Rose
- Salvia
- Tomato
- Vines (most types)
- Willow
- Zonal geranium

❈ Nick the bark off the side of the stem that will touch the ground, and remove the leaves near the nick.

❈ Dust the cut (which has exposed the cambium layer) with rooting hormone, available from garden centers.

❈ Cover the barren and nicked stem with soil. Top it with a rock, or pin it in place with a stake or metal pin.

❈ The branch tip will become the new plant. If it is an upright grower, stake the tip upright to give it a good shape.

❈ Keep the rooting area moist for several months, until roots develop and become large enough to support the new plant.

❈ Cut the new plant free from the parent branch and transplant it to a pot or new site in the garden.

Pests and Other Problems

Some type of pest is bound to "bug" you, no matter how much effort you put into your garden. You may notice yellow patches in the lawn, holes in leaves, or stunted plant growth. The more you water and fertilize, the more you may play host to pests. Or it may be that insects and diseases are making a neglected area even worse. Alas, pests are everywhere, but help is here with organic remedies that are easy on the environment, as well as safety guidelines if you have to resort to chemical methods.

Disease is another problem you may encounter. Plants with enough space are likely to be healthy, but in an overcrowded garden, airflow stagnates, just as it does in an overcrowded room. Without free air circulation, foliage dampened by dew, rain, or sprinkling will stay wet longer and be more susceptible to fungus and other diseases.

INVITING BENEFICIAL GUESTS

Add toad houses to the garden to attract toads for natural pest control. Just as fairy-tale toads can be turned into handsome princes with just a kiss, ordinary toads become plant protectors just by hopping into the garden. They may not be pretty, but toads eat plenty of bugs, so you'll be glad to see them. To encourage toads to come to live in your garden, try the following:

❀ Put several broken clay pots in the garden for toads to hide under.

❀ Water when the ground gets dry to keep the environment pleasant for amphibians.

❀ Avoid spraying toxic chemicals on the garden.

❀ Watch out for toads when tilling, hoeing, or shoveling.

You can also attract beneficial insects that will prey on plant-eating pest insects. Distributing some flowering plants amid the garden helps attract "good bugs" such as ladybugs, spiders, lacewings, and tiny parasitic wasps. The flowers provide shelter plus nectar and pollen, an alternative food source. Once beneficial insects are at home in your garden, keep them there. Remember, they can be killed as quickly as plant pests by broad-spectrum pesticides, which kill all insects indiscriminately. It's best to avoid pesticides or use targeted pesticides

🌿 *This baby deer looks cute, but it's a nuisance in the garden.*

🌿 *You're in luck if you spy ladybugs in your garden. These beneficial insects prey on garden pests.*

such as *Bt* (a bacterial disease of caterpillars that won't harm other insects) to protect beneficial insects.

KEEPING OUT THE REST

Use organic repellents to chase away rodents and deer. Sprays made out of hot peppers, coyote or bobcat urine, rotten eggs, bonemeal, or bloodmeal (even castor oil) can make your garden unappetizing to herbivores. Reapply the repellents frequently, especially after rain. Soap and human hair can also be used to deter deer. Soap can be stuffed in a mesh bag and dangled from branches at the nose height of deer—about three feet. Replenish the soap supply frequently so it won't dissolve away or lose its smell. Human hair stuffed in mesh bags will make deer wonder if you are hiding in the garden.

Grow French or American marigolds to kill any nematodes in the garden soil. Nematodes— microscopic wormlike pests that can damage tomatoes, potatoes, and other crops—are killed by chemicals that are released by marigold roots and decaying foliage. You can plant marigolds in and around other nematode-susceptible plants. Or just till marigolds into

the soil and let them decay before planting potatoes or tomatoes.

Floating row covers will keep pests off vegetables. When draped over plants, these lightweight fabrics allow sun, rain, and fresh air to penetrate but keep flying insects out. Secure them to the ground with rocks, bricks, or long metal staples. They can:

🌼 Eliminate maggots (fly larvae) that tunnel into the roots of radishes, turnips, carrots, and onions. They keep egg-laying flies away. If there are no eggs, there are no maggots.

🌼 Keep potato beetles from eating the foliage off potato leaves and vines. Pin the row cover edges down tightly so the beetles can't crawl under.

SOME DISEASE-RESISTANT CULTIVARS

- Apples: 'Freedom,' 'Jonafree,' 'Liberty,' 'MacFree'
- Beans: 'Buttercrisp,' 'Florence,' 'Jade'
- Cucumbers: 'Fancipack,' 'Homemade Pickles,' 'Park's All-Season Burpless Hybrid,' 'Salad Bush,' 'Sweet Success,' 'Tasty King'
- Peas: 'Green Arrow,' 'Maestro,' 'Sugar Pop,' 'Super Sugar Snap'
- Roses: 'Carefree Delight,' David Austin English Roses, 'The Fairy,' Meidiland roses, 'Red Fairy,' rugosa roses, Town and Country Roses
- Strawberries: 'Allstar,' 'Cavendish,' 'Delite,' 'Guardian,' 'Lateglow,' 'Redchief,' 'Scott,' 'Surecrop'
- Tomatoes: 'Beefmaster,' 'Better Boy,' 'Big Beef,' 'Celebrity,' 'Enchantment,' 'LaRossa,' 'Mountain Delight,' 'Roma,' 'Sunmaster,' 'Sweet Million,' 'Viva Italia'
- Zinnias: 'Cherry Pinwheel,' 'Crystal White,' 'Orange Pinwheel,' 'Rose Pinwheel,' 'Salmon Pinwheel,' 'Star Gold,' 'Star Orange,' 'Star White'

Use sticky red balls for control of apple maggots on apple and plum trees.

✽ Protect cucumbers, squash, and pumpkins from cucumber beetles, which carry a wilt disease capable of killing entire vines. Since flowers of these vines need insect pollination for fruit set, the covers must be lifted for several hours at least every other day for honeybees to do their work.

Use barriers of copper strips or diatomaceous earth to keep slugs away. Slugs eat tender plants down to the ground. They come out from under rocks, logs, or mulch when it's rainy or cool and dark. Diatomaceous earth is a gritty substance that pierces the skin of soft-bodied slugs. Sprinkle it on the soil, encircling plants plagued by slugs. Use the horticultural grade, not the kind sold in swimming pool stores. Copper strips, set around the edge of the garden, prevent slug trespass by creating an unpleasant reaction when touched by slimy

slugs. Set strips on edge an inch deep and several inches high.

Spray aphids off plants with a strong stream of water from the hose. Aphids, small sap-sucking insects with soft bodies, cling to succulent young stems and buds but are easily dislodged. This works best on roses and mature or woody plants that won't be damaged by the force of the water. Repeat every few days or when you see new aphids.

SAFETY WITH PESTICIDE

These days, chemical pesticides come and go. Yes, they kill plant pests, but they often have unforeseen consequences. Several formulations have been taken off the market due to their ill effects. For example, DDT was pulled from the market because it was spreading through the environment, causing death among bug and fish-eating birds, including the American eagle (it made their eggshells too fragile for survival of the young). Unfortunately, there are times when a particular pest, such as fire ants, requires strong measures. Use every caution when you resort to pesticide. Follow the directions on the package, wear protective clothing (and wash it afterward), and take a shower or at least wash your hands and face as soon as possible. Keep in mind that insects and microorganisms sometimes evolve rapidly and become immune to chemical remedies whose damaging effects remain in the environment nonetheless.

ELIMINATING DISEASE

Growing healthy plants is the first step toward a great garden. To achieve this, it's important to prevent diseases through careful plant selection, planting, and care. Choose disease-resistant cultivars whenever possible (see sidebar on page 69 for some suggestions). They are bred to resist infection—an ideal way to avoid diseases. Growing disease-resistant vegetables prevents chemical tainting of your food. Planting disease-resistant varieties of popular flowers such as roses saves you time, trouble, and expense. There are varying levels of protection available:

❀ Some cultivars have multiple disease resistances for maximum protection. The 'Big Beef' tomato, for instance, resists various types of wilts, tobacco mosaic virus, nematodes, and gray leaf spot. Little is left that can harm it.

❀ Some cultivars resist only one disease. But if that disease is a problem in your area, then these plants will be worth their weight in gold.

❀ Other plants are disease tolerant, meaning they may still get the disease but should grow well despite it.

HIGH-SPEED GARDENING: POTTED PLANT SOAP-UP

Potted plants get pests too. Any time yours are suffering from insect damage, you can try the Ivory soap trick. This is an old-time remedy you can use before bringing potted plants indoors after their summer outside.

• Fill a bucket halfway with lukewarm water.

• Get a bar of Ivory soap (which is not a detergent and is milder than most other soaps), lather it up in the water with your hands (just for a minute), and then remove it. The water should not be bubbly, just a little cloudy.

• For small potted plants, dunk the whole pot with its soil and plant under the soapy water for a minute. Then remove it and set it where it can drain. For larger plants, take both the soap mixture and the plant outdoors on a warm day or to the bathtub. Splash and wet every leaf and stem of the plant, and let soapy water go into the potting soil as well. (Do not let potting medium or leaves go down the drain!) Set the plant where it can drain.

• If the plant is infested with a difficult pest, cut off damaged leaves, prune for shape, and repeat the process every few days to make sure you get rid of the last few critters.

COMMON GARDEN PESTS

Here are some common garden pest problems and suggestions about how to deal with them. A reputable garden center sells pesticides, repellents, and fungicides, keeping up with current regulations and usage. Each entry below names the pest, describes the damage, and suggests one or more controls.

Pest	Symptom	Control
Anthracnose	This tree blight of dogwood, ash, willows, and others causes leaves to develop brown spots, giving them a scorched look.	Remove badly diseased branches. Prune for good air circulation.
Aphids	Tiny green, gray, reddish, or brown pear-shape insects suck juices out of plant leaves and stems. You can see them clustering around the tips.	Spray them off with a forceful jet of water, use insecticidal soap or rotenone, or bring in ladybugs to eat the aphids.
Beetles, various	You can sometimes find beetles burrowing into flowers or leaves. They chew away foliage, leaving it very ragged.	Pick them off by hand or spray with rotenone. Look for beetle egg cases on the undersides of leaves and destroy them.
Caterpillars, various	Lacy holes and big bites appear in leaves. Sometimes you can catch criminal caterpillars in the act.	Kill them by hand or spray with *Bacillus thuringiensis* or pyrethrin.
Chinch bugs	Round or irregular yellow patches appear in the lawn in hot, dry weather. This can mean chinch bugs, which are barely visible insects that suck juices from grass blades.	Use an insecticide labeled for this problem and repeat at three-week intervals.
Cutworms	Certain grubs and caterpillars live underground and chew through entire young plants, nipping them off at the base.	Destroy any cutworms you find by searching underground near the damage. Make protective collars for plants out of cardboard tubes two inches tall, setting each one around a plant, halfway into the soil.
Grubs	Patches of dead turf and garden plants that vanish without a trace are signs that you may be dealing with grubs, the larvae of beetles.	Control adult beetles by hand picking. If the problem is severe, use a recommended insecticide in late spring or early summer.
Lace bugs	Leaves of azaleas and other plants become speckled and lose vigor. Lacebugs, with telltale small black specks, are the culprits.	Spray the undersides of leaves with the appropriate remedy, after you have taken an afflicted leaf to the Agricultural Extension agent or garden center expert for confirmation of the diagnosis.

Pest	Symptom	Control
Leaf hoppers	Leaves are peppered with small round holes and begin to curl. Small, triangular hopping insects are the cause.	Spray off light infestations with a garden hose before you turn to stronger remedies.
Leaf miners	There are white, curling trails inside the layers of a leaf. You can sometimes see a dark spot where the leaf miner is doing its damage.	Remove all damaged leaves. Throw them in the trash, not the compost pile.
Mealybugs	A type of white, fuzzy scale insect, mealybugs make sticky clumps on leaves, buds, and stems and seriously weaken plants.	Wash them off with Ivory soap and water solution, paint them with alcohol, or use pyrethrin to get rid of them.
Moles	If you have tunnels under your grass, it could be moles. They are carnivores that eat grubs and earthworms they find underground.	Control insects that they feed on, or trap and remove the moles. Voles sometimes use similar tunnels.
Scale	Like mealybugs, scale insects cluster on stems. Some forms are dark and have a shell about an eighth of an inch long. Juvenile forms can move but adults stay in one place, sucking plant juice and spreading disease.	Wipe branches with alcohol or soapy water, and spray them in early spring with dormant oil.
Slugs and snails	Slimy trails are one clue left by these mollusks, and irregular holes in leaves and stems are another.	Handpick and destroy, or use newer types of slug bait that are earth-friendly. A classic remedy is to trap them in shallow tubs filled with beer, set with the tops at soil level near the damaged plants. Or place a cabbage leaf near the damage, then look under it a day or two layer and find the critters hiding there.
Spider mites	Foggy little webs are nearly invisible, but the damage caused by spider mites can be extensive, killing leaves and plants.	Spray with water often, for they prefer dry, dusty conditions. If the problem is extensive, use a miticide at three-day intervals.
Spittlebugs	In a mass of tiny white bubbles on plant stems, spittlebugs are hiding.	They are not much of a problem, so unless they are pervasive, just spray them off with the hose from time to time.
Whiteflies	Small white insects shaped like houseflies but less than a quarter-inch long make their home on the undersides of leaves, laying eggs and sucking plant juices.	Wash plants off, use yellow sticky traps, improve air circulation, or destroy afflicted plants before the pests spread.

Frequently Asked Questions

Q: I've heard that you can use beer to kill slugs. Is this true?
A: It sounds a little funny, but beer can be the downfall of thirsty slugs. They love beer so much that they can become trapped in deep saucers of it. Bury an empty margarine tub in the garden soil. The top rim should be level with the soil surface. Fill the tub with beer. Any kind will do, but the more aroma it has, the better. Leave it overnight, and the slugs will crawl in and drown. Empty the tub every day or two and refill with beer until the tub makes it through the night empty.

Q: Is it important to collect the grass clippings when cutting the lawn?
A: Remove excessive clippings so that they do not leave thick little clods around the lawn, which will smother the grass underneath. A few species of turfgrass produce heavy thatch buildup near the grass roots—matted, dead grass—that can prevent water, fertilizer, and air from getting into the soil, thus weakening the health of the lawn. But regular cutting of the grass will usually produce only light clippings that quickly decay into the soil, returning valuable nutrients. A mulching mower does a good job of pulverizing the cut grass into an enriching soil booster. When you rake or bag the clippings instead, compost them or use them in a thin layer as garden mulch.

Q: I grew some great marigolds from seed in recycled cell packs. But when I took them out to plant them the roots were all matted together. Can I still plant them?
A: Plants in cell packs can get pretty crowded but they are still good in the garden. Gently break up the root ball. If the roots have overgrown the potting area, pull off the tangles so the roots will be able to grow free into the soil. If roots are wound around the bottom of the root ball, use your finger to gently work the roots free of each other. If they are matted over the entire root ball, you'll need to tear or cut the mats off, leaving the roots below intact.

Q: Does it matter whether I use fresh barnyard wastes and compost as opposed to old, seasoned organic matter?
A: Microorganisms that break down organic matter use some of the available nutrients, especially nitrogen, from the soil. Material will decompose in a compost pile faster than if the matter is directly cultivated into the soil because the microorganisms at work need air. If fresh organic matter is used directly in or on top of the garden, you will need to apply additional nitrogen to protect plants from nutrient deficiency. However, you can use fresh materials on areas that are not yet under cultivation, especially those that will rest for a few months (not counting winter) before being planted.

Q: When should I cut back my ornamental grass?
A: Part of the beauty of ornamental grasses is their attractiveness in the fall and winter garden. The seed plumes and foliage weather to tan and look great in winter. Wear and tear from wind and snow take their

toll, and it's just as well because the old stems should be cut down in early spring, before the plants break dormancy, to avoid damage to the emerging green leaves. A string trimmer handles the job with ease.

Q: What causes the bark of young trees to crack, and how can it be corrected?
A: Vertical cracking, or sunscald, usually appears on the southwest side of the trunk. On warm, sunny winter days, the tree heats up. Then it freezes rapidly when the sun sets. Young trees are most prone to sunscald because of their thin bark. These cracks provide an entry path for diseases and insects. Prevent sunscald by using white plastic tree wraps, available at garden centers, around the trunk.

Q: Can road salt kill the shrubs at the end of my driveway?
A: Salt toxicity is common. The worst damage occurs right where the salt is applied, near roads and walks. Plants display dieback, yellowish foliage, and weak growth. Wash salt residue from plants with a hose, and soak the soil to leach salt from the beds. Rugosa roses, bearberry, and sea thrift manage to thrive in soils that are salty enough to kill other plants. Don't use salt on your sidewalks and driveway at home. Instead, sprinkle granulated fertilizer on the ice; it will be less damaging to nearby plants when it washes off.

Q: When should I prune my trees?
A: Prune to thin out branches in late winter when the sap is rising. The sap "bleeding" helps prevent disease organisms from entering the wound, and the tree will heal quickly at this time of year. Limbs that need to be removed because of storm or disease damage can be pruned any time of year.

Q: What does it mean to have "well-drained soil"?
A: Although it's not necessary for your soil to have water available for your plants, too much water held for long periods of time disturbs the balance of air that is necessary for healthy root growth of most plant species. Without air in the soil, many plants drown. Loam, a balance of sand, clay, and organic matter, is usually well drained. Heavily compacted clay soils are often poorly drained.

Q: I'm looking for a particular cultivar that I can only find through mail order. Is it safe to buy plants from another temperature zone?
A: If you know the type of plant will grow in your climate, you should have no problem—if it's a spring purchase. If the nursery's zone is warmer than yours, specify a safe ship date for your area. The newly installed plant will have all summer to acclimate to your seasons and should survive the upcoming winter.

Q: Although I understand the benefits of using compost in the garden, I will probably never be disciplined enough to build and maintain a pile. What can I use instead?
A: Many municipalities have old piles of leaf mold—from autumn collection—that is free for the taking. Arm yourself with a few plastic bags and a shovel, and head for the lot. Another option is purchasing composted manure from a stable or barnyard. You can also buy dehydrated manure or compost and incorporate it into the soil as you would with fresh compost.

Q: I grow a lot of plants from seeds and cuttings. Is there an inexpensive source for labels?
A: You can buy plastic labels in bulk from greenhouse supply places and some mail-order seed companies. You can also create your own by cutting plastic milk jugs or yogurt cups into strips. But one of the best ways to get labels is to clean up the old ones. A quick scrub with steel wool and soapy water will rub writing or even commercial printing off any plastic label in a jiffy.

CHAPTER 4

Your Landscape Plan

Don't be intimidated by the word *landscape*. A landscape is the sum of its parts: lawn, flower and vegetable gardens, vines and ground covers, shrub borders and hedges, shade or ornamental trees, and pavings and furnishings. Each is an important element in its own right, and each contributes to the beauty and usefulness of the landscape.

A simple assessment of your personal landscape needs is your first step in planning your property. Make a list of the features you want to incorporate into your design. Take notes about special functions or service areas your landscape will need to provide. Then consider the tips in this chapter as you build your landscape. Whether you hope to screen an eyesore or frame a beautiful vista, you'll choose styles, plants, features, and finishing touches that suit your taste and complement the architecture of your home. Here, you'll be living beautifully!

Decisions, Decisions

Growing plants well is a wonderful thing but arranging them in a handsome landscape is even better! A good landscape design plays many roles. It blends the house into the yard, making the entire property look good and increasing property values. Through the design of the landscape, you can create outdoor privacy with vine-covered trellises, hedges, fences, or informal clusters of plants that act like walls of an outdoor room. You can seclude certain areas of the yard or buffer the entire property perimeter.

Landscape designs might include work areas, places for composting or vegetable gardening, even areas for storing trash cans and other less-than-decorative necessities. You can designate places for entertaining—decks, patios, barbecue pits, or perhaps a white garden for guests to enjoy on a moonlit night. You can even have areas designed especially for the dog or the children's play equipment.

WHAT CAN YOUR GARDEN DO FOR YOU?

A beautifully designed landscape may look attractive, but if it doesn't accommodate the needs of the people who use the property, it is not practical. Before finalizing the plan for your space, discuss it with members of your household. Use them as a sounding board as you think about needs and plans for the space, whether it is small or large. Make a list of the functions that you'll want each area of your property to serve. Once you list everything you want, you can begin to find room for it all and start getting the most important elements in place.

POSSIBLE LANDSCAPING FEATURES

- Barbecue area
- Berries for birds
- Children's play areas
- Clothesline area
- Curb appeal
- Dog pen and dog run
- Eyesore screening
- Firewood storage
- Floral display
- Hobby gardening (water gardening, herb gardening, etc.)
- Lawn for recreation
- Noise reduction
- Party or dance area
- Privacy
- Shade to keep the home cooler
- Sitting/dining areas
- Soil retention for a bank
- Swimming pool
- Vegetable garden
- Wind protection

COLOR, TEXTURE, AND FORM

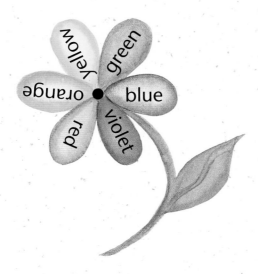

Just as you'd think about color, texture, and form before selecting furnishings and paint for a room, you also need to consider these elements in landscape design. You'll find a wide array of options available in building materials, paving materials, types of leaves and flowers, textures of bark and shapes of trees, and even the types and colors of mulch. Are you interested in a punchy blend of contrasting colors, like rich red with mossy greens? A garden of blue flowers accented with pale yellow ones? A blast of hot-colored azaleas and bulbs in the spring? Soothing greens that last through the year? Warm earth tones? Analogous colors in careful harmony?

Use warm colors and cool colors to give the garden just the right amount of emphasis. Warm colors such as yellow, orange, and red are bold and appear visually to be closer to you than they are. This makes them ideal for a garden located farther away from your house. Cool colors such as blue and purple recede from the eye and look farther away than they really are. They make pleasant, quiet gardens close to the house, but they may be lost if placed farther away.

You can blend cool and warm colors to give a feeling of movement and depth to the garden. Color blends also provide vivid contrast, which some people find exhilarating. Analogous colors, whether warm or cool, are next to one another on a color wheel and effortlessly harmonize together. If you're not born with the kind of flair for color that lets you find unique combinations successfully, find a color theme you like and stay with it throughout the landscape. This will give your property a designed look.

The same goes for textures and forms. The whole design should have cohesiveness, which you can achieve with repetition. If you have a brick walkway, use more brick for other elements such as terraces or built-in planters. It doesn't all have to be brick—you might have a path of "freebie" wood chips, but edge it with two lines of brick just for the sake of continuity. If you have stone in one place, brick over here, railroad ties over there, and round cement pavers in another spot, it all looks too jumbled.

It's a good idea to limit the number of different kinds of hardscapes and materials in any given setting. Here, wood is used for the doorway and post, while brick steps and terra-cotta pots make a pleasant contrast.

 Flowers in a color run of reds and purples pick up on the tones of the antique bricks. The rustic structure of the building and the cottage garden arrangement of the flowers are in good accord here.

Consider varying leaf sizes for more design interest. Large leaves like those on hostas or oak leaf hydrangeas advance and stand out (similar to warm-colored flowers). They are striking in prominent locations, but if overused they will lose their impact.

Small or finely textured leaves, as on thread leaf coreopsis or carrot tops, recede from the eye and look farther away. They can best be appreciated up close. If you are trying to make a garden look deeper, these varieties might be used toward the rear as a floral optical illusion. But when used exclusively, fine-textured leaves may look busy and weedy.

Flower size is another variable for an interesting design. Large flowers are bold and prominent. Smaller flowers and fine flower clusters recede. Blending airy small flower sprays with large, bold flowers combines the best of both textures. Planting larger flowers toward the front of a garden and smaller flowers toward the rear increases visual depth.

WHAT'S YOUR STYLE?

Before you start buying things for your landscape, think about what you like, what goes with your home, and the amount of finishing and trimming you are interested in doing. Stylized topiaries (plants trimmed into geometric or fanciful shapes) must be nipped into shape every month or so, but naturalistic, dwarf plants take care of their shape pretty much by themselves. Styles of gardening vary around the world and in different eras. If attempting a historically correct garden, choose a selection of old-fashioned plants instead of new cultivars that were not available in that period.

There are fashions in plants and garden accessories just as there are fashions in clothing, music, and indoor furnishings. A recent planting fashion combined chartreuse-leaved plants with purple-leaved plants, and suddenly people were doing this everywhere. It's a good idea to think about style and keep the varied parts of your landscape in sync with one another. On a larger property, you can use a formal landscaping style near the home, but as the distance from the home increases, have the style become more informal and natural looking to blend into the surrounding countryside.

PERENNIALS WITH EXCEPTIONALLY LONG BLOOM

These perennials are good in garden designs, because they bloom and sometimes rebloom for many weeks of color, not just a week or two in their season.

- Coreopsis
- Lenten rose
- Orange coneflower
- Purple coneflower
- Rose mallow hibiscus

Formal

A formal garden is neatly trimmed, geometric, and, often, symmetrical. It relies on handsome garden accessories of a classic nature, such as a pair of large urns on either side of the door, planted identically. If there is a path, it is likely to lead to a finely crafted bench or a gazebo. Massed ground covers, lines of trees or shrubs equidistantly planted along a long drive, and tidy lawns fit the scene. Well-kept evergreens such as boxwood are in keeping with formal style. Pavements for pathways and terraces may be of brick, stone, or concrete. Outdoor furniture is classic and looks more civilized than rustic. However, well-made modern furnishings and accessories can also be used in a formal manner. Whimsy is out—no painted plywood cutouts allowed!

🍃 *The style is casual, but the garden does not look disorganized; there is a defined, grassy walkway, and the colors of flowers and foliage are soft and harmonious.*

HIGH-SPEED GARDENING: PASTE UP A QUICK PLAN

🍂

If you're designing a flowerbed and want the quickest possible preview of your combinations of color and shape, try using the color pictures from last year's seed catalogs to test your ideas. Cut out pictures of plants that interest you. Block out the bed on graph paper and try different pictures in different positions. When you find the combinations that work best for you, use them as a basis for your design.

Informal

An informal garden is naturalistic and usually includes asymmetrically placed design elements, naturally shaped plants and beds, curved spaces, rustic-looking furnishings, and more casual pavings, like decking and even wood chips. It can be flowery and colorful or low key to suit the personality of the gardener. Furnishings can be of either traditional or modern design, but they are comfortable looking. This style sometimes employs unusual accents, such as a back-door frame painted to match nearby plantings or a sweep of tall ornamental grasses in a broad, cloudlike band.

A birdbath can be a lovely (and simple) way to modify your garden hardscape. You'll attract lots of garden visitors for added visual interest.

SOFTSCAPES AND HARDSCAPES

A landscape plan may include plants, hedges, mulches, flower and ground-cover beds, and shrub or flower borders, which, together, comprise the softscapes. Planning softscapes requires knowledge of plant material and soil quality, plus a good sense of design.

Hardscapes, the other important part of landscape design, include patios, walkways, stairways, decks, walls, fences, pools, driveways, built-in planters, and parking areas. Major changes in hardscape are feats of engineering, requiring precise measurements and knowledge of foundation footings and soil settlement ratios, so it is wise to have the work designed and supervised by a professional landscape architect (unless you have outstanding skill and experience). Gardeners can manage smaller hardscape projects, such as making paths and edging beds, without too much difficulty.

HIGH-SPEED GARDENING: ADD A BIRDBATH

If there is one thing that quickly adds a focal element plus lots of movement to a garden, it is a birdbath, whether it sits on the ground or on its own pedestal. You may already have an object around the house that makes an excellent bathing bowl for birds. A large terra-cotta flower-pot saucer, about 18 to 24 inches wide and an inch or two high, works well when filled with fresh water. To birds, it is like a puddle, and they like that, because they can tell it's not too deep. They also like to perch on the rim. Your birdbath should be set on a paved terrace or other area you can see from indoors, so you can enjoy the splashing and carrying on and keep track of who flies in for a bath or a drink. Be sure to change the water once a day to keep it clean and to prevent mosquitoes from breeding in it. Why not use the old birdbath water on a deserving plant?

82 ❧ *Your Landscape Plan*

Assessing Existing Features

Draw a map of your property as it is, and use it to decide where the new garden features, beds, and plantings will go. This will keep you from making mistakes when you start buying and planting. The map needs to be to scale—an exact replica of your property in miniature. Many designers use a scale in which ¼ inch on the plan (a single square of graph paper) equals one foot in your landscape. This scale usually provides enough room to show considerable detail but is likely to require the use of over-sized paper to fit everything on one sheet. You can tape several sheets of graph paper together to get the size you need.

MAKE A SCALE DRAWING

Measure the yard using a measuring tape (50-foot lengths work well), and sketch the perimeter on graph paper. Draw in existing trees, shrubs, fences, and other features you intend to keep, using an overhead, bird's-eye view. Trees and shrubs appear to be circular blobs, and fences look rather linear. Draw in the existing lawn. Make some copies so you can experiment with designs. Then pencil in possible bed outlines and imagine how they will look. Once you've decided on the location of the beds, draw in the plants you want to add (at the proper spacing) and get an accurate count of how many plants you'll need. There are computer programs available for home landscapers who want to test various designs from natural as well as overhead views.

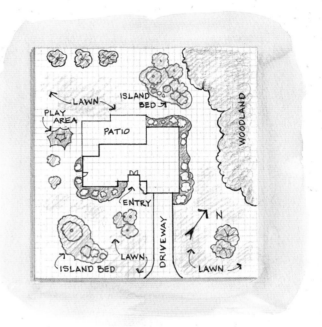

WHAT TO KEEP AND WHAT TO OMIT

What do you like about your home's existing landscape? Perhaps its pavements and patios are already the way you like them, and you just want to expand or beautify the gardens. Perhaps there are treasured old trees that have taken generations to grow. Perhaps the existing shrubs are good but overgrown and need professional pruning, not total replacement. Perhaps your grandmother's iris is overgrowing its space. It can be divided and used as a mass planting elsewhere on the property. Look over everything with a cold eye and evaluate whether it looks good, is in good shape, fits your plan, and should be retained somewhere.

You have four options with every feature: keep it, improve it, move it, or get rid of it. It takes many years for a tree to mature, so think twice before cutting one down. If it's gone, what will the view be like? Its replacement may take too many years to grow to fill the space, so consider whether shaping, thinning, and pruning an existing tree will make it a grand part of your plan. Nonetheless, if a tree is badly diseased or damaged, it may not be salvageable.

Creating a Plan

You have a scale drawing of your existing landscape and have made multiple copies for worksheets. Now draw a simple sketch showing the general location of the elements needed in relation to the house and to one another. For instance, if an outdoor eating area is needed, sketch it near the kitchen or dining room for a good transition between indoors and outdoors. The relationship diagram will help you in the beginning steps of putting a plan together. Your considerations should include the amount of maintenance time you plan to spend in the yard.

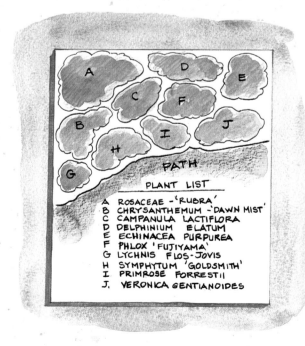

A Place to Garden

Your calculations will have to take the physical limitations of your site into consideration. What are the actual pros and cons of your conditions? Does the land slope or is it level? Is

Here, a stone wall is given a touch of unexpected color. Note how the silver foliage bounces off the gray of the stones, and the dignified stonework gets a lift from effervescent flowers in a medley of bright colors.

Tips for Small Gardens

If your garden space is small, you have to make the most of it. It has the advantage of being easy to maintain to perfection. You will want very rich, deep soil to get maximum growth from the minimum of space. In a crowded environment (a townhouse deck, for instance) there may not be an attractive view beyond the edge of your property. Plant eye-catching tall or climbing plants to fill the scene with color at eye level. Fences and openwork plant supports such as lath panels help a lot. There are containers that fit tightly onto balcony or deck rails.

With a small property, don't automatically assume that you have no room to grow anything. Instead, make the most of what is there. A tiny strip of land next to the house can be fitted with a raised bed and a trellis for growing climbing plants such as roses or clematis. It's a waste to have bare soil or bare walls when you

Using both tall and climbing plants, quite a colorful garden has been created in a very narrow space between the fence and the walkway.

the site sunny or shady? Filled with tree roots or not? Certain kinds of gardens can only be placed in certain kinds of exposures. For instance, you may want to plant an herb garden, which needs full sun, near the kitchen and the deck. But if this area is heavily shaded by an important tree that you wouldn't dream of removing, you'll have to change your plan and either give up on the idea of herbs or place them in a sunny area in another part of your landscape. Sometimes necessities like this lead to wonderfully imaginative solutions. Those herbs could be put into a large planter next to your front door, where you can brush by them every day and enjoy their scent when you come and go. Be sure to match the flowering plant to the site. Most flowers are high-performance plants, especially sensitive to inadequacies in light, moisture, soil, or other elements. Give them exactly what they need to thrive.

DO YOU NEED GRASS?

Some gardeners get pretty emotional about their lawn and feel that it is a necessary part of the landscape. Others are perfectly happy without it. Grass takes a good bit of maintenance, but it offers benefits in return. It looks good and makes a nice, soft surface to walk and play on. Grass makes a nice contrast to pavings, beds of flowers and ground cover, and shrubs and trees. However, given paths and paved areas between the garden beds and features, gardens without grass are pleasant and successful, especially in smaller spaces. Many gardeners prefer to quietly care for garden beds and containers of flowers instead of noisily mowing the lawn. In some shady gardens, moss is used for the carpet of green instead of grass.

can fill them with color and form in your small garden. If there is no soil there at all, container gardening is your answer. Urns and planters are handsome and offer great places to grow plants; hanging baskets raise the level and double the amount you can grow in the same space.

Space is relative, and what is small to one gardener may seem spacious to another. There are gardeners who can make a dazzling display with only a window box and an entranceway planter. On the diagram of your site, sketch in any usable areas: front garden, places for window boxes, narrow strips of ground or pavement at the sides of the building, decks, balconies, atriums, terraces, or a small backyard. You may be surprised at all the planting opportunities you find.

DEVELOPING YOUR GARDEN DESIGN

Take photos and photocopy them. You can shoot the entire front or backyard, the plantings around the house's foundation, or individual gardens. Enlarge the photos, then sketch in prospective new plants to get an idea of how they will look. A great time to do this is in winter. Although the yard may be dormant, you won't forget how it looks in other seasons.

If your house is visible from a road, you have a public view area. Think of your house, or front door, as the focal point of a picture. You'll want to frame the view, to draw attention to your house. Typically, foundation plantings are set at the base of the house to frame the house and connect it to the landscape. Foundation plantings can be a simple mix of small evergreens and flowering shrubs, ornamental trees,

Artfully placed rocks create small waterfalls and a naturalistic planting site. Their parallel lines give them the appearance of a natural outcropping. Low-growing plants were selected, allowing the flowing water and handsome rockery to command the most attention.

ground covers, and herbaceous plants. Consider shade when choosing trees; deciduous trees will shade your home in the summer while allowing sunlight in during the winter. Be sure to screen service areas—trash cans, laundry lines, and the like—from public view with shrubs or fencing.

You'll want to develop other sections of your landscape for outdoor living. You may decide to incorporate a service area—a toolshed or clothesline. It should be convenient to the house yet tucked away from private entertaining and away from public view. Landscape designs might include work areas; places for composting, plant propagation, or vegetable gardening; even areas for storing trash cans and other less-than-decorative necessities. On the other hand, if you have a great view of a lake or a farm, don't cover it up with too many fences and shrubs. Frame your view with careful placement of plantings off to the sides.

If children will be using your landscape, a swing set or sandbox may be in your plans.

There are attractive designs that look natural and fit into the landscape nicely. You'll want this area set aside from heavy traffic yet still in full view for easy supervision. Separate the dining and entertaining area from the children's area with a dwarf shrub border. It will seem more private but will still offer a view of the kids at play. One great idea for a children's sandbox is to make it look like a raised bed, in sight of the outdoor dining area. Instead of mulch and plants, fill it with sand and kids.

LAWNS

We have become accustomed to pampered lawns, but they may be more time-consuming than is necessary. If you want your lawn to be low-maintenance, choose the right kind of grass for the site, plant at the ideal time, and use organic and slow-releasing fertilizers. Here are nine nifty ways to minimize lawn maintenance.

- *Use a mixture of turf grasses for a disease-resistant lawn.* Diseases that attack one type of grass may not affect others, so you are reducing risks. Grass blends also increase versatility. Fine fescues mixed with bluegrass, for instance, are less likely to turn brown in summer heat.

- *Use the right grass for the spot.* Plant creeping red fescue in a lightly shaded lawn where bluegrass is likely to fail. For best results, provide well-drained, slightly acidic soil.

- *Use seed rather than sod to establish grass on poor soils.* Sod roots may never grow into stiff clay soils, which puts a damper on their future if drought strikes. Spend a little extra time and money to improve poor soil with compost and peat moss. Then plant seed of suitable grasses and tend the lawn well (feeding, watering, raking, and weeding, as necessary) until it is growing strongly.

- *Use edgings to keep grass out of garden beds.* A physical barrier can prevent sprigs of grass from spreading to areas where they can make bed edges look ragged. A line of bricks or stones flush with the lawn can be mowed over and has an elegant look. Useful edgings can also be made of five- to six-inch-wide strips of fiberglass, metal, or plastic. Let the upper edge emerge a little above the soil (well below the mower level) and sink the lower edge underground.

- *Use long-lasting fertilizer.* Top-dress the lawn with screened compost or rotted manure to keep it healthy, and fertilize with slow-release nitrogen fertilizer. Moderate amounts of nutrients will be released at a steady pace over time, for better growth that is deep rooted but not rampant.

- *Fill in low spots.* If the surface of the lawn is uneven, spread sand over it evenly with a metal rake. You can sprinkle grass seed on the sand or wait for the surrounding grasses to spread.

- *Leave grass blades longer for more drought resistance and better root growth.* Longer blades shade the soil and roots, keeping them cooler and moister, and the grass roots may grow deeper. In contrast, close-cropped lawns can dry out quickly in summer heat. The stubby blades expose grass-free openings where crabgrass and other weeds can grow.

- *Keep your lawn-mower blades sharp.* With sharp blades, your mower will slice through grass blades, giving a clean, level cut. Dull blades tear grasses, which increases their susceptibility to disease.

- *Don't overdo lawn care during a drought.* Without rainfall, the grass is unlikely to grow much, if at all. Water sparingly. Providing half an inch of water every two weeks keeps grass alive without encouraging growth.

A private entertaining and dining area is among the most common functions of a well-planned landscape. Design it as you would a comfortable room in your house. The size of the area should be determined by the number of people who will be accommodated. A patio with an adjacent lawn for occasional spillover works well. Shade, as well as privacy, can be achieved through proper selection and placement of screening materials and a canopy of trees. All the furnishings and materials should complement the style of the house, whether it is modern or traditional.

SHAPING YOUR PLAN

Plan the shape of the lawn, which is usually the biggest feature in a yard. The lawn's shape should set the tone for the shape of the beds. If it's designed with straight or gradually curving lines, the lawn can make a pretty picture and remain easy to mow. Avoid sharp turns, wiggly edges, and jagged corners that are irritating to the eye and extra work to mow. Your lawn is an important part of the landscape. However, if

space is tight you can replace lawn with pavement or decking for your outdoor living area or with ground covers and paths.

Shapes

The shapes of the garden beds, paved areas, and lawn areas all contribute to the overall look of your garden. Don't muddy the design with too many small shapes or too many kinds of shapes; make sure shapes relate to one another and the property itself. Rectangles alternated with kidney bean shapes can get pretty weird looking. A sloping, hilly property usually is easiest to landscape with simple, flowing, curved bed and walkway shapes that relate to its contours. To do otherwise could involve lots of professionally built, straight-edged terraces, steps, retaining walls, and other expensive hardscapes. But the landscape does not have to be all one shape. Most plots of land are rectangular, with a house in the middle somewhere. The garden beds at the edges can either be gently curved or follow the straight lines of the overall plot. Or a large circle or

Using a wooden fence that looks equally attractive from the front and the back, this gardener has divided the garden into sections, sometimes referred to as garden rooms. At the same time, he or she has provided an excellent backdrop for the colorful border of perennial flowers.

oval of grass can be completely surrounded with pavements and plantings out to the edge of the property line.

Proportions

Proportions of garden features are even trickier than shapes. Don't clutter the view with a lot of little shapes. Here are some general guidelines.

Island Beds

Make island beds half as wide as the distance from where you view them. Island beds, often oval or kidney-shaped, are situated in areas of lawn where they can be viewed from all sides. They may be near a corner of your yard or by your driveway or entrance walk. No matter where you put it, an island bed needs to be wide enough to look substantial from your house, patio, or kitchen window—wherever you usually are when you see it. A tiny garden located far from the house is more comical than beautiful. So, for example, if an island bed is 20 feet away, make it 10 feet across. In very large yards, keep island beds closer to the house if you don't have time to tend a large island bed.

Borders

Borders can take up to half of the space in a small- or medium-size yard. For example, a 40-foot-wide yard could have one border 20 feet wide or two borders 10 feet wide. Borders—traditional gardens usually set at the edge of a yard, fence, or hedge—also need enough size to be in scale and make an impact in the yard. Wider borders can accommodate taller plants, including trees, shrubs, and large clumps of perennials and ornamental grasses, taking on a rich diversity.

Paths and Pavings

Build garden paths anywhere that gets enough foot traffic to wear out the grass. Paths make pleasant straight or curving lines through the yard and make it easier to get where you need to go in wet weather. They also save you the trouble of having to constantly reseed barren, foot-worn areas.

If you have a large lot, make paths wide enough for two people to walk side by side. If your path is of grass, make it wide enough to accommodate a lawn mower. Give your paths turns or curves so that part of the scene comes as a surprise as you stroll. Terraces and patios, too, should have an uncrowded feeling, with plenty of space for the furniture plus more for walking around the tables and chairs. Include extra space for container gardens.

Banks of flowers closely line both sides of the path. Note how the grass strips effectively widen the stone path.

Paving materials range in style, price, ease of installation and maintenance, and appearance. Here are four popular options.

Irregular flagstones create a casual but handsome appearance. The walkway is leveled and laid out carefully on a gravel bed, with or without mortar. For a more formal appearance, rectangular stones are used.

Professionally laid brick paving is durable and rather formal. There are several possible patterns and edgings, but simpler styles look best. Paving bricks are flatter and broader than bricks for buildings. Recycled or antique bricks can be used for pavings and edgings.

An ordinary concrete sidewalk, plain and simple, is a good-looking and practical choice and is usually less expensive than stone or brick. Be sure to make the path sufficiently broad or it may look too cramped.

Where a path is needed, and a casual look is desired, wood or bark chips can be used. This kind of path is permeable, so water does not run off, which makes it environmentally friendly. Because the chips break down, a new layer must be added from time to time to refresh the path. The old, decomposing chips can be left in place under the new ones or used for mulching or soil enrichments.

Fencing

Fences can be made of wood or lookalike plastic timber. Different sizes and patterns affect the style and function. No fence lasts forever, but better woods like cedar and redwood have longer lives.

A stockade fence like this is practical for total privacy, for it makes a solid wall. It is often used near a busy street and to keep pets and children inside the yard. Usually made of unpainted cedar, this fence requires little maintenance.

Picket fences are more for design than practicality. Traditional in New England and other places, picket fences, short or tall, have a friendly feeling but still mark property lines and boundaries. They are usually painted white and utilize boards that are pointed at the top.

This kind of rustic cedar split-rail fence is often used on farms and properties with lots of acreage. Simple and inexpensive, it marks the property line and, at the right height, can be used to outline pastures for cattle and horses. Individual rails can be replaced if necessary, without redoing the entire fence.

While many board fences have a front side and a back side, this type of fence alternates the fronts and the backs, so it looks the same from both sides. That is why it is referred to as a "good neighbor" fence. It is not uncommon for neighbors to decide to install this type of fence on their mutual property line and share the cost.

🌿 *Plant butterfly weed to attract some animated color to your garden.*

Seasonal Timing

Select flowering plants with a range of bloom times to keep the garden interesting through the seasons. Many perennials, shrubs, and trees will flower for a maximum of three weeks per year, but there are some exceptions. Take pictures of your garden at all times of year. On paper, list those plants that bloom in early and late spring, early and late summer, and early and late fall. Then when you plant your garden, you can develop a sequence so one kind of flower will fade as another begins to open. Wherever you have an important blooming shrub, surround it with a ground cover or ground-hugging perennial that blooms at the same time to maximize its impact. If this is a vacation home, you may want to concentrate on plants that bloom during the season you will be there. If you like to give an outdoor party at a particular time of year (someone's birthday, for instance), especially in the summer, keep track of plants that are in bloom or look especially good on that date, and cluster them near your outdoor living areas.

Plan ahead to cover the gaps left by perennials that go dormant in summer. Two of the most common now-you-see-them-now-you-don't perennials are sun-loving Oriental poppies and shade-loving old-fashioned bleeding hearts. When they finish blooming, both plants lose their old foliage and hibernate underground. This creates vacant places in the garden. But with a little planning, you can easily work around them.

❀ Plant Oriental poppies or bleeding hearts individually instead of in large clumps or drifts, which leave larger holes.

❀ Organize gardens so that neighboring plants can fill in and cover for the missing greenery. In shade, the ample foliage of hostas and ferns can move into voids left when old-fashioned bleeding hearts go dormant. In sun, hardy geraniums, frothy baby's breath flowers, and spreaders like dragon's blood sedum can fill in for Oriental poppies.

❀ Fill in the temporary opening with a potted plant, such as a houseplant spending the summer outdoors.

NOISE REDUCTION

Noise is a nuisance that limits garden enjoyment. Noise from the street or neighborhood is a common offender. Solid walls and dense foliage help break up and block the noise. Berms—mounds of dirt planted with shrubs and perennials—are good for deflecting noise; they also offer a sense of privacy. Other noises come from lawnmowers, power trimmers, chippers, chain saws, and leaf blowers. We didn't always have these conveniences, so if the noise distresses you, go back to the tools of earlier days: reel mowers, handsaws, hand shears, and garden rakes. Or replace the lawn with pavement or ground cover and the hedge with a fence or a planting of dwarf shrubs.

Annual flowers are great for filling the gaps. Pansies, sweet alyssum, and calendula thrive in cool spring and fall weather. Petunias, marigolds, zinnias, geraniums, and other annuals will fill the frost-free summer months with color. And tender bulbs such as dahlias and cannas can also provide bright color through much of the warm summer season.

You can also easily brighten dull spots in the garden with pots of tender bulbs such as agapanthus, tuberous begonias, caladiums, pineapple lilies, or dahlias. The versatility of pots combined with the bright blooms of summer-flowering bulbs keeps gardens looking exceptional all summer and fall.

Be sure to choose flowering plants with good foliage as well as flowers. The foliage will still be on display long after the flowers are gone. For starters, find plants with foliage that stays healthy, lush, and green and won't become off-colored, ragged, or diseased after flowering. Then you can add plants with golden, silver, bronze, blue, or multicolored leaves that fit the garden color scheme.

Garden Accents

Containers, raised beds, accent plantings, and decorative structures like trellises and gazebos give an extra dose of color and texture to your garden. Garden sculptures are often the finishing touch of a perfect garden.

CONTAINERS

Containers are an excellent way to learn about gardening because they're easy to plant and give great results quickly. They also provide color to highlight patios, steps, garden gates, or any other drab area. Choose containers in styles and materials that harmonize with your landscape. Containers can be placed on paved areas and under trees whose roots fill the ground. In addition, pots are the best places to show off rare and exotic plants. Hanging bas-

 A weathered wheelbarrow adds a touch of country charm to this yard.

kets ornament porches and decks, even where there is not much space for plants. The larger and less crowded the container, the less frequently it will need to be watered. In any raised container, whether it is a tall pot or a hanging basket, plants should trail downward, spread sideways, and grow upward, for the most impact in a small space.

An effective window box combination is ivy or variegated vinca trailing down, petunias filling the middle area, and zonal geraniums standing up. Window boxes should have matching plantings for coherent design. If your containers are weatherproof, you can use perennial plants and dwarf shrubs in them as well as annuals.

Containers eliminate much of the guesswork in gardening. There is no need to tolerate difficult soil or make do with marginal sites. You can start with any potting mix, choosing the perfect blend for the plants you want to grow. You can set the pot where it will have the ideal amount of sun or shade. You provide water when nature comes up short, and you schedule the fertilization. There is nothing left to chance, assuming that you take the time to tend the

potted plant. In return, containers become living flower arrangements. With lively color schemes, varied textures, and handsome containers, potted plants grow, flower, and flourish close at hand where they are easily enjoyed.

Protecting Containers in Winter

Moisture expands when it freezes. Damp soil also expands when it freezes, causing many kinds of containers to break during the freezes and thaws of winter. Terra-cotta, ceramic, and even synthetic stone and concrete containers can easily chip or crack. To prevent this, empty your pots and store them in a dry place such as the garage or basement. Empty heavy urns and pots that are too bulky to carry indoors, and wrap them in plastic for winter protection. Do this on a dry autumn day, securing the plastic across the top, bottom, and sides of the pots to prevent moisture from getting inside.

BUILT-IN RAISED BEDS

Like containers, built-in raised beds are excellent for accent plantings, especially near doorways, where you may wish to add shrubs for framing the entryway, and atop paved areas, where it would otherwise be difficult to garden. They generally offer excellent drainage and deep soil that is free from competing tree roots. If your home has existing raised beds,

YEARLONG COLOR

Keep a succession of new flowers blooming in pots throughout the seasons, so your home and yard will never be short on color. You can place pots directly in your planters and change them with the seasons. In spring, enjoy cool-season flowers like forced bulbs, primroses, and pansies. In summer, grow tender perennials and annuals like impatiens and begonias. In fall, enjoy late bloomers like asters and mums.

check their design and condition. If they are too small, too low, or not attractively made, you should consider replacing them. An advantage of raised beds is that the gardener can tend the plants in them with a lot less bending and kneeling.

PLANT SUPPORTS

Arbors and pergolas are sturdy supports, often used for growing massive grapevines, wisteria, and trumpet vines. They can be used as a focal point at the end of a walkway and to provide shade and privacy in narrow spaces where you do not want to plant trees.

Create a shade garden without trees by planting under a vine-covered arbor. Shade gardens can feature serene blends of ferns, hostas, and woodland wildflowers, plus a few dazzling bloomers such as azaleas and rhododendrons. Although these plants usually grow amid trees and shrubs, they can thrive in shadows cast by other structures—walls, fences, houses, or a vine-covered arbor. The advantage of an arbor shade garden is that fewer roots are competing for moisture and nutrients. And unlike a planting close to a wall or building, the arbor shade garden has plenty of fresh air circulation. In addi-

MATERIALS FOR CONTAINERS

Brass
Bronze
Cedar
Ceramic
Clay
Compressed fibers
Compressed peat moss
Concrete
Fiberglass
Plastic
Redwood
Stone
Tin

tion, an arbor looks great when clad in flowers and handsome foliage.

Add height to a perennial border with annual or perennial vines on wire cages, tepees, or scrims. All kinds of eclectic treasures can be used. When you want a dynamic high point for a flower garden, an upward-trained vine will be effective throughout the growing season and sometimes beyond. In contrast, many of the tallest perennials reach their maximum height only when in flower, which may last for just a few weeks. Here are some support options to consider:

* Wire cages: These work like tomato cages but can be made from wire mesh in any height or shape. A narrow, upright pillar shape is elegant in a formal garden.

* Tepees: Make a support of angled posts tied together at the top. Plant one or several vines at the base and let them twine up and fill out to cover each post.

* Scrims: These are open-structured, see-through supports that vines can climb and still provide a veiled view of the scene beyond. With imagination, scrims can be made of braided wire or other creative materials.

Time and Money

Since none of us have infinite amounts of either time or money, emphasize the most important parts of your plan first. Work on improving the soil, because it is the foundation for everything else. Lay out the design, even if the intended terrace has to be grass for a few years, until you can afford brick or flagstone. If you are buying or building a house, see if you can get money for landscaping worked into your mortgage.

Plant trees and shrubs first, then add flower gardens. Woody plants are the bones of the garden, the bold foundation that will be there summer and winter to enclose your yard or blend your house into the property. They are also the most expensive and permanent features and, as such, need to be given special priority. Plan well, find top-quality trees and shrubs, and plant them properly where they can thrive.

MINIMIZING UPKEEP

If you are used to cutting your lawn every week and shearing your shrubs once a month, you may be relieved to know that there are easier ways to keep your yard looking nice. Low-maintenance gardening begins with choosing plants ideally suited for your yard's conditions so they won't need coaxing to stay alive.

Beyond that, some plants are naturally easier to keep, requiring little but suitable soil and sun exposure to grow and prosper. You can plant them and let them be without worrying about pests and diseases or extensive pruning, watering, fertilizing, or staking. Spending a little time finding these easy-care plants will prevent hours of maintenance in coming years.

Selecting the right style of planting for any given area can also reduce maintenance. Choose dwarf and slow-growing plants to eliminate the need for pruning and pinching. Tall shrubs just keep growing, and growing, and growing... sometimes getting too big for their place in the landscape. Lilacs, for example, commonly grow to 12 feet high. If planted by the house, they can cut off the view from the window. The only solution is regular trimming or replacement. A better option is to grow dwarf shrubs or special compact varieties that will only grow two to four feet high. They may never need pruning and won't have to be sheared into artificial globes. Also, some flowers with extra layers of petals, such as double peonies, become so heavy that stems always require staking. Choose single-flower types instead, for they are less likely to need props and supports.

Use plants adapted to dry conditions in drought-prone climates. Perennials such as butterfly weed have deep or moisture-storing roots that allow them to weather dry conditions. Other drought-survival specialists have

Group your pots of annuals together for more visual impact. It is also convenient to have them together for grooming and maintenance.

leaves that are modified to reduce moisture loss. Silver leaves reflect hot sunlight, and needle-shaped leaves have less surface area for moisture loss. Moisture is stored inside succulent leaves, and moisture loss for furry leaves is slowed by their furry coating.

Avoid planting large-fruited trees over patios and decks. Large crabapples, apples, pears, and other fruits and berries can mar the patio and furniture, drop on people, and make steps slippery. Sweet, ripe fruit can attract yellow jackets and other critters. Let large fruits look pretty from afar, where they can drop unheeded in mulch, lawn, or ground cover.

Don't plant salt-susceptible evergreens near the street in cold climates. Salt used for snow and ice control will splash up on the needles and drip into the soil. It won't be long before a thriving tree begins to brown out and then fail. Look for trees that can withstand salt spray. An example of a salt-susceptible evergreen is white pine. Salt-tolerant trees include sycamore maple, Austrian black pine, Japanese black pine, red mulberry, and sour gum.

Avoid fast-spreading and aggressive perennials such as yarrow, plume poppy, 'Silver King' artemisia, and bee balm. Although these plants are lovely, they have creeping stems that can spread through the garden, conquering more and more space and arising in the middle of neighboring plants. Keeping them contained in their own place requires dividing—digging up the plants and splitting them into smaller pieces for replanting. This may need to be done as often as once a year. It's better to just avoid them, or grow them only in containers.

Also avoid delicate plants such as delphiniums and hollyhocks, which need extra care and staking. Although spectacular in bloom, these prima donnas require constant protection from pests and diseases, plus pampered, rich, moist soil and, often, staking to keep them from falling over. If you simply have to have them, look for compact and/or disease-resistant cultivars, which are easier to care for.

Choose plants that are right for your garden, and you'll have more free time to relax and enjoy your yard!

MONEY-SAVING TIPS

Instead of buying new hanging baskets and containers, recycle the old ones. Sterilize old pots with a ten percent bleach solution before using them for other plants. Saving old pots from flowers, vegetables, poinsettias, even shrubs transplanted into the yard, is a great way to economize. But you have to be certain to eliminate any disease spores that may have come with the previous occupant. Begin by washing out excess soil, bits of roots, and other debris with warm soapy water. Mix one part household bleach with nine parts water and use the solution to wipe out the pot. Rinse again, and the pot is ready to plant.

Would you like an inexpensive source of perennials? Try a seed packet of mixed perennials that bloom the first or second year from seed. Follow the directions on the packet, whether you are growing the seeds indoors or out. If growing them outside, make the rows straight so you can tell your seedlings from the weeds. Make one or two additional sowings from the packet if you have enough seeds, because your results may vary somewhat. The plants that grow best for you will be well suited to your site and will be inclined to self-sow and give you a continued supply of plants in the future. Mixes like this are often composed of perennials such as rudbeckias and columbines that are relatively short-lived, but they are attractive and can fill the space while you wait for more permanent hostas, irises, and shrubs to grow.

Frequently Asked Questions

Q: What can I do with a narrow, shady area between my house and the neighbor's fence?
A: Your area may be rather cool, crowded, dark, and moist, with little room for larger plants. Yet it can still be attractive. Pave a pathway next to your house, and surround it with plants that thrive in shade. Don't even try to grow grass. Ferns, hostas, shade-loving wildflowers, and ground covers are your best bets. Accent them during warm months with impatiens and caladiums. Enrich the soil with compost to keep everything green and healthy.

Q: It will be years before our trees grow large enough to shade our deck. Is there anything to do in the meantime?
A: An overhead trellis or arbor will provide shade and interest. You can use it as a support for fast-growing annual vines, such as morning glory and nasturtium, or for perennials, such as clematis. An overhead structure identifies a comfortable living space while affording protection from the sun, appreciated by both plants and people. Be sure to build the structure high enough for comfort, while realizing that cascading vines will take space.

Q: What time of year should I start a new lawn from seed?
A: It depends on the type of grass you plan to grow. Most likely, if you're planting seed, you'll be using a cool-season grass. It's best to prepare the soil at the end of the summer and sow seed about six weeks before the first average frost in your area. The seed will sprout during the remaining warm weeks and continue to develop deep roots through autumn and into winter. By mid-spring the lawn will be well established.

Q: How can I make a design for my property that is drawn to scale?
A: First, make a nonscaled sketch of your area, noting the dimensions of existing details. Next, use graph paper to sketch the plan to scale using each square to represent a certain distance (for example, one square equals one foot). Photocopy your sketch so you're able to use it to try several ideas without having to repeat the process. Remember that plants will grow, so sketch your layout as it will look about ten years from now. By using scale during the planning stage, you'll get a good perspective on your garden design.

Q: How should I eliminate the existing moss to rejuvenate the lawn?
A: The presence of moss is telling you something. It tends to grow where soil is shaded, acidic, compacted, low in fertility, and moist. These are very difficult conditions for lawn grass. You have two choices here. Is this an area where lawn is needed? If not, you may save yourself a lot of trouble by changing the landscape design and having pavement, moss, ferns, or ground cover there instead of grass. But if you want lawn grass to grow, remove the moss and rejuvenate the soil. Raise the pH by adding ground limestone and also add fertilizer, organic matter, and sand, if needed, for better drainage and aeration. Reseed or install sod of a shade-resistant turf species.

Q: A lecturer at our garden club said to plant bulbs in clusters. Is this correct?
A: In most cases, yes. Bulbs look better when clumped together in groups of five or more. If you plant them in a straight, thin line, they don't show up as well, and if one of them doesn't bloom, gets eaten by a squirrel, or blooms at the wrong time, your line won't look right. In future years, the line may disintegrate further if fewer of the bulbs come back. However, if you prefer straight lines in design, plant your bulbs in a broad band, ten deep or so, like they do in public gardens. You'll have a wonderful, showy mass of color in the spring.

Q: When is the best time to dig and separate bulbs?
A: The foliage of most spring bulbs will naturally turn yellow about six weeks after flowering. This is a good indication that the plant has produced and stored enough energy to survive and bloom the next season. When leaves are halfway to yellow or brown, dig deeply to remove the entire clump. Gently shake the soil from the bulbs and break individual bulbs from the clump. Immediately replant the bulbs in good soil at improved spacing.

Q: The outer edges of my property have lots of shrubs and roots, and a friend suggests I put an island bed in a sunny spot in the lawn. Any tips?
A: Island beds—plantings that are centrally placed and viewed from all sides—require a different design approach than side beds. To be effective from every direction, it's necessary to lay them out so that the tallest plants are located in the middle of the bed. It is useful to have more plants of low and intermediate height than tall ones in these plantings. Since the beds are surrounded by lawn, they may be meant to be seen from a distance. If so, select large-flowered or colorful plants.

Q: There's a spot in my garden that always stays soggy, and I can't grow grass there. How can I fix it?
A: Turn a low, moist spot into a bog garden for plants that need extra moisture. You can even excavate down a little to create a natural pond. Plant the moist banks with variegated cattails, sagittaria, cardinal flower, hostas, ferns, bog primroses, marsh marigolds, and other moisture-loving plants.

Q: I am trying to grow shrubs in the back left corner of the yard, but they keep getting mowed down even though they have plant markers. Help!
A: You need to defend your shrubs by defining their space and marking it well. Turn the area into a corner bed by enlarging the garden area near the immature shrubs and mulching it evenly all across, under the shrubs, too. Add some annual flowers inside the mulched bed to make the spot more colorful while the shrubs are growing. Make a nice, even edge of mulch so that there is no way to mistake your garden bed for part of the lawn.

Q: I have several large patio containers of trees and shrubs growing with mixed annuals. How do I overwinter these containers?
A: Remove the annuals from the containers at the end of the season. Move the containers to a location protected from the warming sun and winter wind. Insulate the soil with mulch—compost, bark, or leaves—and make sure the containers receive adequate water during dry spells. In fall when you move the pots, try planting some spring flowering bulbs in them in place of the annuals, to enjoy some early season color next year.

CHAPTER 5

Annual Plants

The world of annuals includes high-performance plants that give you speedy garden results. These plants, whether small or large, are primed to germinate quickly when conditions are right, grow speedily, and then do what they do so well—make loads of flowers, fruits, roots, and seeds for the duration of the growing period. Many of our most useful vegetables are annuals and are similar to annual flowers in their needs. Many of the best flowers for bedding and containers are annuals. They can be used alone or in combination with perennials, shrubs, and trees.

Annuals generally need sunshine and rich, moist soil for all that growth, but there are types that have adapted to dry or shady conditions. Look at any popular seed catalog to get a quick glimpse at the astonishing bounty of annuals within your reach. Annuals are great for beginning gardeners, but experts grow them, too.

What Is an Annual?

Annuals are flowers that bloom the first year they are planted, often flowering only a few months after sowing. Then they die the same year. Annuals can be tender or hardy (defined below) and prefer different climates and temperatures.

Tender annuals are killed by frost. They grow in hot weather and are started indoors or in greenhouses and then set out into the garden after the danger of frost passes. Some of the faster-growing tender annuals such as zinnias and marigolds can be sown directly into garden beds, after the frost in spring, for bloom or use all summer long. This depends on many factors, including where you live and how long summer weather lasts. *Hardy annuals* have some built-in frost tolerance. They are often, but not always, planted outside from seed a few weeks before the final frost, but sometimes they are started indoors in warmer conditions, hardened off for a good adjustment, and planted outside during spring (or in winter in Zones 8 to 10). *Biennials* such as sweet William are similar to hardy annuals; it can sometimes be hard to say which is which, because local climate plays a key role in their behavior. Biennials are sown in summer or fall. They develop their roots and foliage and live through winter. Then they come quickly into a spectacular but short-lived period of bloom in spring. They tend to self-sow, providing a constant supply of plants. Hardy annuals grow like biennials where winters are not too cold. *Tender perennials* include other plants that are mainly used as annuals. In colder climates, tender perennials such as wax begonia and some species of impatiens will behave like annuals and must be cultivated as such. These same plants, however, will grow as perennials in their native hot climates, living for several years.

Some annual plants are ornamental, some are edible, including many garden vegetables, and some are both. The mission of an annual is to make seeds for the next generation. Pinching the dying flowers off before the seeds form stimulates side branches as the plants try to bloom again.

A meadow garden of poppies and daisies has natural charm. Most mixes of meadow flowers come with instructions on soil preparation and planting time.

 A "Garden of Eden" effect is sometimes achieved when you mix edible plants with ornamental ones in a beautiful garden, as it is in this display garden. Here, delicious looking pears growing on a trellis are in harmony with rows of flowers and neatly maintained vegetables.

EDIBLE ANNUALS

Most annuals like the same basic garden conditions: full sun and level, moist, rich, well-drained soil with a neutral pH. These conditions are exactly the ones preferred by most of our best garden vegetables and herbs. There is no reason to avoid combining vegetables, herbs, and flowers in the same garden or

BIENNIALS

Biennials such as cup and saucer campanula (Canterbury bells), money plant (lunaria), some foxgloves, forget-me-nots, sweet William, fall-planted larkspur, and some hollyhocks produce only greenery the first year. During the second year of growth, they flower and set seed destined to become the next generation. If you allow plants to self-sow for at least two years, you will have a steady supply of blooming plants.

group of containers. Breeders have developed colorful types and also dwarf types to help everyone fit vegetables into the scene. You can have an ornamental garden that includes attractive edible plants, or you can have a traditional vegetable garden with a few rows for flowers or with a double row of French marigolds as a border. Here are some quick tips for incorporating something edible into your landscape:

❀ **Lettuce** grows during cool weather in spring or fall. Even when crowded, it will produce usable leaves, but plants grow better when widely spaced. In flowerbeds, an edging or clump of lettuce does double duty. Leaves can be green or red, frilled or plain, depending on the cultivar.

❀ **Radish** is another cool-weather crop. You can grow some nice spring radishes in the space you will use later for zinnias or other summer flowers—or for tomatoes.

Growing your own vegetables organically ensures fresh and flavorful produce and saves you the high prices of organically grown produce at the grocery store.

- **Beans** can sprawl and aren't particularly ornamental. They do not tolerate frost. If you choose climbing types, you can train them on tepees and pergolas for nice garden accents. Scarlet runner beans have great flowers and edible beans, and string beans and limas are favorites everywhere.
- **Cucumbers and squash** include climbing or vining types for trellises as well as dwarf forms that squeeze into containers and tight spaces. Pumpkins take lots more space and a longer season, so they may not work as well for some gardeners. None of these plants tolerates frost.
- **Parsley, dill, fennel, and basil** have aromatic foliage that is handsome enough for any garden. Basil is tender, but the others will survive a touch of frost.
- **Corn** needs space and is planted in blocks for pollination, so the tender plants usually are seen only in proper vegetable gardens. However, breeders offer types with red or variegated foliage that can do double duty as ornamental grass.
- **The tomato** is on everyone's list, because there is nothing like a fresh, sun-warmed tomato. There are many types to consider, from beefsteak to cherry to heirloom varieties. There are also petite types bred for hanging baskets. Tall and rangy cherry types

Tomatoes are grown just like many other annual plants, in rich, loose soil in a sunny spot. They offer a juicy reward to the gardener who gets it right.

Peppers range from sweet to mildly spicy to super hot—something for everyone's taste buds!

Annuals in Warm Climates

Gardeners who live in warm climates with little frost (mainly Zones 9 to 11) can do really interesting things with annuals and grow them throughout the year, using tender annuals and perennials in spring, summer, and fall. They may need seasonal replacement, for annuals cannot live forever, even in Florida. In winter, hardy annuals can be put to great use. Plant seeds of shirley poppies, larkspur, pansies and violas, baby's breath, cornflowers, sweet peas, and other hardy annuals directly in the sunny garden in November or December, after the weather cools. Thin the seedlings if they are crowded. They'll grow through the shifts of cool and warm weather of the South's winter. A few months later, in early spring, fabulously colorful blooms will be delightful and amazing.

can be trained up a trellis or over an arch. In fact, in the 1800s, tomatoes were grown only as ornamentals (often near outhouses) because people thought they were toxic. Tomatoes do not tolerate frost.

❧ **Peppers** of all types (see page 115) have good form, are not too rangy, and are color-ful and attractive. They prefer hot weather and have no frost tolerance.

❧ **Eggplants** exhibit preferences similar to peppers. They are very good-looking in any garden because of their purple flowers and colorful fruits. There are purple, white, or streaked fruits, elongated or globular, and even a red form.

Design and Color

Designing with annuals gives lots of impor-tance to flower color. Annuals offer flower color for a longer period of time than other plant types, for they are constantly in bloom. They are

❧ *A curve of color in a sea of green, this trim border of pink, rose, and white impatiens blooms from late spring until frost. It is never in disarray and is the ideal companion to the well-kept lawn and foundation planting.*

ANNUALS THAT DO WELL IN CONTAINERS
Fibrous-rooted begonia
Calendula
Coleus
Dracaena
Impatiens
Lobelia
Marigold
Nasturtium
Ornamental pepper
Pansy
Perilla
Phlox (*P. drummondii*)
Sweet pea
Verbena
Viola
Zonal geranium

often used in complex plans. Clumps look better than rows or thin lines. Arrange tall types toward the back and shorter types in front. In island beds, taller types go in the center because the beds are seen from all sides. Random mix-tures of like plants in different colors are usually

Casual in style yet very tidy, this rock-lined annual border of pansies and snapdragons is perky and colorful for weeks on end.

less successful than clumps of one color contrasted with clumps of another, in the color scheme you have chosen (see Chapter 4).

Keep design factors such as color, form, texture, and scale in mind with the assurance that annuals will perform their role in the design in a stable fashion, not changing that much from week to week. Whatever your style, whether casual or formal, annuals are excellent sources of accents and colors for great garden effects.

DESIGN TIPS

Use pale sand to outline the plant groupings before planting when laying out annual beds. This is like making a pencil sketch of a painting before stroking on the oil paints. Whether you're planning to put blue ageratums in edging rows, make a teardrop of red zinnias, or create a sweeping mass of pink impatiens, you can adjust and fine-tune the overall shapes before filling them in with colorful flowers. After making the sand outlines, stand back and look at the results objectively. If you don't like the first attempt, cover the sand with soil and try again.

Plant staggered rows of annuals to create a fuller look. A single marching line of annuals such as French marigolds set side by side can look weak in a bigger garden. You can beef up their impact by planting a second row behind the first, with the rear plants centered on the openings between the front-row plants. Staggered rows are also nice for showcasing taller annuals, such as blue salvia or snapdragons, set in the rear of a garden. A double row of spider flowers (cleome) can become so full and bushy it resembles a flowering hedge. In large gardens, try a triple row.

Use a spacing aid to plant annual displays and cutting gardens in even rows. Even the most beautifully grown annuals can be distracting if they are spaced erratically. Fortunately, spacing is one element you can easily control. Here are some options:

❀ Make a planting grid by stapling a large piece of wire mesh over a wooden frame. If the mesh openings are two inches square and you want to plant ageratums six inches apart, you can put one seedling in every third hole.

❀ Make a spacing rope. Tie knots in the rope to mark specific measurements, for instance, noting every four or six inches. You can

---

SELF-BRANCHING ANNUALS

Many modern types of impatiens, begonias, multiflora petunias, marigolds, and other annuals have been bred to be self-branching. They stay fuller naturally and will need little, if any, pinching.

stretch the rope between two stakes to make even measurements along a straight line.

❀ Take a yardstick with you when you go to plant. Measure the distance between each plant in a row and between rows rather than simply eyeballing it.

ANNUALS IN THE SHADE

Choose shade-tolerant or shade-loving annuals for a lightly shaded garden. Among the annuals that prefer shade are impatiens, browallia, and torenia. Other annuals, the most versatile of the bunch, will grow in sun or light shade. They include wax begonias, sweet alyssum, ageratum, coleus, forget-me-nots, and pansies.

Create the most excitement from your shade garden by choosing flowers with white,

pastel, or brightly colored blossoms. Dark burgundy leaves and cool blue or purple flowers won't shine the way brighter blooms do from shady garden depths.

ANNUALS SUITABLE FOR LATE SUMMER STEM CUTTINGS

Coleus

Fibrous-rooted begonia

Geraniums, ivy-leaf and standard

Impatiens

Petunia

Portulaca

Verbena

Care and Feeding

Fertilize annuals periodically during the growing season to keep them producing. This is particularly helpful after the first flush of blooming flowers begins to fade (which often marks the beginning of a quiet garden during hot summer months). For best results, follow the directions on the fertilizer package label for application instructions. "Blossom Booster" types of fertilizer such as 10-20-20 are great for annuals.

Snip back leggy annuals when you plant to encourage bushy new growth. Don't hesitate—it's really for the best! Removing the growing tip of a stem stimulates side shoots to sprout, which makes annuals fuller. Since each side shoot can be full of flowers, the whole plant will look better.

Remove spent blossoms from geraniums and other annuals to keep them blooming and tidy. The bigger the flower, the worse it can look when faded, brown, and mushy. Large, globular geranium flowers are particularly prominent when they begin to discolor. Snip off the entire flower cluster. Take off the stem, too, if no other flower buds are waiting to bloom. This process, called *deadheading*, is more than mere housekeeping. By removing the old flowers, you prevent seed production, which consumes a huge amount of energy from the plant. Energy saved can be channeled instead into producing new blooms. Happily, the same effect is achieved when you cut annual flowers in bloom for bouquets.

PEST PREVENTION

Make a daily or weekly checkup, and look for signs of pest damage. Common offenders range from cute bunnies and chipmunks to slimy slugs and creepy caterpillars. If you are uncertain what is causing damage to your plants, take a specimen to your garden center or local Agricultural Extension Agent. Quick action prevents future damage. Remedies range from barriers and netting to earth-friendly pesticides (see Chapter 3).

Increasing Annuals

Take stem cuttings of tender flowers in late summer before temperatures drop below 50 degrees Fahrenheit. You can root them indoors and enjoy their greenery and perhaps a few flowers during winter. Then you can take more cuttings of these plants to set out next spring. Cuttings are more compact and versatile than old garden plants dug up and squeezed into a pot. They can thrive with less effort and space.

Fresh-cut annual stems may root if you put them in a vase of clean water. But stems can root more reliably in a sterile, peat-based mix. Have flowers blooming in sunny windows during fall and winter by starting new seedlings outdoors in pots in mid- to late summer. Bring them indoors several weeks before the first autumn frost. They will begin to bloom as frost arrives, perfect for brightening the autumn transition period. This works well with French marigolds, pansies, petunias, nasturtiums, violas, impatiens, compact cockscomb, and annual asters. Simply discard the plants later when they get ratty looking.

SAVING SEEDS

Annuals make seeds, if allowed to, and they will grow for you. Watch the pods as they develop. They will often turn from green to tan as the seeds become ripe. Seeds are not viable unless they are fully formed. If the seedpods tend to open or even explode when ripe, slip a net of cheesecloth or a bit of old pantyhose over them to trap the seeds. Store them in labeled envelopes for planting the next year. Seeds of biennials and, sometimes, hardy annuals, can be planted immediately.

Other Ways to Use Annuals

Since annuals are plants that grow fast, they have many practical uses in and out of the garden. Annuals can be used to fill gardens that will later be used for perennial borders when the budget permits or the plants have multiplied enough to fill the space. Because annuals stay in bloom for several months at a time, they are used for constancy in gardens where other plants come in and go out of bloom. This is why they are so often an important element in decorative containers and flowerbeds where high impact is wanted. There are annuals that evoke different styles and historical eras, used in theme gardens.

Some annuals are less showy but great for fragrance. Nasturtiums and violas are edible, so they are used as colorful garnishes for food. Annual grasses and strawflowers are used in bouquets, fresh or dried. Containers of living annuals, small or large, can be used for many decorative purposes, with the small ones serving as table centerpieces or take-home gifts for guests.

A half whiskey barrel is deep and wide and can be used in place of a garden or in addition to one. Here, the gardener has made the container into a charming cottage garden with dusty miller, delphinium, petunia, campanula, and dianthus.

WINTER ARRANGEMENTS OF DRIED FLOWERS

Grow some annuals with everlasting flowers to dry for winter arrangements. There are many wonderful annuals to choose from. Those listed in the sidebar on page 111 are easily dried if spread out in a warm, dark, airy place. Grow a few for yourself and some extras to give away as gifts. If seedlings of everlasting annuals are not available at your local garden center, consider starting your own seedlings indoors.

ANNUAL FLOWERS FOR CUTTING

Annuals make great "cuts" because they are so productive. The flowers you cut for bouquets will soon be replaced by new flower growth. If you have a choice, plant long-stem types for bouquets. Harvest in the morning, removing lower foliage on stems and putting them in deep room-temperature water in a bucket for several hours. Here are some annuals that look great in a vase:

- basil
- calendula
- capsicum
- cleome
- coleus
- cornflower
- cosmos
- dahlia
- lantana
- larkspur
- lisianthus
- love-in-a-mist
- nasturtium
- nicotiana
- perilla
- petunia
- poppy
- salvia
- snapdragon
- sunflower
- sweet pea
- tithonia
- verbena
- zinnia

ANNUAL FLOWERS FOR FRAGRANCE

Why not plant some perfumed flowers under an open window or beside the patio? Here are some good choices:
- Heliotrope
- Lemon and orange gem marigold
- Moonflower
- Petunia
- Pink
- Stock
- Sweet pea
- Fragrant white flowering tobacco

A BIT OF THE PAST

Relive a little slice of history by growing a few heirloom flowers. These are flowers your ancestors may have enjoyed. Many of these plants are returning to popularity, thanks to their interesting appearances. Some heirlooms are only slightly different from modern flowers—taller, larger- or smaller-flowered, or more fragrant. But other heirlooms are quite distinct and unusual. Here are some examples:

ers, California poppies, and verbenas; and open-pollinated annuals such as snapdragons, portulaca, cockscomb, balsam, shirley poppies, larkspur, viola, and spider flowers (cleome). You can help them along by clearing away weeds and competing plants and lightly tilling the soil near the parent plants where you want the volunteers to grow.

❁ Balsam: This impatiens relative sprinkles flowers amid the foliage along the stems.

❁ Love-lies-bleeding: Long, dangling, crimson-red seed heads form colorful streamers.

❁ Kiss-me-over-the-garden-gate: These six-foot-tall plants have pendulous pink flowers.

❁ Sweet pea: Vining pea-shape plants that bear colorful pink, white, purple, and red flowers with delightful fragrances.

SELF-SOWN ANNUALS

In informal gardens, plant annuals, especially those that are not hybrids, that may return from self-sown seeds allowed to mature and fall to the ground. Suitable annuals include the heirlooms love-lies-bleeding and kiss-me-over-the-garden-gate; wildflowers such as cornflow-

SOME EVERLASTING ANNUALS AND BIENNIALS

- Cockscomb: plume or comb-shaped flowers in bright red, orange, or yellow

- Annual baby's breath: cloudlike drifts of small white flowers

- Bells of Ireland: spikes of green trumpet-shape flowers

- Globe amaranth: ball-shape flowers of white, pink, purple, and orange

- Love-in-a-mist: maroon-striped seedpods

- Statice: bright sprays of pink, purple, yellow, white, and blue flowers

- Strawflowers: double daisylike flowers with straw-textured petals in red, pink, white, gold, and bronze

Excellent Annuals

The plants selected for this directory are suited to a wide range of conditions and purposes, but they can all be used as annuals to provide seasonal color outdoors. Many kinds are listed here, enough for you to try different ones in different years or positions. Whether you live in a country home or a multistory condo with a windy balcony, you will find plants here that will work for you.

Each plant listing includes its common name or names first, followed by botanical names, descriptions, care, propagation, uses, and related species and varieties. A color photo illustrates each entry. Propagation times are estimates, for plants behave differently in varying situations.

Most of these plants can be found in bloom in pots or market packs at garden centers and other stores. A few will have to be grown from seed, either from mail order or local seed sources. Some are slow from seed, some are quick. Browse through and familiarize yourself with annuals that will work in your location and provide the attributes you are looking for.

Ageratum, Floss Flower

Ageratum houstonianum

These fluffy flowers in white, lavender-blue, and pink are favorites for summer gardens and containers.

Description: Ageratum plants are covered with clusters of small, fuzzy flowers. Most types are mounding plants six to ten inches tall and wide, but there are taller types. Plants bloom from spring planting until frost in fall.

How to grow: Grow in any well-drained soil in full sun or partial shade. Space six to ten inches apart for solid color. Deadhead or shear back slightly if plants become untidy.

Propagation: Start seeds indoors six to eight weeks before planting. Seeds germinate in five to eight days at 70°F.

Uses: Place in the front of borders and beds. Use them for their scarce blue color, which is seldom found in annuals. Taller, sometimes older, varieties make good cut flowers.

Related species: Golden ageratum, *Lonas inodora*, has the same flower effect in bright yellow.

Related varieties: The blues include 'Blue Horizon' for cutting and 'Blue Lagoon' and 'Blue Danube' for pots and bedding.

Sweet Alyssum

Lobularia maritima

Alyssum flowers for months, even through the winter in milder climates. A member of the mustard family, alyssum is quite fragrant.

Description: Alyssum grows only a few inches high but spreads as much as a foot in diameter. The tiny flowers are closely packed around small racemes that grow upward as lower flowers fade. Although white is the most planted color, pink, lavender, and darker shades of violet are also available.

How to grow: Alyssum grows best in full sun in cool weather, but it will tolerate partial shade. The plants will survive light frosts. Space from six to eight inches apart. Alyssum will reseed vigorously.

Propagation: Sow seeds outdoors as soon as the ground can be worked. Seeds germinate in 7 to 14 days at 65° to 70°F.

Uses: Alyssum is traditionally used for edging beds, borders, and as annual ground cover.

Related varieties: 'New Carpet of Snow' is the most planted, but the 'Wonderland' series consists of 'White,' 'Rosy-Red,' and 'Deep Purple.' White 'Snow Crystals' is wide, low, and vigorous.

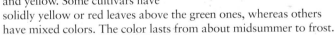

Amaranthus, Summer Poinsettia

Amaranthus tricolor

Capped with a swirling crown of brilliantly hot-colored leaves, these tall, striking plants are grown for their foliage.

Description: When plants have grown, the upper third of the foliage takes on hot colors of red and yellow. Some cultivars have solidly yellow or red leaves above the green ones, whereas others have mixed colors. The color lasts from about midsummer to frost.

How to grow: Grow in any fertile, well-drained soil in full sun. Space two feet apart. Plants require hot weather and will tolerate drought once they are established. Do not deadhead or shear back these plants or you may lose the colorful tops.

Propagation: Start the small seeds indoors eight weeks before planting. Seeds germinate in ten days at 70°F. In regions with long, hot summers, sow directly where they will grow.

Uses: Place in masses, especially in island beds and at the back of borders.

Related species: *Amaranthus caudatus*, known as love-lies-bleeding, is grown for its dramatically trailing seedpods in reddish tones. Amaranthus 'Pygmy Torch' is 18 inches tall with purple leaves and curved, cranberry-red seed spikes.

Related varieties: 'Aurora' is green with a crown of golden leaves. 'Illumination' is coppery red, and 'Summer Poinsettia Perfecta' has multicolored red, yellow, and green leaves at the top.

Bachelor's Button, Cornflower

Centaurea cyanus

This favorite got its name from its use as a boutonniere flower.

Description: Bachelor's buttons grow one to three feet tall with innumerable fluffy but trim round flowers held above the rather sparse, long and narrow gray-green leaves. The habit of growth is relatively loose, except with compact new cultivars.

How to grow: Full sun in average soil is good. For earliest bloom, sow seeds outdoors in the fall so they will start to grow before the first frost and bloom the next spring. Otherwise, sow seeds outdoors as early in the spring as the soil can be worked. Thin to 8 to 12 inches apart.

Propagation: To grow seedlings indoors, germinate at 65°F four weeks before planting out. Germination time is 7 to 14 days.

Uses: Bachelor's buttons lend themselves to informal planting, particularly with other annuals and perennials in beds and borders.

Related species: *Centaurea montana*, blue-flowered perennial.

Related varieties: 'Blue Boy' grows to more than two feet. 'Polka Dot Mix' comes with flowers of many colors. 'Dwarf Midget' produces bushy plants a foot high.

Basil
Ocimum basilicum

Basil plants are grown not only as herbs for culinary purposes, but also for their good looks. There are basils of varying leaf colors and sizes, and they combine nicely with other garden plants. Basil grows well near tomatoes and also pairs beautifully with them in many recipes.

Description: Most types of basil grow 16 to 24 inches tall and wide, with oval green leaves about two inches long. There is a purple-leaved form and a tiny-leaved dwarf form. Plants are at their most attractive during warm weather and are killed by frost.

How to grow: Grow basil in well-drained soil of average fertility in full sun. Space plants about ten inches apart. Pinch tips for bushiness and side growth. You can cook with the pieces you trim off. Water the soil around plants, not the leaves, to prevent leaf spots.

Propagation: Start seeds indoors six weeks before planting or outdoors when soil is warm and the danger of frost has passed. Seeds germinate in ten days at 70°F. Thin or transplant the seedlings when they are three or four inches tall. Basil also grows from tip cuttings.

Uses: Grow basil in vegetable garden rows, in herb gardens, as clumps in flower borders, and as container plants. Their nice leaves and good form help them blend in everywhere. Leaves can be used fresh or dried.

Browallia, Sapphire Flower
Browallia speciosa, B. viscosa

Flowers bloom heavily from early spring to fall frost and year-round in sunny windows or greenhouses. They're at their best in cool or coastal gardens, but with partial shade or an eastern exposure they will consistently grow well elsewhere.

Description: *B. speciosa* varieties grow in a loose mound up to 18 inches high and as wide, their lax habit allowing them to trail. The popular variety of *B. viscosa* 'Sapphire' is a compact, rather stiff plant that doesn't trail.

How to grow: Plant in rich, well-drained soil but keep moist. Plant large varieties ten inches apart and dwarf ones six inches apart. Browallia is a good shade plant, though with a looser habit and sparser flowers.

Propagation: Start seeds indoors six to eight weeks prior to planting out after the last frost. At temperatures of 70° to 75°F, they'll take 14 to 21 days to germinate.

Uses: The sapphire-blue flowers are grown in beds, borders, or rock gardens. Compact plants make good edges for a tall border and are excellent container plants.

Related varieties: 'Sky Blue' has great color and thrives in pots. 'Jingle Bells' is a mix of white and blue shades.

Wax Begonia, Fibrous Begonia
Begonia semperflorens

The brightly colored bedding begonias are equally at home in full sun (except where temperatures stay above 90°F for days on end) or full but bright shade (where trees are pruned high). From first setting them out until they are laid low by frost, they'll be packed with white, pink, rose, or red blossoms. Virtually untouched by bugs or blight, their only shortcoming is a relatively narrow color range. They are widely available in market packs.

Description: Uniformity is the trademark of most begonias—tight mounds of closely packed leaves covered with blossoms. All four flower colors are available with your choice of leaf color: chocolaty-red or shades of green. The deeper-colored or bronze-leaved varieties offer especially eye-catching contrast with flowers. There are also varieties with double flowers that resemble fat little rosebuds and others with variegated foliage.

How to grow: Begonias perform well in rich, well-drained soil, but the soil must be allowed to dry between waterings. They'll form tight, compact plants in full sun, with increasingly looser form and fewer flowers as you move them deeper into the shade. Most hybrids will grow six to nine inches high and spread as wide.

Propagation: Most hybrids are grown from seed, but great patience is required. Dustlike seeds (two million per ounce) must be sown in December or January for large, husky plants by May. Germination temperature is 70° to 85°F and requires 14 to 21 days. Cuttings root readily, so an easier way to start plants is on a sunny windowsill during fall and winter.

Uses: Wax-leaved begonias lend themselves to large, formal plantings because of their uniform size and shapeliness. They're also suitable in front of summer annual borders and combine well with other cool-colored flowers in mixed plantings and containers.

Related varieties: Popular, dark-leaved kinds are the 'Cocktail' series: 'Brandy,' 'Vodka,' 'Whiskey,' and 'Gin.' Good green-leaved varieties are found in the 'Lotto' and 'Pizzazz' series. 'Avalanche' begonias in pink or white are rangier, suited for containers and hanging baskets, where their arching growth habit is handsome.

Calendula, Pot Marigold
Calendula officinalis

This old-fashioned herb is a hardy annual that has been updated with large-flowered cultivars in sunny shades of yellow, buff, orange, and apricot. Seeds are large and easy to grow.

Description: Leaves are green rosettes that sport multiple stems of single or double daisylike flowers, which are sometimes crested in form. Height can be anywhere from one to two feet, and flowers may be two to four inches wide. Plants bloom and grow best during cool weather, but flowers close on cloudy days.

How to grow: Grow plants in any well-drained soil in full sun or bright partial shade. Space 12 inches apart. Deadhead regularly to promote the formation of new blossoms and to keep plants neat.

Propagation: In regions with hot summers, 90°F or higher, start seeds indoors in summer for fall plants. In areas with mild summers, sow seeds directly in the ground in spring, after the danger of frost passes. In areas with mild winters, sow seeds in the ground or in pots in December. Seeds germinate in eight to ten days at 70°F.

Uses: Use in beds, containers, and toward the front of borders. The flowers appear on strong stems and make good cut flowers. The edible petals can be used either fresh or dry to add color to rice and salads.

California Poppy
Eschscholzia californica

In the wild, these orange flowers carpet California hillsides in early spring. Garden forms are hardy annuals that grow in a broad range of colors.

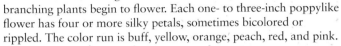

Description: Leaves are thread-like and lacy, growing in one-foot mounds that elongate as branching plants begin to flower. Each one- to three-inch poppylike flower has four or more silky petals, sometimes bicolored or rippled. The color run is buff, yellow, orange, peach, red, and pink.

How to grow: Grow in any well-drained soil in full sun. Thin to ten inches apart. Pinch back and deadhead to prolong flowering.

Propagation: Start seeds outdoors where they will grow, about four weeks before the danger of frost ends in spring. In climates with mild winters, plant seeds in late fall.

Uses: Excellent for drifts of color in beds, borders, and meadow gardens. Flowers self-sow freely when planted where they are well suited.

Related species: *E. caespitosa* 'Sundew' is only six inches tall and loaded with little yellow flowers on feathery tufts of greenish-white foliage. *E. mexicana* has large reddish-orange flowers and self-sows strongly.

Related varieties: 'Thai Silk' is a standard mix of large poppies in varied colors. 'Champagne and Roses' has large pink blooms with fluted petals.

Capsicum, peppers
Capsicum annuum

Colorful ornamental peppers last longer than flowers and add festive color and texture to beds and borders.

Description: Plants range from six inches to several feet tall and have a tidy growth habit. The glossy fruits grow from an inch or less in length to more than six inches and can be pointy, round, or blocky. They have bright colors and waxy coats. Foliage may be green or purple, and peppers range from cream through yellow, orange, red, purple, and brownish-black.

How to grow: Grow peppers during warm weather in full sun, after the danger of frost has passed. Fertilize the soil and give plants ample space. Pinch the central tip to promote side branches. Do not let young plants become stressed by cold weather or drought.

Propagation: Start seeds indoors eight weeks before planting. Seeds germinate in 15 to 20 days at 75°F.

Uses: It's fun to see colorful peppers as pot plants. They work well in flower borders and vegetable garden rows. When cooking, beware and taste the peppers. Heat is concentrated in the inner veins and seeds.

Related varieties: 'Chilly Chili' has nonfiery-tasting pointy little multicolored peppers, facing upward in a swirling manner. 'Prairie Fire' has blockier small peppers. 'Thai Dragon' has long, red, hot peppers on prolific plants. Many heirloom types plus bell peppers are widely available.

Celosia
Celosia argentea

The silky blooms of celosia get attention wherever they grow. You have a wide choice of appearance, size, and color.

Description: Celosia offers large flower clusters on top of green or reddish leaves. Colors include yellow, gold, red, pink, orange, and wine. Velvety crested types (cockscomb) are rippled, whereas others are shaped like plumes or spikes. Heights range from 6 to 36 inches; flower size is not determined by height.

How to grow: Grow in rich to average well-drained soil in full sun. Space 6 to 24 inches apart. Outdoors, sow seeds or set out plants during warm weather, after the danger of frost has passed.

Propagation: Start seeds indoors six to eight weeks before outdoor planting time. Seeds germinate in ten days at 70°F.

Uses: Use dwarf types in containers and as edgings. Mass tall types in borders or grow them in garden rows for use as cut or dried flowers. To dry, pick before flowers open fully and hang upside down in a cool, dark place.

Related varieties: 'Amigo Mix' has huge crests on dwarf plants. 'Bombay Pink' is a rippled pink and white marvel. 'Century Fire' has big red plumes on 20-inch plants and blooms early.

Cleome, Spider Flower
Cleome hasslerana

What gives the beautiful spider flower its name? Those exceedingly long seedpods that develop below the flowers as bloom progresses upward on the stalk give the plants a spidery look, as do the projecting stamens of the flowers.

Description: Cleome flowers, with many opening at once, grow in airy racemes six to eight inches in diameter. Flowers—white, pink, or lavender in color—perch atop stems that grow up to six feet high.

How to grow: Cleome grows well in average soil located in full or nearly full sun. It is very drought-tolerant, though it will look and grow better if it is watered well. Space plants one to three feet apart.

Propagation: Sow after the last frost when the ground is warm. Cleomes may also be started indoors four to six weeks earlier at a temperature of at least 70°F. Germination time is 10 to 14 days. In the garden, it reseeds prolifically and should be thinned.

Uses: Plant cleome for its height, to back up borders, in the center of island beds, or in any spot where its dramatic quality stands out.

Related varieties: 'Helen Campbell' is a popular white variety. 'Rose Queen' is salmon-pink, and 'Ruby Queen' is rose colored. 'Sparkler' is a newer strain that grows three to four feet tall, not six.

Coleus
Solenostemon scutellaroides

An annual member of the mint family, coleus is a colorful classic with serrated leaves on branching plants.

Description: Plants show their colors when small. Leaves are banded and veined with multiple improbable colors like purple, lime, red, brown, white, and copper, in a variety of lacy or plain shapes. Leaf size can be from 1 to 6 inches, and plants have a mounded shape anywhere from 6 to 36 inches tall and almost as wide.

How to grow: Grow plants in moist, rich soil in partial shade. Space ten or more inches apart. Protect plants from frost and drought. Pinch back tips for bushiness. Remove flower spikes before they open.

Propagation: Start seeds indoors eight weeks before planting. Seeds germinate in 10 to 12 days at 72°F. Root tip cuttings for a week or two in moist soil, vermiculite, or even plain water.

Uses: Group identically colored plants together for better design. Use plants in containers, bedding designs, and borders. Side branches, cut, have been known to make roots while still in bouquets.

Related varieties: Breeders love the many variations of color and form. Solid purple and velvety 'Palisandra' is great for combinations. Countless named types in all colors have tiny, huge, frilled, or serrated leaves and have led to a craze for coleus.

Coreopsis
Coreopsis tinctoria

The gold, brown, and rusty-red flower colors of coreopsis are warm and distinctive. Plants grow quickly and easily from seed. Plants sometimes live through winter and come back taller and fuller the next year.

Description: Small, daisy-flowered plants appear in summer in most areas, in spring in the Deep South. Each flower is half an inch wide, on wiry, branched stems. Clusters can be a foot across. Cultivars range from under a foot to four feet tall.

How to grow: Plants grow best in full sun. Soil can be of average fertility, well-drained. Space plants a foot apart. Deadhead or remove plants when they become untidy. Let flowers go to seed in places where you want self-sown plants.

Propagation: Start seeds indoors six weeks before the last expected frost, or start them outdoors in beds around the time of last frost. Seeds germinate in a week at 72°F. Thin seedlings.

Uses: Coreopsis is excellent in meadow gardens, borders, and flowerbeds. Dwarf types are good in pots. Use it in bouquets because of its wiry stems and lasting flowers.

Related varieties: 'Mahogany Midget' has red petals around golden eyes and grows ten inches tall. 'Tiger Flowered' is the same size with splotched red and yellow petals. The *C. tinctoria* species is four feet tall with gold and red petals on two-inch flowers.

Cosmos
Cosmos bipinnatus

Cosmos is one of the fastest-growing annuals. Some varieties reach up to six feet by summer's end.

Description: Cosmos forms a lacy, open plant with flowers three to four inches in diameter. These "daisies" come in pink, red, white, and lavender with a contrasting yellow center.

How to grow: Cosmos grows best in full sun, but it will bloom acceptably in partial shade. Space at least 12 inches apart.

Propagation: Because it grows so fast, sow cosmos outdoors after danger of frost has passed or three weeks earlier, indoors. Barely cover seeds; they need light to germinate. Germination takes three to seven days at 70° to 75°F.

Uses: Because of its height, cosmos should be planted at the back of borders and grouped against fences or other places as a covering.

Related species: *Cosmos sulphureus* is the source of the hot red and yellow colors of cosmos. Blooms come quickly after planting seed and continue until frost.

Related varieties: 'Sensation' series is four feet tall and comes in mixed colors. 'Purity' is similar in pure white. 'Gazebo' is a two-foot mix.

Dahlberg Daisy, Golden Fleece

Dyssodia tenuiloba

A charming little plant with sunny flowers, the Dahlberg daisy is now becoming widely available at garden centers.

Description: This species of daisy bears many golden-yellow, upright flowers measuring a half an inch in diameter. The long, narrow leaves are divided, giving a feathery appearance. Plants grow from 6 to 12 inches high and spread as much as 18 inches.

How to grow: Dahlberg daisies grow well in full sun and well-drained, moderately fertile soil. However, they will also grow and bloom abundantly in poor soil and hot weather. Plant outdoors when the soil is warm and the danger of frost has passed. Space 6 to 12 inches apart.

Propagation: Sow seeds in place when the ground is warm. For earlier bloom, start seeds indoors six to eight weeks prior to planting. Germination takes 8 to 12 days at 60° to 80°F.

Uses: Dahlberg daisy can be planted in rock gardens or in pockets among paving stones or patio blocks. It makes a superb edging for beds and borders and can be used as a ground cover plant for sunny areas. Its reseeding habit makes it ideal for naturalized gardens.

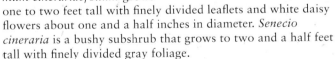

Dusty Miller

Senecio cineraria, Chrysanthemum cinerariaefolium

The common name, dusty miller, is used for several additional similar, silvery types of plants including *Artemisia*, *Centaurea*, and *Lychnis*.

Description: *Chrysanthemum cinerariaefolium* grows one to two feet tall with finely divided leaflets and white daisy flowers about one and a half inches in diameter. *Senecio cineraria* is a bushy subshrub that grows to two and a half feet tall with finely divided gray foliage.

How to grow: Dusty millers prefer full sun and ordinary, well-drained soil, though they will grow in lightly shaded areas, too, brightening them with their silver color. Set plants into the garden when the soil has warmed and after the danger of frost has passed. Space eight to ten inches apart.

Propagation: Germinate seeds of *Senecio cineraria* at 75° to 80°F and those of *Chrysanthemum cinerariaefolium* at 65° to 75°F. Germination will take 10 to 15 days. Sow seeds 12 to 14 weeks before planting outside.

Uses: Excellent in containers, they're especially good to use as a bridge between two clashing colors.

Related varieties: 'Silver Lace' has dissected, feathery leaves. 'Diamond' and 'Silver Dust' develop finely divided silvery leaves.

Dahlia

Dahlia hybrids

From huge, dinner-plate-size blooms down to midget pompons only two inches in diameter, dahlias show as much diversity as any summer flowering plant can have.

Description: Dahlias grow from one to five feet tall. Flowers come in every color except blue, and the form is varied: peonylike; anemone-flowered; singles; shaggy mops; formal, ball-shaped; and twisted, curled petals. The flowers are carried on long stems above the erect plants. The American Dahlia Society has classified dahlias by both type and size. There are 12 different flower types: single, anemone-flowered, collarette, peony-flowered, formal decorative, informal decorative, ball, pompon, incurved cactus, straight cactus, semi-cactus, and orchid-flowered.

How to grow: Dahlias are sun lovers and need air circulation around them. Soil should be fertile, high in organic matter, and moist but well-drained. Plant the tubers so that the eye is two to three inches below ground level. Do not plant container-grown dahlias any deeper than the level they were growing in their pot. Space tall varieties 12 to 18 inches apart, reducing the spacing for dwarf plants to as little as 8 inches. Dahlias are not cold-hardy but can live for years if the roots are dug and saved (see below).

Propagation: Most of the large-flowered varieties are grown from tuberous roots available at garden centers or specialist growers. At the end of a summer's growing season, dig clumps of tubers and store in a cool but frost-free location until spring. Sow dahlia seeds four to six weeks prior to planting out at 70°F. Germination will take 5 to 14 days.

Uses: Taller varieties can be planted as a hedge with shorter flowers growing in front of them. Groups of three plants can be effective at the back of the border or in the center of large island beds. You can also feature compact varieties in the front of beds and borders.

Related varieties: There are hundreds of named varieties in every style and color; consult your garden center, specialist catalogs, or a specialist grower. Seed-grown varieties are available as started plants or can be grown from seeds at home. 'Diablo' is a compact variety that grows up to 15 inches tall and wide. Its bronze foliage contrasts with its many different flower colors. 'Double Pompon' has perfectly round, two-inch flowers on plants two feet tall.

Gazania, Treasure Flower
Gazania ringens

This South African flower likes hot, dry summers. Gardeners treasure it for its strangely patterned daisylike flowers.

Description: Gazanias grow in rosette form with attractive notched leaves. Flowers rise 8 to 12 inches on short stems. They're white, pink, bronze, red, yellow, orange, and white with banded markings. Flowers close on cloudy days.

How to grow: Gazanias prefer full sun and moderately fertile but well-drained soil. They don't like heavy soil in hot, humid climates. Plant out as soon as the danger of frost has passed at 8 to 15 inches apart.

Propagation: Sow seeds outdoors after final frost or plant them indoors four to six weeks earlier. Seeds germinate in 15 to 20 days at 70°F. Cuttings taken in the summer root quickly.

Uses: Plant gazanias in the front of beds and borders. Use them as a ground cover in sunny, dry areas or in rock gardens.

Related varieties: 'Sundance Mixed' has multicolored striping and patterning in all colors. 'Talent Mix' has gray foliage and tolerates wind and drought. The 'Daybreak' series includes pink, yellow, orange, red, and white.

Globe Amaranth
Gomphrena globosa

This tropical native has small, cloverlike, papery flowers that continually bloom throughout summer.

Description: Globe amaranth can grow up to two feet with newer, smaller varieties that are bushy dwarfs. The flowers are about an inch in diameter and can be red, purple, magenta, orange, or off-white.

How to grow: Plants require full sun and excellent drainage. Average to fertile garden soil is fine. Set plants into the garden after the last frost and space from 10 to 15 inches apart.

Propagation: Soak seeds in water for three to four days before sowing. Sow seeds in place in the garden after last frost. Seeds germinate in 14 to 21 days at 65° to 75°F.

Uses: The tall varieties are ideal for midborder. Use dwarf varieties for edging beds or borders or as a colorful ground cover.

Related species: Gomphrena haageana has yellow to orange, pinecone-shaped flowers.

Related varieties: 'Gnome' is a compact, purple-flowering variety, growing only 9 to 12 inches tall. 'Strawberry Fields' is bright red.

Geranium, Zonal
Pelargonium x hortorum

These mainstay garden flowers, named for the horseshoe-shaped band of dark color in the leaves of most varieties, are tender perennials that must be replanted each year except in mild climates.

Pelargonium species come from South Africa, but through hundreds of years of breeding, the parentage of today's varieties has been obscured.

Description: Zonal geraniums are upright bushes covered with red, pink, salmon, white, rose, cherry-red, or bicolored flowers on long stems held above the plant. Flower clusters (umbels) contain many individual flowers and give a burst of color. Plants from four-inch pots transplanted to the garden in spring will reach up to 18 inches tall and wide by the end of summer.

How to grow: Zonal geraniums benefit from full sun and moderate to rich, well-drained, moist soil. Incorporate a slow-release fertilizer into the soil at planting time. Plant after all danger of frost has passed and the soil is warm. Space them 12 inches apart. Remove spent blooms.

Propagation: Cuttings root easily. Make cuttings eight to ten weeks prior to planting out for husky plants. Seed-grown varieties should be started 10 to 12 weeks prior to garden planting. Seeds germinate in seven to ten days at 70° to 75°F.

Uses: Zonal geraniums provide pockets of color in any sunny spot. Group three or more together for color impact in flower borders or along walks and pathways. They're classics in containers, by themselves or mixed with other plants. They will bloom through the winter in sunny windows. Zonal geraniums are also grown as standards—a single stem is trained to the desired height with a bushy globe of flowers and leaves above it.

Related species: Pelargonium x peltatum, the ivy-leaved geranium, has pendulous branches loaded with flowers and excels in window boxes and hanging baskets. Scented geraniums (Pelargonium species) have small or large leaves that may smell like roses or lemons and are grown as herbs. Martha Washington geraniums have showy, large flowers and are used as pot plants.

Related varieties: There are many varieties available at garden centers in the spring, in the whole color range of flower and leaf. Seed-grown singles will be virus free and can be found in many colors. Widely planted are 'Orbit,' 'Maverick,' 'Ringo,' 'Bandit,' and 'Regalia' varieties. 'Black Magic' contrasts dark foliage with pink and white flowers.

Heliotrope, Cherry Pie

Heliotropium arborescens

Fragrance is one of the most alluring attributes of heliotrope. Flowers bloom in splendid clusters of deep blue, violet, lavender, or white florets during the summer.

Description: Heliotrope has long, gray-green leaves with deep veins; reaching a height of one foot with an equal spread is reasonable. Many tiny flowers are clustered in the large heads carried well above the foliage.

How to grow: Any good garden soil with medium fertility in full sun will grow good heliotropes. Normally, plants are started early indoors (from seeds or cuttings) and transplanted outdoors when danger of frost has passed and the ground is warm. Depending on the size of transplants, space from 8 to 15 inches apart.

Propagation: Sow seeds 10 to 12 weeks before planting out. Seeds germinate in 7 to 21 days at 70° to 85°F. Root cuttings in four-inch pots in February to have husky plants for May planting.

Uses: Tuck heliotropes into rock gardens, or grow them in the front of borders or in mixed containers.

Impatiens, Busy Lizzie, Patience

Impatiens wallerana

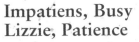

With nonstop flowers in many colors, impatiens is one of the most popular annuals. Its tidy, mounding form and self-cleaning flowers make it an ideal low-maintenance plant.

Description: Breeders have developed compact, branching plants whose flowers are borne above the foliage. Flowers are white, pink, rose, orange, scarlet, burgundy, and violet, with many bicolored variants. Foliage is deep, glossy green or bronze in color. Most specimens grow 12 to 15 inches high.

Propagation: Sow seeds 10 to 12 weeks before the last frost date. Germination takes 10 to 20 days at 75°F. Use a sterile soil mix, because young impatiens seedlings are subject to damping off. A fungicide is recommended. Cuttings root in 10 to 14 days.

How to grow: Impatiens will grow in any average soil and prefers dappled shade. It requires lots of moisture and fertilizer to bloom well. In deep shade, bloom diminishes.

Uses: Impatiens can be used in beds, borders, planting strips, and containers. The plants are beautiful in hanging baskets and planters.

Related species: New Guinea impatiens grows in full sun and has larger and showier flowers. Leaves can be green or variegated.

Lantana

Lantana hybrida

These shrubby plants are abundantly covered through the summer with brightly colored blossoms. The garden varieties bear white, yellow, gold, orange, and red flowers; usually the older flowers in each cluster are a different color than the younger ones.

Description: Lantanas are woody shrubs with large, rough leaves. They grow about three feet tall and equally wide over a summer. When protected against frost, they can grow to 15 feet or more in height over a period of years.

How to grow: Lantanas need full sun and hot weather—and actually poor soil—to give their best performance. They are frost-sensitive, so plant outdoors after the ground has warmed thoroughly. Space the plants about 18 inches apart.

Propagation: Take cuttings in February for spring planting.

Uses: Lantanas are most often used in containers. They grow well in sunny window boxes, hanging baskets, or patio planters.

Related species: *Lantana montevidensis* is a widely grown, pink-lavender flowering species. Its growth is more trailing. *Lantana camara* can be grown from seed.

Related varieties: 'New Gold' with yellow flowers grows 18 to 24 inches tall.

Lavatera, Rose Mallow

Lavatera trimestris

Lavatera is related to both hibiscus and hollyhock.

Description: Rose mallow grows to three to five feet by the end of summer. It branches vigorously to form a sturdy bush. The flowers, borne in leaf axils, are three to four inches in diameter.

How to grow: Grow rose mallow in full sun and average, well-drained soil. Plant outdoors as soon as the ground can be worked in the spring. Space approximately one foot apart.

Propagation: Sow directly in the garden where the plants will stay; it is difficult to successfully transplant seedlings. For earlier bloom, sow indoors six to eight weeks prior to outdoor planting. Seeds germinate in 14 to 21 days at 70°F.

Uses: Lavatera can be used along pathways or walks, or grow a row of them from the middle to the rear of a border bed, depending on border height. The pink and white colors mix well with other flower colors. Lavatera makes good cut flowers.

Related varieties: 'Mont Blanc' has pure-white flowers; 'Mont Rose' is rose-pink; and 'Silver Cup' has large, pink flowers.

Lisianthus, Prairie Gentian
Eustoma grandiflorum

Roselike flowers of lisianthus are loved all the more because each blossom lasts for several weeks, and plants bloom nonstop. Popular cultivars are hybridized from native prairie gentians.

Description: Cultivated types of lisianthus range from one to four feet tall, with two- to four-inch single or double flowers of white, pink, lavender, blue, deep rose, and cream. Some have white petals edged in a contrasting color. Plants set out in spring bloom until frost in fall.

How to grow: Grow in rich, well-drained soil in full sun. Water regularly to make sure young plants do not dry out. Space 12 to 24 inches apart. Deadhead or cut blooms for bouquets to stimulate growth. Stake tall plants.

Propagation: Most gardeners buy plants. Dustlike seeds take more than three weeks to germinate and several months under lights to reach outdoor planting size.

Uses: Use shorter types in the front of borders and beds and in containers. Grow tall types in masses toward the back of borders, and cut flowers for long-lasting bouquets.

Related varieties: 'Forever Blue' is an ever-flowering award winner, a foot tall. 'Mermaid' is similar but comes in many colors. 'Heidi' hybrids have huge blooms on taller plants.

Lobelia
Lobelia erinus

Few flowers have the intense blue provided by certain annual varieties of lobelia.

Description: Lobelias have small, round leaves and flowers up to ½ inch in diameter. Some varieties are compact and mound to six inches; others are definite trailers.

How to grow: Lobelia grows best in cool areas. Space four to six inches apart in the garden or in containers.

Propagation: Seeds are tiny and should be started indoors 10 to 12 weeks before planting outdoors. Seeds germinate in 20 days at 70° to 80°F. Seedling growth is slow, and the early stages should be watched carefully to prevent damping off.

Uses: Use the mounding forms for edgings, as pockets in rock gardens, or in front of taller plantings beside walks and pathways. The trailing varieties are among the best for containers of all kinds.

Related varieties: Mounding forms include: 'Crystal Palace,' deep-blue flowers and bronze foliage; 'Cambridge Blue,' sky-blue flowers; and 'Rosamund,' cherry-red. Some trailers include: 'Blue Fountain,' deep-blue with white eyes; 'Blue Cascade,' light blue; and 'White Cascade.'

Marigold
Tagetes patula, Tagetes erecta

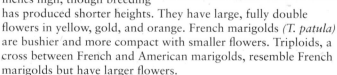

Bright marigolds bloom so well over a long season that they're a mainstay of gardeners everywhere.

Description: American marigolds *(T. erecta)* can be tall plants, growing up to 36 inches high, though breeding has produced shorter heights. They have large, fully double flowers in yellow, gold, and orange. French marigolds *(T. patula)* are bushier and more compact with smaller flowers. Triploids, a cross between French and American marigolds, resemble French marigolds but have larger flowers.

How to grow: Marigolds grow best in full sun with moist, well-drained soil, though they will tolerate drier conditions. Plant them outdoors as soon as all danger of frost has passed. Space French marigolds 6 to 10 inches apart, Americans 10 to 18 inches apart.

Propagation: Seeds may be sown in place after the danger of frost or four weeks earlier indoors. Seeds germinate in five to seven days at 65° to 75°F.

Uses: Grow taller ones to the center or rear of beds and borders or as planting pockets in full sun or in containers.

Melampodium
Melampodium paludosum

Mounded plants with bright green leaves have many yellow, daisylike flowers peering forth all summer long. Plants are exceptionally tidy looking at all times.

Description: Melampodium will form a vigorous, bushy plant 10 to 15 inches high, and about as wide, in the garden. The flowers are small, up to an inch in diameter.

How to grow: Melampodium needs full sun. An average to rich, moist but well-drained soil is satisfactory. Plants should not be allowed to dry out. Plant outdoors as soon as all danger of frost has passed and the ground is warm. Space 10 to 15 inches apart.

Propagation: Sow seeds indoors seven to ten weeks prior to planting outdoors. Seeds germinate in seven to ten days at 65°F.

Uses: Plant melampodium where you want some contrast between flowers and foliage. Melampodium can be used as a sunny ground cover or be planted toward the front of flower borders.

Related varieties: 'Million Gold' is an award-winning variety. It grows up to ten inches tall, and as wide, and is covered with small, golden-yellow flowers all summer.

Nasturtium

Tropaeolum majus

Nearly every child who's been introduced to gardening has grown a nasturtium. And salad-savvy adults have probably enjoyed the peppery tang of nasturtium leaves and flowers among their greens.

Description: Nasturtiums are vigorous and can grow as either vinelike or compact bushy plants. The leaves are nearly round, and the flowers are bright oranges and yellows with long spurs behind them.

How to grow: Nasturtiums need full sun in a dry, sandy, well-drained soil. They're at their best in regions with cool, dry summers, though they will grow elsewhere, too. Bushy types get viny or stringy if they have too little sun. Sow seeds outdoors in the ground after the last frost. Depending on variety, space them 8 to 12 inches apart.

Propagation: Sow seeds where they will grow; germination takes 7 to 12 days at 65°F. Do not cover the seeds; they need light to germinate.

Uses: Dwarf varieties are good for flower borders, beds and edging paths, and walks. Vining varieties can be tied to fences or posts and trailed from window boxes and hanging baskets.

Related varieties: 'Dwarf Double Jewel,' in separate colors and a mix, has light yellow, gold, orange, rose, and crimson flowers. 'Milkmaid' is a fashionable shade of pale butter-yellow.

Nicotiana, Flowering Tobacco

Nicotiana alata grandiflora

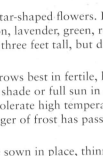

Related to the tobacco plants of commerce, flowering tobacco has been bred for its ornamental value.

Description: A low rosette of large, flat, velvety leaves supports the tall flowering stems covered with many star-shaped flowers. Flower colors include white, pink, maroon, lavender, green, red, and yellow. The plants can grow up to three feet tall, but dwarf forms are also popular.

How to grow: Nicotiana grows best in fertile, humus-rich, moist, well-drained soil in partial shade or full sun in cooler areas. They are tough plants that will tolerate high temperatures. Transplant to the garden when all danger of frost has passed, spacing 8 to 12 inches apart.

Propagation: Seeds may be sown in place, thinning the seedlings to the right spacing. Otherwise, start the plants indoors six to eight weeks prior to planting out. Seeds germinate in 10 to 20 days at 70°F. Don't cover seeds; they need light to germinate.

Uses: Nicotiana is a plant that can give much-needed height to beds and borders. Group it in clusters for more impact. Avoid planting it in dusty places.

Nierembergia, Cup Flower

Nierembergia hippomanica violacea

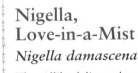

The common name of "Cup Flower," though rarely used, refers to the shape of the flower, which is somewhat like an open-faced bowl.

Description: Nierembergia has attractive, thin, narrow leaves topped at the ends with bluish or purple flowers. The plants develop outward rather than upward, up to six inches high, and will spread a foot.

How to grow: Grow nierembergia in full sun and well-drained soil with adequate moisture. Medium fertility is adequate to grow them well. Transplant to the garden when all danger of frost has passed. For full coverage, plant them five to six inches apart.

Propagation: Sow seeds indoors 10 to 12 weeks prior to planting in the garden after the last frost. Seeds germinate in 14 to 21 days at 70° to 75°F.

Uses: Grow nierembergia as a flowering ground cover in full sun, massed in large patches or beds. It's an ideal edging plant for beds and borders and for lining paths and walkways with ease.

Nigella, Love-in-a-Mist

Nigella damascena

Threadlike foliage above each flower gives you the 'mist' of love-in-a-mist. Easily grown blossoms in soft colors have a delicate look.

Description: Plants range in size from about 15 to 30 inches in height. Single or double flowers an inch or two wide may be blue, pink, purple, or greenish-white. They are followed by two-inch balloonlike seedpods with purple stripes.

How to grow: Grow in rich, well-drained soil in full sun, using seed or transplants. Clear a sizable space for plants so they can become established and return every year.

Propagation: Sow seeds outdoors a week or two before the last expected frost or indoors about six weeks before frost ends. Seeds germinate in a week at 72°F. In Zones 9 and 10, sow seeds outdoors in November or December.

Uses: The flowers are good for bedding and cutting. Seedpods, fresh or dry, are used in flower arrangements. In the garden, plants are often allowed to self-sow.

Related species: *Nigella sativa*, or fennel flower, has blue flowers and black seeds used for seasoning.

Related varieties: 'Persian Jewels' is a classic type with flowers in mixed colors and big pods. 'Oxford Blue' and 'Miss Jekyll' are strong growers with blue flowers.

Pansy, Viola
Viola x wittrockiana, Viola x hybrida

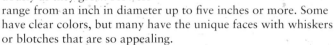

Pansies and smaller violas are related to violets and bloom during cool seasons of the year. In the Deep South, they are used for winter bedding.

Description: Pansies and violas produce flowers continuously as they grow. Flowers range from an inch in diameter up to five inches or more. Some have clear colors, but many have the unique faces with whiskers or blotches that are so appealing.

How to grow: In mild winter areas, set out plants as soon as the weather cools in late summer. Even areas with short freezes can enjoy winter pansies; once the weather warms, they'll start blooming. Elsewhere, enjoy them for several months in the spring, setting them out two to four weeks before the last frost is expected. Space six to nine inches apart.

Propagation: Start seeds eight weeks prior to planting out. They will germinate in 10 to 15 days at 68°F.

Uses: Pansies and violas are suitable for the front of borders and beds, in small groups among other flowers, and in containers.

Related species: 'Johnny Jump Up' is a tiny yellow and purple viola of mixed heritage. Its cultivars include 'Helen Mount' and 'Penny Orange Jump Up.'

Petunia
Petunia x hybrida

A plant that has captivated breeders, petunias have funnel-shaped flowers that have been coaxed into crisped, curled, waved, and doubled variations. The run of color goes from pink through red, lavender, purple, peach, white, cream, and even yellow.

Description: Garden petunias are divided into two types: multifloras and grandifloras. Each has single and double forms, with grandiflora petunias being larger (though new hybrids have blurred this distinction). Singles are more weatherproof than doubles.

How to grow: Well-drained soil in full sun suits petunias best. They grow well in cool temperatures and will stand a few degrees of frost if plants are well-hardened before planting. Space petunias 12 inches apart. To promote more branching and increased bloom, shear plants back halfway in midsummer.

Propagation: Start seeds indoors 10 to 12 weeks prior to planting outdoors. Seeds germinate in 10 to 12 days at 70° to 75°F.

Uses: Beds, borders, walkways, paths, containers—all will accommodate an abundance of petunias. Some varieties are especially recommended for containers, since they mound up and billow over the edges.

Perilla
Perilla frutescens

Frilly purple leaves are the main feature of these easily grown plants. Perhaps they grow too easily, for they self-sow all over the place.

Description: Resembling purple basil, perilla plants grow two to three feet tall. Large, oval leaves can have a metallic sheen and some rippling. Most types are purple, but there are green forms. Showiness is at its height near the end of summer.

How to grow: Set out plants after the danger of frost ends, in good garden soil in partial shade to full sun. Space them eight to ten inches apart. In a few weeks they will make an attractive mass of color. Pinch them back once to develop bushy side branches. Remove flowers for neater looking plants, but leave a few on for seeds for future plants.

Propagation: Sow seeds outdoors just after the last expected frost or indoors a few weeks earlier. Seeds germinate in a week at 70°F. You can also start plants from tip cuttings.

Uses: Use plants for purple color in pots, beds, and borders. Transplant volunteers while they are small, to fill bare spaces in the garden. Use leaves in salad or stir-fry, and add some to white vinegar in a bottle to tint it pink and flavor it.

Related varieties: 'Checkerboard' has densely crinkled foliage. 'Atropurpurea' has deeply purple leaves.

Portulaca, Moss Rose
Portulaca grandiflora

Portulaca's profusion of sunny flower colors combined with its toughness make it a natural for difficult garden sites. It will do even better under less difficult conditions.

Description: Moss roses grow nearly prostrate—a mat of fleshy leaves with stems topped by flowers. Newer varieties are available in a myriad of jewellike colors—yellow, gold, orange, crimson, pink, lavender, purple, and white.

How to grow: Full sun, sandy soil, and good drainage are musts for portulaca. Since they are frost-tender, they should not be planted outdoors until the danger of frost has passed. Space them one to two feet apart.

Propagation: Sow in place as soon as danger of frost has passed and the soil is warm. For earlier bloom, start indoors four to six weeks ahead. Seeds germinate in 10 to 15 days at 70° to 80°F.

Uses: Reserve your problem areas for portulaca. They are notoriously good container plants that do not languish if you forget to water them one day.

Salvia, Scarlet Sage
Salvia splendens

Salvias are best known for their spiky form and bright color that is dependable in any climate and adaptable to full sun or partial shade with equal ease. Salvia comes in brilliant red, creamy white, rose-colored, and purplish variants.

Description: Depending upon variety, salvia will grow from eight inches to three feet tall. The spikes of flowers are composed of bright bracts with flowers in the center of each. They are either the same color or contrasting.

How to grow: Salvia is a good dual-purpose plant that will perform dutifully in full sun or partial shade. It needs average soil and continuous moisture to perform its best. Transplant seedlings to the garden after danger of frost has passed. Depending on variety, space from 8 to 12 inches apart.

Propagation: Although seeds can be sown directly in the garden when the soil is warm, sowing indoors in advance will bring earlier flowering. Sow the seeds six to eight weeks before the final frost. Seeds germinate in 12 to 15 days at 70° to 75°F.

Uses: Salvia provides some of the purest reds and scarlets in the garden world, and their vertical growth makes them superb accents in the garden. Plant them as spots of color against other colors. They're a classic combination with blue and white for patriotic plantings. Their ability to bloom well in light shade makes them especially useful with pastel colors that tend to fade in the sun. They also make good container plants.

Related species: *Salvia farinacea* is a perennial in milder climates that is now widely used as an annual throughout the country. Its common name is "mealycup sage" for the grayish bloom on its stems and foliage. It grows 18 to 24 inches tall and produces either blue or white flowers. 'Victoria' is the most popular blue; its counterpart is 'Victoria White.' *Salvia patens*, gentian sage, is named for its rich indigo-blue flowers that have a long blooming season.

Related varieties: 'Vista' grows to 12 inches and has purple shades in addition to red. 'Flare' is taller and blooms somewhat later. The tallest reds, 'America' and 'Bonfire,' will grow to two feet in the garden.

Sanvitalia, Creeping Zinnia
Sanvitalia procumbens

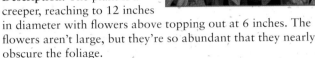

Although not a true zinnia, sanvitalia has enough resemblance to one to be called "creeping zinnia." Golden-yellow flowers bloom nonstop all summer until frost.

Description: The plant is a creeper, reaching to 12 inches in diameter with flowers above topping out at 6 inches. The flowers aren't large, but they're so abundant that they nearly obscure the foliage.

How to grow: Sanvitalia prefers full sun but will adapt to partial shade with less flowering. It is tolerant of most garden conditions. Plant outdoors when all danger of frost has passed and the soil is warm. Space plants four to six inches apart.

Propagation: Sow seeds in place when ground has warmed. For earlier bloom, start indoors four to six weeks before outdoor planting. Seeds germinate in 10 to 15 days at 70°F.

Uses: Use it as an edging for the front of borders, along sidewalks and paths, and in rock gardens. Sanvitalia trails well from containers.

Related varieties: 'Mandarin Orange' brings a different color to sanvitalia. 'Irish Eyes' has green centers and gold petals.

Shirley Poppy
Papaver rhoeas

Glowing in sunlight, large, silky blooms atop straight stems make shirley poppies desirable in the garden.

Description: Plants start as basal rosettes and bloom in spring. They grow one to three feet in height, with flowers two to four inches. Plants hate high heat.

How to grow: Protect from rabbits and slugs. Thin to 12 inches apart. Pinch once for bushiness. Deadhead or harvest to prolong flowering. Allow seeds to ripen and self-sow.

Propagation: Poppies are hard to transplant. Plant seeds outdoors four weeks before the danger of frost ends, in well-drained, rich beds in full sun. Or start seeds indoors in individual pots six weeks earlier. Seeds take eight days to germinate at 70°F, longer in cooler temperatures. In Zones 8 to 10, plant in fall for early spring bloom. In cool climates, make successive sowings.

Uses: Grow in borders, beds, and meadows. For bouquets, cut in early morning. Singe the stem base with a flame to seal it before putting it in water.

Related species: Hybrids were developed from common European corn poppies, the famous flowers of Flanders Fields. 'Lady Bird,' with red petals and black basal blotches, is this type.

Related varieties: 'Angels' Choir' has three-inch double flowers in a range of colors and bicolors; 'Cedric Morris' comes in soft pastel shades.

Snapdragon
Antirrhinum majus

Children love snapdragons because they can snap open the flowers like puppets. Snapdragons endure cool weather and are widely planted for winter color in mild-winter areas.

Description: Snapdragons uniformly bear a whorl of flowers atop slender stalks. The best known are ones with snappable flowers, but others have open-faced flowers including double forms. Colors include white, yellow, burgundy, red, pink, orange, and bronze.

How to grow: Plant in rich, well-drained soil with plenty of organic matter. Grow in full sun. Space tall varieties 12 inches apart, small varieties 6 inches apart. Pinch tips of young plants to encourage branching. For cool season bloom in Zones 9 and 10, plant snapdragons in September.

Propagation: Germination takes an average of eight days at 70°F. For early bloom, sow seeds indoors six to eight weeks before setting outdoors after last frost.

Uses: Use the tall varieties for the back of the floral border and for cut flowers. Short varieties are good in borders and as edgings.

Sunflower
Helianthus annuus

Whether giants of the garden at 15 feet tall or dwarf bedders only a foot tall, these natives of North America come in a vast variety of colors and forms.

Description: Breeders have given us sunflowers in shades of cream, yellow, orange, red, rust, and brown, with and without pollen. Pollen stains are a problem with cut flowers. Leaves are large and coarse. Bedding types are well branched.

How to grow: Sunflowers prefer full sun and rich, well-drained soil. They're tolerant of heat and drought. Plant the tall varieties 12 to 18 inches apart, dwarf ones at 9- to 12-inch spacings. Pinch the central tip of bedding types for more branching.

Propagation: Sow seeds outdoors after final frost. Seeds germinate in 10 to 20 days at 70° to 85°F.

Uses: The dwarf kinds can be used in beds and borders, while the taller varieties are best at the back of the border. All are great in bouquets. Seeds of sunflower are used as food for animals, birds, and people. Leave the seed heads on your sunflowers and watch the birds have a treat.

Swan River Daisy
Brachycome iberidifolia

Variable in nature, flowers are blue, pink, white, and purple, each one centered with either yellow or black.

Description: The Swan River daisy forms a loose mound up to 18 inches tall with equal spread. A plant with numerous branches, it holds its one-inch flowers upright on slender stems.

How to grow: Brachycome needs full sun and a rich but well-drained soil. To encourage bushiness, young plants should be pinched once. Space plants nine inches apart in the garden.

Propagation: For early bloom, sow seeds indoors at 70°F six weeks prior to planting out after danger of frost has passed. Germination will take 10 to 18 days. Seeds may also be sown outdoors after the frost-free date. Cuttings will root in 15 days and are useful for multiplying good forms of brachycome.

Uses: Because of its mounding habit, brachycome is an ideal hanging basket or container plant. It also is useful for edging tall borders.

Related varieties: 'Purple Splendor' will give shades of blue to purple. For a range of all colors, plant 'Mixed Colors.'

Sweet Pea
Lathyrus odoratus

In cool maritime or mountain climates, sweet peas will bring forth their beauty all summer. In Zones 9 and 10, they're best in cool seasons like winter and early spring.

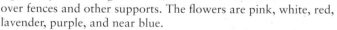

Description: Sweet peas are vining plants that climb vigorously—six to eight feet over fences and other supports. The flowers are pink, white, red, lavender, purple, and near blue.

How to grow: In mild winter areas, sow seeds outdoors in the fall. Elsewhere, plant as soon as ground can be worked. Sweet peas need full sun and a deep, rich soil. The shortest varieties need no support.

Propagation: Nick seed coats with a knife, and soak seeds overnight in water. Before planting, treat with a culture of nitrogen-fixing bacteria available at garden stores. Seeds will germinate in 10 to 14 days at 55° to 65°F.

Uses: Grow climbing types against fences and over trellises, arches, and pergolas. The dwarf varieties can be planted in a border.

Related varieties: 'Early Mammoth Mixed' has many colors. 'Explorer' is a variety with a bushy habit, growing up to three feet without support.

Torenia, Wishbone Flower

Torenia fournieri

Torenia is a colorful plant that thrives in shade and hot, humid weather.

Description: Torenia forms a compact mound about a foot high with many branches. Leaves are oval or heart-shaped. The flowers look a bit like open-faced snapdragons with prominent markings on the petals. The most predominant color has been blue, but newer varieties are pink, rose, light blue, and white.

How to grow: Torenias grow best in rich, moist, well-drained soil. They thrive during summer in partial shade. They like high humidity and won't tolerate being dry. Plant outdoors after all danger of frost has passed, spacing plants six to eight inches apart.

Propagation: Sow seeds 10 to 12 weeks prior to outdoor planting. Germination takes 10 to 15 days at 70°F.

Uses: Plant torenia in groups of three or more in woodland bowers; grow clumps along paths or walkways. Because it grows evenly, it's a good candidate for formal beds in sun or partial shade.

Related species: *Torenia concolor* is a tender trailing perennial.

Verbena

Verbena x *hybrida*

Verbenas are garden treasures in areas where few other plants will grow. Some varieties trail; others form mounds of color.

Description: The trailing varieties may reach 18 inches in diameter, while the mounding types will grow to about a foot high and wide. The flowers bloom in clusters and come in strong and pastel shades including blue, red, purple, peach, and white.

How to grow: Verbenas prefer well-drained, sandy soil with good fertility. Plant after all danger of frost has passed. Space plants 12 (upright types) to 18 (trailing types) inches apart.

Propagation: Verbenas are slow in the early stages. Sow seeds 12 to 14 weeks prior to planting in the garden. Germination takes three to four weeks at 75° to 80°F.

Uses: The trailing types are ideal for rock gardens, for trailing over walls, and as edgings for garden beds and borders. Use mounding types in beds and borders. Verbena also trails nicely from containers.

Related varieties: 'Blaze' is a red variety. 'Peaches and Cream' is tinted peach, pink, and white. Other named forms are constantly introduced in a rainbow of colors.

Vinca, Madagascar Periwinkle

Catharanthus roseus

These tropical plants flower constantly and stand up well to heat and humidity.

Description: Vinca flowers are divided but round, one to two inches in diameter, and borne at the tips of branches or shoots that bear glossy green leaves. The flowers of many varieties also have a contrasting eye in the center of the bloom. Colors include white, red, pink, and lavender.

How to grow: Vinca is at its best in hot conditions—full sun, heat, and high humidity. Set out plants at 8 to 12 inches apart, after the soil has warmed.

Propagation: Sow seeds 12 weeks prior to setting out after last frost. Germination takes 14 to 21 days at a temperature above 70°F. Maintain warm temperatures after germination and don't overwater.

Uses: Vinca is good for massing and edging and exceptional as a container plant. It is extremely heat tolerant.

Related varieties: Popular varieties include the 'Pretty In' series with clear tones and good shape.

Zinnia

Zinnia elegans

Zinnias are among the favorite American garden flowers, loved for their sturdy and colorful blooms.

Description: Zinnias can be grouped into three classes: tall (to 30 inches), intermediate (to 20 inches), and dwarf (to 12 inches). Flowers come in almost every color except blue and in many textures.

How to grow: Zinnias need full sun and rich, fertile soil. They grow best in hot, dry climates after the final frost, when the soil is warm. Depending on the size of the variety, space 6 to 12 inches apart. Powdery mildew can be a problem in humid locations.

Propagation: Zinnias grow fast, and early bloom can be achieved in most climates by sowing seeds directly into the soil. Seeds germinate in five to seven days at 70° to 75°F.

Uses: Dwarf and intermediate varieties can be used in beds and borders or in container plantings. Taller varieties should be moved to the back of the border or the cutting garden.

Related varieties: The tall variety includes 'Giant Cactus' hybrids that come in many separate colors and in a mix. 'Peter Pan' hybrids are dwarf plants with large flowers on short stems.

Frequently Asked Questions

Q: Which annuals require the least amount of maintenance?
A: Choose annuals that do not require deadheading or very much irrigation. Some annuals drop their flowers naturally, whereas others put energy into seed production. Those seed capsules must be removed for continual bloom. Ageratum, alyssum, begonia, dusty miller, impatiens, and vinca are self-cleaning annuals; ageratum, marigold, ornamental peppers, portulaca, melampodium, and vinca are among the most drought-tolerant species. Prepare your soil well, using lots of compost, to increase the intervals between waterings and save on maintenance time.

Q: What should be done this fall to prepare a bed of annuals for next spring?
A: When this year's plants have died from frost, cut them to the ground and, to prevent this year's pests from overwintering, remove all debris from the area. Have your soil tested now. Add lime if necessary, but wait until spring to fertilize. Cultivate organic matter into the soil and apply a fresh layer of mulch to prevent winter weeds from germinating. Your bed should be ready for spring planting.

Q: What is the best way to stake my tall and floppy annuals?
A: Use materials that will be unobtrusive in the garden. Natural brush and twigs blend in well with plants. Green bamboo stakes are available at garden centers. It is best to set up the stakes during planting so the roots of the annuals are not damaged when you insert them. Tie the plants loosely with garden twine, yarn, or even leaves of ornamental grass. Avoid wires because they slice through slender green stems with ease.

Q: It seems that the only bedding plants available are short varieties suited for the front of the border. What can I do to get some height for the back of the border?
A: Look for plants at better garden centers, for they are starting to carry taller annuals that are grown in larger pots, not multicelled market packs. An even greater selection of varieties is available if you grow them from seed. You can buy seed locally, but for the best and widest selection, use a mail-order seed company. Any garden magazine will have advertisements and catalog request coupons for them. Some companies sell starter plants as well as seeds. You may find you enjoy raising plants from seed. Allow plenty of time for them to grow, starting small seeds indoors, a few weeks before planting them outside.

Q: My hanging baskets of annuals look great each spring when I purchase them, but by midsummer they look dried up and have few blooms. How can I keep them fresh and full of flowers?
A: Follow three basic principles when growing flowering baskets—water, fertilize, and groom. The soil mass in a basket is very small, so it heats up and dries out quickly. Daily watering may be needed. Fertilize the plant with a liquid balanced fertilizer every two weeks. Groom the plants often—deadhead and pinch back leggy growth to promote heavier flowering and branching. If you are still having poor results, shift the plants to larger containers.

Q: I have trouble growing flowers in my shade garden. Are there any colorful, shade-tolerant plants that I can use?

A: Shade-loving perennials bloom very briefly, so for continued color through the season use shade-tolerant annuals. Your best choices are coleus (grown for its leaves), wax begonias, torenia, and impatiens. Caladiums may also be successful for you. If the shade is not too deep, you may also be able to grow alyssum and ageratum.

Q: Do you have any suggestions for helping children to enjoy gardening?

A: Success is the best motivator. Encourage children to have a space of their own, but work with them to ensure success. Grow plants such as nasturtium from large seeds, or use transplants. Container gardening is a great activity for instant results. Get a large container (two feet high and wide), fill it with all-purpose potting soil that includes fertilizer, and set in flowers or vegetables from market packs, at the same depth at which they were grown. The soil level should be about an inch below the pot rim. Pat them in, water them, and your child has a garden to be proud of.

Q: I'd like to grow annuals for cutting and arranging. What types make the best cut flowers, and where should I plant them?

A: Look for varieties that have tall stems but that also have the flower colors you would like for arranging. Many annuals, such as zinnias and ageratums, come in an array of shapes, sizes, and colors. Some types of zinnias and ageratums are short and bushy, and these are good for massing in beds. Other types of zinnias and, more rarely, ageratums, are tall, and these are good for arranging. You can buy seed packets or market packs of a single species that are either mixed or all of one color. You can also buy premixed packets of seed for cut flowers. Many kinds of tall annuals are great for cutting. Most of them prefer to grow during warm seasons in full sun. You'll want to cut them for bouquets without spoiling the way the garden looks, so grow them toward the back of garden beds or in their own row in a vegetable garden.

Q: When can I safely plant seeds of hardy annuals in the spring?

A: Where do you live? Hardy annuals such as shirley poppies and larkspur need cool weather for germination and growth. Plant them outdoors where they will grow about the same time as you would lettuce, that is, around the time when frost becomes rare, and temperatures are around 50 to 65 degrees. In Zones 9 and 10, they can be planted around Thanksgiving for spring bloom. In Zones 8 to 2, they can go out a few weeks before the last frost in spring. They need time to grow foliage before the long days of summer arrive, because the extra light triggers their bloom whether the plants are still tiny or well grown. The bigger the plants, the better they will flower.

Q: When should I plant zinnia and marigold seeds?

A: Zinnias and marigolds are easy to grow from seed, but they need warm weather. They are easily killed by frost. Find out the date of your area's average last frost from your local Agricultural Extension Office. A week or two after that, planting should be safe, whether you plant seed directly in the garden or set in purchased transplants. Remember, this date is an average, so some years will have frost later than that date. When you purchase annuals, condition them to the sunlight, wind, and night temperature for a few days before planting them in the garden. Be prepared to protect them from a late season freeze.

CHAPTER SIX

Perennial Plants

Durable yet ever-changing, perennials are a mainstay of ornamental gardens. Gardening with perennials is a fun way to make a personal and lasting impact on the landscape. And it is a collector's joy, as many passionate gardeners know, for the world of perennials is endlessly diverse; new hybrids gain popularity all the time. Additional species are constantly being brought from other parts of the world for use as garden plants, throwing their genes into the mix. And such a mix it is, with diversity of leaves and flowers in their form, color, texture, size, hardiness, and behavior. Every gardener becomes an artist when orchestrating a beautiful medley of perennials.

This chapter explains how perennials grow and how to use them in your garden. The directory of featured plants, Those Fabulous Perennials (see page 146), is a guide to the name, appearance, uses, and characteristics of easy yet worthy perennial choices.

Perennials, Defined

Perennials live for more than two growing seasons. They are distinct from annuals in that they return year after year, eliminating the need to buy new flowers every spring. They differ from shrubs in that they are not woody. Once mature, they do not get taller each year, though they often spread and become more numerous.

Perennials vary in their ability to tolerate heat and cold. A few types of hardy herbaceous perennials have evergreen foliage, but most die all the way back to the ground in winter, with their roots and buds below ground, awaiting spring and a return to their active period of growth. There are short-lived hardy perennials (for instance some types of rudbeckia and columbine) that live two or three years and long-lived perennials (such as peony and iris) that last decades. You can find Victorian houses where the original peonies still hold forth every June, more than a century after they were planted. People who garden often pass divisions of their favorite irises along from generation to generation.

Perennial plants come in all shapes and sizes. There are tall perennials, such as *Aster tataricus*, that delight gardeners with their six-foot stems of lavender flowers; and low plants, such as ajuga and *Phlox subulata*, that carpet the ground. Foliage may be large or small, smooth or rough, plain or variegated, and narrow or round. Flowers, too, are available in many colors, shapes, and sizes.

For every garden purpose, there are perennials. Countless perennials are ornamental plants for borders, bedding, containers, bog gardens, bulb gardens, shade gardens, and ground covers. Edible perennials include asparagus, strawberries, and herbs such as oregano and mint.

SEASONAL CHANGES

Perennials usually have a period of bloom that lasts only a week or two, though there are many exceptions. Some perennials have a much longer bloom period or a recurring one. There are spring bloomers, summer bloomers, fall bloomers, and even winter bloomers. When they're not in flower, perennials are enjoyed for their foliage, which is at least as important a consideration as the blooms. It is exciting to watch the perennial garden change from week to week, as one flower finishes its annual show and another starts. Keep track of these changes in your garden journal as a basis for making new and better plant combinations for next year's garden. Take photos and keep them with your notes.

Flowers that are native to densely shaded woodland, like these Virginia bluebells, bloom early in spring to catch the sun before the deciduous leaves appear in the forest canopy above them.

Perennials may grow and expand each year, eventually filling more space than you expect. To grow well, many perennials need division from time to time (dig up the root clump, divide it into sections, and replant the best sections in freshened soil). This can provide a harvest of new plants for use elsewhere in the garden.

Design Details

Plant form, color, and texture are important factors when designing with perennials. But the main difference between designing with annuals and designing with perennials is bloom sequence. Annuals tend to bloom all at once, but perennial plants will be in bloom for only a short part of the growing season. One perennial follows another in the annual sequence of bloom, so the focus shifts as the garden changes. It is important to know when to expect each type of plant to flower and which ones are blooming at the same time.

If you would like flower color throughout the entire growing season, plan on a succession of bloom provided by different species. You can do this entirely with perennials, or mix in annuals for additional color from mid-summer to frost. Both tender (such as dahlia) and hardy (such as daffodil) bulbous plants offer additional possibilities. Throughout

THE VARIED APPEARANCE OF PERENNIALS

Form: Plant shape is an important consideration when designing with perennials. If you select plants with varying forms, the garden will be more interesting. Ground-hugging mats; tall, spiked growth; and arching or rounded plants provide visual variety whether the plants are in bloom or not.

Texture: A variety of textures adds to a garden's beauty. Placing plants with feathery foliage next to ones with large, bold leaves will produce a more dramatic garden. To test how plants will look when planted together, place potted samples side by side and evaluate them.

Pattern: Some plants have foliage or flowers with stripes, spots, and splotches of color, which provide variety to the basic forms. Some flowers are two-toned, with outer petals of one color and inner ones of another, or with several colors on the same petal. Others, like iris, may have upper petals of one color and lower ones of another. Anthers or other flower parts may have colors that contrast with petals.

summer, hardy lilies—with their varied colors, heights, and forms—are especially effective in perennial borders.

Each plant has a flowering height and a foliage height. A plant's flowers are usually held up much higher than its leaves. As you plan the placement of plants, design the garden so that the flowers show and are not covered up by the foliage and flowers of plants in front of them.

Ground covers can be used in masses or lines. This edging of liriope makes a trim and attractive finish between the brick walk and the lawn. The grass can be mowed right up to the edge of the liriope without any problem.

PERENNIALS FOR MEADOW GARDENS

These are easy, sun-loving plants that combine well in broad perennial beds or in fields or meadows. They can even be used instead of a lawn—if the neighbors don't mind. The soil usually needs some improvement, as it does for any other garden. Cut back the plants after they flower, but leave some of the flower heads on to ripen for self-sown plants, food for the birds, and texture in fall and winter. Cut remaining stalks down to a few inches high, and remove dead leaves in late winter or early spring. Here are some perennials that make a good meadow:

- Aster
- Black-eyed Susan
- Blanket flower
- Butterfly flower
- Coneflower
- Coreopsis
- Dame's rocket
- Evening primrose
- Gayfeather
- Maiden pink
- Penstemon
- Rock cress
- Shasta daisy
- Snow-in-summer
- Wild lupine
- Yarrow

When the plants in bloom finish flowering and are deadheaded, the unfolding foliage and flowers of other plants help to camoflauge the remaining foliage. Long, narrow bands of the same plant give you the most oomph in the least space, as one species supplants another.

Another factor is the attractiveness of the foliage itself, with more and more attention being paid to having gardens of leaves of many colors and forms. There are wonderful gardens composed mainly of hostas. Late-emerging hostas combine well with spring wildflowers and bulbs that bloom before the hostas come up. Then the hostas hide the dying foliage of the ephemeral spring plants. From mats of ground-cover ajuga or ginger to towering canna lilies with striped leaves, foliage is a great element of design.

Perennial gardeners strive for a mix of early, midseason, and late bloomers throughout the garden to keep it in constant bloom. As with any artistic endeavor, the right balance is a personal and somewhat subjective decision. For a powerful display, choose two or more plants that will bloom together in a good color combination. Also try to select flowers for all the seasons. Don't clump all the plants that bloom at once in only one part of the garden.

Observe your plantings through the seasons and note where color needs improved balance. Plant large blocks, three or more (many more) plants of just a few varieties together, per bloom period. The bigger the garden, the larger these blocks of plants should be. The balanced masses of color make the garden successful. Note how the garden changes in both color scheme and balance from week to week. A yellow, blue, pale green, and white spring garden may transform into a red, purple, violet, and forest-green one by July, and then go to gold, rusty-red, purple, and bronze shades in September.

Intermixing and underplanting perennials can get complex. It helps to draw up a plan on paper before digging and planting. On graph paper, draw in the band or blob for each group of perennials. After the garden is planted, it will take another year or more to fill in and get established. Spaces between clumps can be filled with annuals while the garden develops.

If your color combinations are not as good as you'd like, move the plants around. If a plant does not thrive, see if it works better under different conditions. If there's a plant you hate or one that dies, get rid of it. If you see a gorgeous perennial that you've never noticed and it grows in your zone and exposure, give it a try. Take a stroll though a botanical garden in your region for ideas about interesting perennials and ways to combine them. Be warned: Words like "addiction" and "obsession" are often used in discussions of gardening with perennials!

Planting Perennials

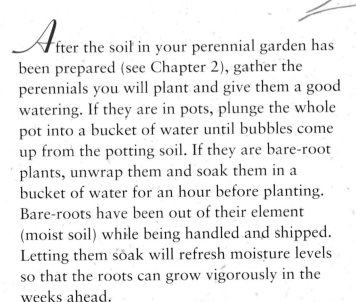

After the soil in your perennial garden has been prepared (see Chapter 2), gather the perennials you will plant and give them a good watering. If they are in pots, plunge the whole pot into a bucket of water until bubbles come up from the potting soil. If they are bare-root plants, unwrap them and soak them in a bucket of water for an hour before planting. Bare-roots have been out of their element (moist soil) while being handled and shipped. Letting them soak will refresh moisture levels so that the roots can grow vigorously in the weeks ahead.

Make the planting hole big enough to set in the plants at the same depth at which they grew when potted (see Chapter 3). The shape

DROUGHT-TOLERANT PERENNIALS

Artemisia
Aster
Butterfly flower
Epimedium
Gayfeather
Lavender
Orange coneflower
Purple coneflower
Russian sage
Sea pink
Sedum
Yarrow
Yucca

of the pot is a good match for the hole you dig. Put the plants in place, fill the remaining spaces with soil, then water.

The procedure is a little different for bare-root plants. For these, you should mold the planting hole to provide the proper support for the spreading roots.

❀ Dig a wide, shallow hole in well-prepared soil.

❀ Form a cone of soil in the center of the hole. Make the cone high enough to hold the crown (where the shoots emerge from the roots) at the soil surface.

❀ Spread the roots around the perimeter of the cone so that each has its own space. The hole should be deep enough to accommodate the entire root length without a lot of cramming, twisting, and turning.

❀ Fill in around the roots with soil, and keep it moist.

If you think the potting mix is too dry and peaty, you can shake it off the roots of potted perennials and plant them like bare-root perennials. Larger perennials sold in one- or two-quart-size containers are perfect candidates for this. Roots of perennials grown in

peat-based mixes can have difficulty growing out of the peat and penetrating into the native soil. In addition, peat can quickly become parched in drying soils, causing root damage. Getting the peat out eliminates both of these problems and can help new perennials get established very quickly.

Once you've planted a perennial, you hope it will succeed. But what if it doesn't take off? Grow a plant for at least two or three years before you decide to remove it. It can take that long for a perennial plant to get comfortable in a new home and begin to really show what it can do. Allowing a trial period of several years also lets the plant get beyond setbacks from difficult weather—for instance, slow growth after an exceptionally cold winter or poor flowering during a long drought.

Don't assume you can't grow a plant if it dies once. If you like that plant and are willing to buy another one, put it in a different place—one better suited for its light and soil needs.

MULCHING PERENNIALS

If you plant perennials in the fall, mulch new plants with straw or chopped leaves to prevent root damage during winter. A little mulch used immediately after planting can help to keep the soil moist and encourage continued root growth. But the main reason to mulch lies

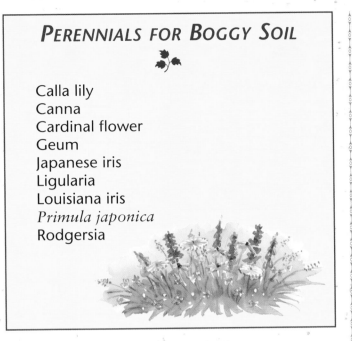

Calla lily
Canna
Cardinal flower
Geum
Japanese iris
Ligularia
Louisiana iris
Primula japonica
Rodgersia

ahead, in winter. Alternately freezing and thawing, expanding and contracting soil can break new roots or even push new plantings out of the ground, a process called *soil heaving*. By mulching generously with an airy material like straw when the soil first freezes, you can help keep the soil frozen until winter ends, at which point the mulch can be removed.

In winter, mulch evergreen perennials and ground covers with evergreen boughs to protect them from winter burn (the cold weather opposite of sunburn). When the soil is frozen, the wind is strong, and the sun is bright, moisture is pulled out of the vulnerable leaves and cannot be replaced by the frozen roots. A protective layer of evergreen boughs, possibly obtained by recycling the branches of a Christmas tree, forms a protective shield over vulnerable greenery. Straw will also do the job, especially in colder areas where there is less chance of rot in winter.

PERENNIALS FROM SEED

You can grow perennials from seed—it's not that hard (see Chapter 3 on propagation). Perennial seeds are more varied in their germination requirements than those of most annual plants. The sprouts need the right cue

from nature before they venture out of their seeds. Some need a cold treatment, which signals winter, followed by a moist, warm period, which signals that spring has arrived. Garden centers, mail-order catalogs and Web sites, and plant societies have good perennial seeds to sell or trade. Some perennials (foxglove is one) have seeds that sprout in days if they are fresh off the plant but go into dormancy if they dry out.

Perennials can be sown indoors or out, but outdoor-sown seeds have a higher attrition rate due to pests and other factors. If you plant seeds of a named cultivar, such as *Hosta* 'Frances Williams,' which is variegated, you will get baby hostas, but they most definitely will not have precisely the same color and leaf size and shape as their parent. They may grow up to be attractive but different. They will also differ from one another in subtle and not so subtle ways, so a breeder's excitement comes in looking for those few that may be of special interest.

Sow perennial and wildflower seeds outdoors in raised beds or spacious nursery pots (the kind you get big flowers in at the nursery), and let nature get them ready to sprout. Hardy perennials and wildflowers often have a special defense called *dormancy* that keeps them from sprouting prematurely during a temporary midwinter thaw (which would be damaging

when the frost returned). They require a certain amount of cold—or alternating freezing and thawing—to indicate that winter is truly over and spring has begun. The easiest way to accommodate the cold requirement is by putting them outdoors.

Another way to give plants a cold treatment is to stratify perennial seeds that require it. Sow them in a community flat of moist seed-starting mix. Label each row with the date planted, the seed source, and the plant name. Wrap the entire flat in a plastic bag and close with a twist tie. Set the flat in the refrigerator for the time indicated on the seed packet or in a seed-sowing handbook. When the recommended stratification time is up, move the flat into warmth and bright light so the seeds can sprout and grow.

PERENNIALS THAT DON'T NEED STRATIFICATION TO GERMINATE

Butterfly weed
Catmint (*Nepeta* species)
Chives
Coneflower
Coreopsis
Fennel
Germander
Lavender
Lemon balm
Mountain bluet
Oregano
Rock cress
Sage
Shasta daisy

Caring for Perennials

Maintaining perennials is similar to caring for other plants (see Chapter 3), but there are a few special requirements. Perennials stay in the same site, feeding from the same soil, for years. Good, deep soil preparation is the basis for healthy perennial gardens. Double digging is a lot of work, and it is mainly perennials that offer the motivation for such effort.

The foliage of perennials is growing and changing during a long span of time, so the supply of fertilizer and water must be adequate. In winter, perennials are still alive but may be completely invisible, for without woody parts, the entire plant can be underground (as buds and roots) in winter, or it can be reduced to a small mat of leaves that start to grow in spring. Do not remove or disturb any green leaves in winter or early spring, for they are part of the plant's survival strategy. If the plants have become too crowded, divide them and replant them (see Chapter 3). For

PERENNIALS THAT OFTEN NEED SUPPORT

Aster
Balloon flower
Bellflowers (tall types)
Foxglove
Garden phlox
Hollyhock
Pyrethrum daisy
Sedum (tall types)
Shasta daisy
Yarrow

most perennials, early spring, when new growth begins, is the best time to do this.

Trimming and deadheading are important in perennial gardens, as in others. If the brown stalks of daylilies or hostas are left on after the flowers fade, it spoils the look of the whole bed because the untidiness is distracting. It's also important to direct the plant's energy toward leaf and root growth rather than making seeds. You can always leave just a few fading flowers on low parts of the plant if you want some seeds. A few seeds go a long way, and you don't need them all.

Staking perennials is another issue. An optimist might figure that the new flower spikes rising from the hollyhocks can take care of themselves. But maybe not. You won't know the answer until it is too late. In advance, use slender tree prunings, wire perennial supports, or bamboo stakes to keep tall perennials upright and prevent spoiling the best sights in the garden. In direct sunlight, plants are less leggy than they are in partial shade.

Pests damage perennials just as they do other plants, and it seems that each kind of plant is susceptible to an array of poachers. Deer and moose are the worst, for they gobble everything wholesale. It can take a nine-foot-high fence to keep them out. Animals have personal flavor preferences, just like us. Some of the perennials they love most are English ivy, asters, hosta, phlox, lilies, tulips, crocuses, and daylilies. A few plants are toxic enough to ward them off. The best of these are daffodils and other narcissi, hellebore, and monkshood.

Bulbs in the Perennial Garden

Bulbs are long-lived and rewarding. They are easy on the gardener, and planting them is a good way to ensure both successive bloom and a low-maintenance garden. Even the planting time fits the gardener's schedule, since most spring-flowering bulbs are planted after the annuals have died from frost and the general growing season is over.

What Is a Bulb?

In everyday speech, any plant with an underground storage organ is referred to as a bulb, even at garden centers. There are many categories, technically speaking, with different names for different structures.

True bulbs, such as tulips, are made of modified leaves that are attached to a flat basal plate. They surround the following season's flower bud. Some bulbs (such as daffodils and tulips) are surrounded by a papery tunic, and some (such as lilies and fritillarias) are covered by fleshy scales. *Corms* look much like bulbs but when cut open, they have a solid starchy interior stem. Crocuses grow from corms. *Tubers* are modified stems with starchy interiors but no basal plate or tunic. Both roots and shoots sprout from the same growth buds,

🌿 *For bulbs to flower another year, dead-head the flowers after they bloom and leave the foliage in place until it turns yellow. Daffodils (back) bloom a little earlier than tulips (center) and hyacinths (front).*

called *eyes*. The potato is a typical tuber. Tuberous roots are similar but are actually swollen roots, not stems. Dahlias produce tuberous roots. *Rhizomes* are thickened underground stems. They grow in a horizontal manner, sprouting new sections as they spread. The bearded iris is a typical rhizome.

GARDENING WITH BULBS

Bulbs are grouped according to their flowering season. There are late winter, spring, summer, and fall flowering bulbs. Within each seasonal group, there are early, mid-season, and late bloomers. Crocuses and snowdrops bloom earlier than most tulips. But within each type there are early, mid-season, and late varieties. An early-blooming variety of tulip may precede a late variety of crocus. The early types of lilies can bloom several months before the late types.

Bulbs grow in nearly any soil, but it must be well drained. Raised beds can improve drainage in places where the ground stays too wet.

Many spring-blooming bulbs lose their leaves in early summer, so plan ahead to fill the gaps. Ground covers and bulbs make a good combination, if the ground cover is not so thickly planted that the bulbs have trouble getting through when they sprout. The ground cover conceals the fading bulb foliage after the blooms have finished. Annuals can be planted among the bulbs, and they too will help hide the fading bulb foliage. Some gardeners plant annuals that bloom in the same color as the bulbs they are following as a reminder of where the bulbs are, underground, and what color they will be next spring.

Bulbs look best planted in large groups or in straight bands several flowers wide, not in a single line where it is too easy to spot a place where one is missing. More is better, but plant at least 3 to 5 large bulbs (such as lilies), 7 to 10 medium-size ones (such as tulips and daffodils), and 12 or more small ones (such as crocus). Bulbs can also be naturalized in a random manner in lawns or meadows. Choose bulbs that will multiply on their own. Narcissus is a good choice, because it is not eaten by deer or rabbits, and it increases nicely. The foliage should be left alone to ripen and nurture the bulbs enough for them to divide. It may take all kinds of patience to keep from mowing the foliage down too soon.

PERENNIALS FOR DEEP SHADE

Ajuga
Bleeding heart
Brunnera
Epimedium
Ferns (most types)
Hepatica
Hosta
Jack-in-the-pulpit
Virginia bluebell
Wild ginger
Wild violet

PURCHASING BULBS

When purchasing bulbs by mail, order from reliable, well-known sources. When purchasing them locally, look them over. Do not buy any that are squishy or moldy. Bulbs should feel firm and solid. Ideally, they should not be sprouted, but sometimes this is acceptable for summer-flowering types. If sprouts show, they should be short and straight. If they are long and twisted, the bulbs will not grow properly. Worst of all, if there is a visible sprout that has dried and died, there's little chance of getting a live plant, let alone an attractive one.

HIGH-SPEED GARDENING: PLANTING BULBS QUICKLY

Use a dibble stick to plant small bulbs extra fast. A dibble stick (see page 27) is similar to a trowel but much narrower. It's basically a stout stick that is rounded at one end and attached to a handle at the other. Where the garden bed has already been prepared and enriched (for instance in a place where you grew annuals in the summer), there's no need to do a total excavation in the fall just to plant bulbs. Instead, stick in the dibble to the depth needed for the bulbs, work the stick back and forth, and quickly make a deep, narrow hole. (You can do the same thing with a sturdy, narrow trowel.) Drop in the bulb and go on to the next. Before you know it, the job is finished. Smooth it all over, pat it down, and water.

In a small garden, bulbs in pots make an ongoing spring statement. When the daffodils shown here are past their prime, pots of tulips or other bulbs with a later bloom time will take their place.

PLANTING BULBS

Plant hardy bulbs in fall and tender bulbs in late spring, in USDA Zones 8 to 3. Farther south, hardy bulbs such as tulips will not grow without special treatment. They need too much cold weather. There, plant tender bulbs in winter for bloom in spring and summer, and enjoy amaryllis as perennials instead of daffodils. Prepare a planting hole several inches deeper than the recommended planting depth, and mix organic matter into the soil. Add bulb fertilizer and enough soil to bring the hole to the proper planting depth, which is listed on the bulb package. Set the bulb in place and fill the hole with fresh soil. Firm the soil and then water. The underground bulb will start growing roots long before you can see anything happen above ground.

Ground Covers

Using ground cover creatively can solve many garden problems and highlight the shape of garden beds. Ground covers are perennial plants or, sometimes, mat-forming shrubs, that form a stable, solid mat of growth, replacing either lawn or other garden beds. The lawn itself (see page 87 in Chapter 4) is one kind of ground cover that is a landscaping standby, even in areas where it is not that easy to keep lawn grass alive. It is best not to mix too many kinds of ground covers into the same area, for they will start spreading and becoming inter-mixed in a way that is hard to handle.

No one can give you a list of all possible ground-cover plants. Ground covering is a way of using plants, not the plants themselves. To function well, a ground cover should grow thickly enough to block out most competing weeds, look good for all or most of the year, prevent erosion, and not be in constant need of

Ground covers are often used to cover a spot that is difficult to mow or hard to use for grass or other plants because of tree roots and shade. The square form of this ground-cover bed is an excellent design element.

HIGH-SPEED GARDENING: BULBS IN POTS

You can plant hardy bulbs in a pot more easily than in the ground, and you can fit more flowers into the same space. In the fall, get a large, deep, weatherproof container, about a foot wide and eight to ten inches deep or larger (with a drainage hole). Cover the hole with a pebble to keep the soil in. Put in a layer of potting soil two to three inches deep. Place a layer of bulbs of the same type on it, at close spacing. Tulips, hyacinths, and daffodils are great in north-ern climates. Cover them with a layer of potting soil that drains well, and add another layer of the same type of bulbs at staggered spacing, not directly above the first bulbs. Add more soil to cover the bulbs, but level it half an inch lower than the pot lip. Water well—the bulbs need moisture to grow their roots. Label the pots with the date and plant name and place them in the garden, with heaps of leaves or branches around them for insulation. Let them go through winter outdoors as if they were in the ground. If it doesn't rain, water them. In early spring, you should see sprouts. At this point, uncover the sprouts and make sure the pot is in full sun so they get enough light. If you like, you can shift them to a coldframe or sunroom for earlier blooms. Or you can leave them outside for a cheery container of flowers. Once they bloom, move them away from direct sunlight and sources of heat—they'll last a few days longer. Discard them after they flower, or plant them in your garden, where they may eventually recover from their crowded con-ditions and bloom another year.

Ajuga is a fast-spreading ground-cover plant with many virtues. The foliage always stays low, the plants spread quickly, and the blue, pink, or (rarely) white flower spikes bloom at the same time as azaleas every spring.

repositioning. There are flowering and non-flowering ground covers. Many ground covers are tough enough to grow in root-filled soil in shade, under trees.

Ground covers can be taller or shorter, as you please. Typically, ground covers should not be used in dinky clumps. Rather, mass them generously over wider areas. Climate is another factor. Liriope, a grasslike plant with glossy leaves, makes a great ground cover in warmer zones, where it stays green all year. In cold-winter areas, it either turns brown or dies altogether, making it a nuisance or an eyesore.

Maintain ground cover by trimming off brown or unsightly parts and excessive growth. If you let the ivy or pachysandra escape its

---

A GIFT OF GROUND COVER

Ground covers spread fast. People with established gardens often have ground cover to spare, because it needs thinning or trimming anyway. See if a neighboring gardener or even a groundskeeper at the park will fill a big plastic trash bag with starts of ivy, periwinkle vine, or pachysandra for you. It will save you some serious money, compared to buying flats at the garden center or hiring a landscaper to do the job.

---

bounds, you'll forever be pulling it out of the lawn or flowerbed. Add a topdressing of compost every fall. Thin the plants in the spring if they are too crowded. Fertilize several times a year to keep growth healthy and steady. Water if necessary, and remove weeds and garden litter.

Each region has ground-cover plants that are right for the climate, either in sun or shade, and serve well to fill in around shrubs, provide contrast, grow in spots that are hard to mow (such as steep slopes), or grow where lawn grass or other plants will not thrive.

PLANTING GROUND COVER

Ground-cover plantings should be evenly thick. It helps to set plants in place at regular spacing in the first place. Begin by preparing the ground as for any garden bed. Then use a wire or string grid with regularly spaced openings at three-inch intervals (or other size if appropriate) to help you distribute the plants. Firm plants into the soil and water them.

Help vining types of ground covers, such as ivy and periwinkle vine, spread by covering barren parts of the stems with soil and keeping them moist. This is a form of layering, and roots and new shoots will sprout where there is contact with soil. This works with pachysandra, too.

Lily of the valley may be too invasive for the flower border, but it is perfect in deep shade as a ground-cover plant. Sweetly scented flower spikes appear in spring, followed by low-growing leathery leaves that last until fall.

Perennial Edibles

A few vegetables, strawberries, and a number of herbs are herbaceous perennials that return every year. Vegetables and strawberries need fertile soil; herbs do well in average soil that is not too rich. All these plants prefer full sun.

ARTICHOKES

In regions with warm winters (Zones 7–11) you may be able to grow true artichokes (*Cynara scolymus*), as they do in California. Each artichoke is actually the flower of this six-foot perennial, which has what landscapers call "architectural form"—that is, it is large and bold. Harvest artichokes before the flowers open. If you wait too long, use them in flower arrangements instead of for dinner. Artichokes usually flower their second year and afterward. There are also Jerusalem artichokes (*Helianthus tuberosus*), which are sunflowers with fleshy, edible tubers. These plants grow 6 to 12 feet tall in Zones 3–10, but there are some shorter cultivars. The late-blooming yellow flowers are attractive. Plants spread quickly.

STRAWBERRIES

Strawberries (*Fragraria* species, Zones 3–10 with different types for different zones) are fun to have around for garden tastes, even if the crop is not that large. Various raiders such as birds and squirrels will get most of the crop if you don't keep them out with netting or repellants. The plants like full sun or bright partial shade and moist, rich soil. Buy from local sources for types that thrive in your climate.

If you'd like a summer-long harvest, grow day-neutral strawberries. While June-bearing strawberries bear fruit heavily in early summer and ever-bearing strawberries bear in June and

DISEASE-RESISTANT STRAWBERRIES

'Allstar'
'Cavendish'
'Delite'
'Guardian'
'Lateglow'
'Redchief'
'Scott'
'Surecrop'

 Straw helps berries stay healthy and attractive.

again in fall, day-neutrals can keep flowering and fruiting throughout much of the summer.

Plant day-neutral strawberries as early in spring as possible and pinch off all the flower buds for six weeks afterward. This lets the plants grow strong before they begin to fruit. Once the plants are flowering, fertilize them monthly to keep the plants vigorous and productive. Heavy producers such as these may not keep up the pace year after year. When you notice berry production diminishing, consider starting a new strawberry patch with fresh plants.

HIGH-SPEED GARDENING: SIMPLE STRAWBERRIES

Plant strawberries in a strawberry jar for an edible feast on a patio. Strawberry jars stand about two feet high and have openings along the side, perfect for planting with strawberry plants. They look especially charming when little plantlets sprout on runners and dangle down the sides.

Plant in peat-based potting soil mixed with extra compost. To make watering easier, run a perforated plastic tube down the center of the pot before planting. You can pour water down the tube to moisten the entire container from the inside out.

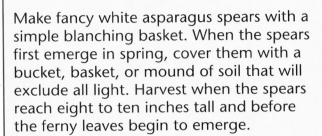

FANCY WHITE ASPARAGUS

Make fancy white asparagus spears with a simple blanching basket. When the spears first emerge in spring, cover them with a bucket, basket, or mound of soil that will exclude all light. Harvest when the spears reach eight to ten inches tall and before the ferny leaves begin to emerge.

ASPARAGUS

Once planted, asparagus (*Asparagus officinalis*, Zones 3–8) takes about four years to become established. It grows best in rich soil in full sun. The plants can last dozens of years, and a good asparagus bed is quite a treasure. The spears of established plants are harvested when they are under a foot tall, in spring. At least half of the spears are left to grow into fernlike, leafy stems about four feet tall. In flower borders, fit in clumps of five to seven asparagus plants for double duty as edibles and ornamentals. Do not plow asparagus once it has been planted.

Mulch asparagus every spring with several inches of compost or decayed livestock manure. Asparagus, a greedy feeder, will use all the nutrients it can get its roots on and grow that much better for it. By mulching in the spring, you can fertilize, help keep the soil moist, and reduce weed germination all in one effort. The shoots that arise through the mulch will grow especially plump and succulent.

HERBS

Plant herbs that double as perennials in beds and borders in sunny places. Pinch back the tips for bushy plants, but use the parts pinched off for cooking or aroma. Herbs are attractive, easy to grow almost everywhere, and have many uses:

❁ Sweetly fragrant bee balm has flowers and foliage wonderful for tea or drying for potpourri.

SAVORY STEPS

Remove a few bricks in a garden path to make places for low-growing thyme or oregano. Either herb will thrive in this warm, well-drained location and will give a charming natural look and wonderful fragrance to the walkway.

Thyme will thrive when planted in well-drained, peat-based potting mix—and it looks great, too!

❁ Oregano can be short or tall. The leaves have great flavor and are used in stews and pasta dishes. Marjoram has similar growth form and uses.

❁ Mint comes in many flavors and types, and it's always nice to have peppermint around for tea. It is rampant in the garden, spreading on long underground runners, so grow it in pots or place it where its spread will not be a problem.

❁ Tarragon has narrow leaves and is not as hardy or long-lived as other herbs. It is a good pot plant.

❁ Culinary sage plants can have purple leaves; variegated gold leaves; tricolor green, white, and pink leaves; or whitish-green leaves that are a cooling contrast to other plants.

❁ Thyme makes hardy mats with many small flowers in summer. The aroma is nice, and the herb is delicious in soups and stews and with beans. There are creeping and upright forms of thyme, and all make good garden plants.

❁ Savory has small, delicious leaves that are similar in flavor to thyme. It looks great in a container, by itself or with other herbs.

❁ Lavender has flowers for sachets and also for use in herb mixtures, imparting an interesting flavor that people cannot place.

HERBS FOR LIGHT, SANDY SOIL

Hyssop
Lavender
Marjoram
Oregano
Sage
Santolina
Sweet fennel
Tarragon
Thyme
Winter savory

Lavender's fragrant flowers can be dried for potpourri.

POPULAR GROUND COVERS

Here are some of the most popular and dependable ground-cover plants, the main USDA plant hardiness zones for them, their appearance, and their preferred exposure.

Ajuga reptans. Zones 5–9. Has blue, white, or pink flowers on spikes in spring, loses leaves in winter. Moist, loamy soil in full to partial shade. Foliage stays low.

Daylily (*Hemerocallis* species, see also page 152). Zones 3–9. Flowers in summer in North, spring and fall in South. Arching leaves, long and narrow. Full to partial sun, moist to average soil. Nearly evergreen.

Epimedium species (see also page 153). Zones 4–8. Leaves elongated but heart-shaped. Good in partial to full shade, loamy soil, average moisture. Nearly evergreen.

Ivy (*Hedera helix*). Zones 5–9. Trailing or climbing vines, lobed heart-shaped leaves, often variegated. Grows in sun or shade, any soil. Evergreen.

Lamium (*Lamium maculatum* and others). Zones 3–8. Vines with heart-shaped leaves. Rampant growth can be a problem. Dry shade to partial shade. Not evergreen.

Lily of the valley (*Convallaria majus*). Zones 3–9. Elliptic green leaves, white bell flowers in spring. Moist to dry shade or partial shade. Nearly evergreen.

Liriope muscari. Zones 6–9. Grassy leaves, purple flowers on spikes. Moist soil. Partial to full shade. Evergreen in Zones 8–9, subject to winter leaf damage elsewhere.

Moss Pink (*Phlox subulata*). Zones 2–9. Dense low mats bloom in reds, whites, and blues in spring. Full sun to partial shade. Well-drained soil, good on slopes. Nearly evergreen.

Pachysandra terminalis. Zones 3–9. Short stems, scalloped leaves in rosettes. Good soil, not too dry, in full to partial shade. Fully evergreen.

Sweet Woodruff (*Galium odoratum*). Zones 4–8. Lacy leaves, white flowers in spring. Grows in loamy, moist soil in partial to full shade. Nearly evergreen.

Thyme, creeping (*Thymus serpyllum*). Zones 3–9. Tiny leaves on low-growing mats. Small flowers in spring. Grows in full sun in dry to average soil. Nearly evergreen.

Vinca, trailing myrtle (*Vinca minor*). Zones 3–8. Trailing vine with blue flowers, tidy growth. Grows in deep to partial shade, any soil. Nearly evergreen.

Wild ginger (*Asarum canadense*). Zones 2–8. Rounded leaves, good for moist or dry shade, loamy soil. Nearly evergreen.

Liriope can be plain green or variegated with green and white stripes. In areas with very cold winters, it will survive but the foliage will be damaged. Farther south, it is more evergreen as a ground cover.

Those Fabulous Perennials

The adaptability of perennials truly makes them all-purpose plants. If you select and plant perennials carefully, you'll be rewarded with many years of interest from their colors, forms, and textures. And if you like what you created, you have the satisfaction of knowing that with minimal effort your garden can flourish year after year!

The following encyclopedia was designed to help gardeners in all regions of North America make the best perennial selections possible. Botanical and common names, compatible USDA zones, descriptions, ease of care, how-to-grow techniques, propagation, uses, and related species and varieties are all dealt with in detail. Photos are included for each entry. Listed here are some especially hardy and low-maintenance varieties of proven perennials.

Agapanthus, Lily of the Nile

Agapanthus africanus

Zones: USDA 8–11

Gorgeous blue or white florets arranged in large globes make this tender perennial a wonderful addition to the garden. It is very popular in California and other places where it is fully hardy. Newer types have been bred for additional hardiness. The roots are large and fleshy, and the leaves are straplike, arising directly from the roots. Flower heads appear, one to a stalk, in clumps of two-foot stalks.

How to grow: Full sun and well-drained, rich soil are needed for agapanthus. It can be grown in large pots and planters. Make every effort not to disturb the roots. In northern gardens, bring in the pots at the end of summer, and grow the plants in a greenhouse or bright sunroom; or trim back any stalks and foliage, and keep them indoors in a dormant state until it is time for the pots to go back outdoors in spring, after the danger of frost ends.

Propagation: By division in spring or fall, also from seed

Uses: Where it is hardy, agapanthus is used in borders and for ground cover. Elsewhere, it is an accent plant in containers.

Alstroemeria, Lily of Peru

Alstroemeria species

Zones: USDA 7–10

Beautifully spotted and marked, alstroemerias are lilylike flowers with deep, thick roots. They grow two to three feet tall on strong, branched stems. Each trumpet-shaped flower is an inch or two in diameter. Flowers come in pink, rose, purple, yellow, cream, orange, and white and are spotted or streaked with contrasting colors.

How to grow: Provide a sunny location in areas with cool summers, but in Florida and other hot summer regions, plant in shade. The roots must be well below the surface of the soil or the plants will not last long. Enrich soil with compost and manure. If soil is not well drained, or if you live in a cold climate where plants are not hardy, grow them in pots in well-drained soil. Store the root-filled pots indoors in a moderately cool but not freezing place for winter, and set them outside again in spring after the danger of frost passes.

Propagation: By division and also from seed, which is very slow (1 to 12 months) to germinate

Uses: Excellent in garden containers and in flowerbeds and borders. They are long-lasting as cut flowers and are often seen on restaurant tables.

Amsonia, Bluestar

Amsonia tabernaemontana

Zones: USDA 4–8

Bluestars are native wildflowers found in wooded areas and on river banks from New Jersey to Tennessee to Texas, and they are popular garden plants as well. Blooming in May and June, each flower has five pale blue petals and blooms in clusters on two- to three-foot stems. The upright stems with narrow leaves are attractive all summer and turn a beautiful butterscotch-yellow in the fall.

How to grow: Plants are easy to grow in full sun or partial shade, in any reasonably fertile garden soil. They are somewhat tolerant of dry soil. They will self-sow, with seedlings becoming bushy clumps in a few years.

Propagation: By division in the early spring

Uses: Bluestars belong in any wild garden and look good in groups of three or more in mixed borders and flowerbeds.

Related species: *Amsonia hubrichtii* is a similar but smaller plant. Its very slender leaves turn shades of gold and burnt-orange in fall, so it is planted in feathery masses for fall color.

Anemone, Japanese

Anemone species

Zones: USDA 4–7

This plant's name comes from the Greek word for "wind," and some other anemone species are called wind flowers. The Japanese anemone's strong-stemmed, showy, poppylike flowers can reach a height of four to five feet, in white, pink, or lavender. Each flower has five or more petallike sepals that enclose numerous golden stamens. The compound, green leaves are about two feet tall and turn wine-red in autumn.

How to grow: Anemones are easily grown in fertile, moist soil with plenty of organic matter mixed in. They prefer full sun in northern gardens but will adjust to partial shade. Anemones need partial shade in southern gardens. Protect anemones from slugs. In areas that have severe winters with little snow cover, plants should be mulched in late fall. They bloom late in summer and in fall, so protect flowers from early frosts in colder areas.

Propagation: By division in early spring or by root division

Uses: Anemones are especially beautiful when grown in large clumps.

Artemisia, Wormwood

Artemisia species

Zones: USDA 3–9

Artemisias are rugged herbs with varied leaf forms that are usually selected for their silvery foliage color. The flowers are insignificant yellowish daisies. Some types are woodier or shrubbier than others. Size ranges from four inches to over four feet.

How to grow: Artemisias tolerate drought, heat, and cold but not wet feet in winter. They grow in any decent garden soil with good drainage. Plants perform best in full sun and become somewhat leggy in partial shade.

Propagation: By division in early spring, also from seed

Uses: Low-growing types of artemisia can be used at the front of borders and in rock gardens. Tall types are good toward the back in flower borders and can be massed by themselves.

Related species: *Artemisia absinthium* is the common herbal (but somewhat toxic) wormwood, called absinthe. *A. ludoviciana* is known as southernwood and white sage—'Silver King' is a popular cultivar. *A. frigida* forms low mats and can be pruned to shape.

Astilbe, Garden Spirea

Astilbe species

Zones: USDA 4–8

Beautiful plants for the garden, the astilbes available to gardeners today are usually the result of hybridization and are often listed as *Astilbe* x *arendsii* in garden books and nursery catalogs. They are grown for their dark green, fernlike foliage and their long panicles (or spikes) of flowers that resemble feathery plumes. Some have denser plumes. Color may be white, pink, lavender, or cranberry. Depending on the type, they can bloom from spring until the end of August. Blooms last about three weeks, but foliage looks great for the duration of the growing season.

How to grow: Astilbes are easily grown in partial shade, especially in the southern parts of the country. In areas with cool summers they thrive in full sun. The soil should be moist with plenty of organic matter mixed in.

Propagation: By division in early spring

Uses: The larger varieties work well in the garden border as specimen plants. Colors include white, pink, red, rose, and lilac. Heights vary from 12 to 40 inches. They also make an effective ground cover.

Aster, Michaelmas Daisy

Aster species

Zone: USDA 5

An aster is a type of daisy, and you will find garden asters in many sizes and colors. Flowers usually bloom in late summer or fall in clusters, with each blossom from half an inch to several inches wide, on stems six inches to several feet tall. Ray petals are white, blue, deep purple, or pink, and central disks are golden. Many asters are North American natives and grow in wayside places with no care at all.

How to grow: Asters grow best in full sun in good garden soil but also tolerate sandy and clay soils that are difficult for other plants. Divide them every three years and refresh the soil to keep plants healthy. Pinch tall asters back quite hard in midsummer to promote branching and flowering on shorter stems that need no staking.

Propagation: By division in spring, also from seed

Uses: Asters are excellent in garden borders and mass plantings. Containers of asters in bloom are popular in fall. Asters make good cut flowers.

Related species: *Aster tataricus* is a seven-foot species with clusters of lavender flowers. *A. novae angliae* can be the tall wild type but has also been bred into dwarf forms that stay low without pinching. *A. tongolensis* is a small rock-garden perennial.

Balloon Flower

Platycodon grandiflorus

Zones: USDA 3–7

The unopened flowers of platycodons resemble hot-air balloons, for which they are named. Balloon flowers are clump-forming perennials with alternate leaves of light green on stems that usually grow between one and three feet tall. They bear two- to three-inch balloon-shaped buds that open to bell-shaped flowers with five points, in pink, blue, and white.

How to grow: Balloon flowers like moist, well-drained soil in full sun or partial shade. They prefer places with cool summers but are easy to grow in other areas, too. Plan the plant's position carefully and mark it, for spring growth is late to appear.

Propagation: By division in mid-spring or by seed indoors in winter or outdoors

Uses: Blooming for most of the summer, balloon flowers are attractive in borders, with the smaller types growing best along garden edges.

Related varieties: 'Fuji White' is dwarf and bears white flowers; 'Mariesii' has blue flowers on 12- to 16-inch stems; and 'Shell Pink' bears soft-pink flowers.

Baptisia, False Indigo, Wild Indigo

Baptisia australis

Zones: USDA 4–8

A beautiful plant in leaf, in flower, and after going to seed, false indigo was originally planted to produce blue dye for early American colonists. Clump-forming plants grow two to four feet in height. The blue-green, compound leaves on stout stems look fresh all summer, and the showy blue, white, or yellow pealike flowers are followed by ornamental black pods.

How to grow: Baptisia takes a few years to get well established, but it is easy to grow. It needs well-drained soil in full sun but will accept some partial shade. White baptisia needs more shade than blue baptisia. A member of the legume family, baptisia will do well in poor soil. The root systems of older plants become so extensive that they are difficult to move.

Propagation: By division or from seed

Uses: One baptisia plant will in time cover an area several feet in diameter with gracefully arching foliage. These plants are excellent in borders, meadow gardens, and along the edge of woodlands.

Basket-of-Gold, Goldentuft

Aurinia saxatilis

Zones: USDA 4–8

Once included in the Alyssum genus, these charming flowers of spring now belong to the mustard family. Attractive low gray foliage growing in dense mats gives support to clusters of golden-yellow, four-petaled flowers floating 6 to 12 inches above the plants.

How to grow: Aurinias are easy to grow in full sun in well-drained, average soil, but plants will rot in damp locations and resent high humidity. Shear off the stalks after plants bloom.

Propagation: By cuttings, division, or seed

Uses: Aurinias are quite happy growing in the spaces between stone walks, carpeting a rock garden, or growing in pockets in stone walls where their flowers become tumbling falls of gold.

Related varieties: 'Mountain Gold' has silvery evergreen leaves and fragrant bright yellow flowers. 'Citrina' bears lemon-yellow flowers.

Bergamot, Bee Balm, Oswego-Tea

Monarda didyma

Zones: USDA 3–7

These hardy native American plants have been garden favorites for decades. Sturdy, square stems growing to four feet tall have simple leaves. They are topped by crowns studded with lipped, usually bright red, pink, purple, or white flowers blooming from summer into fall.

How to grow: At ease in almost any soil, bergamots prefer a slightly moist spot with full sun; they become somewhat floppy when grown in the shade. These plants are vigorous spreaders, so excess plants should be removed from time to time. Plant where air circulation is good, because mildew can be a problem.

Propagation: From seed or by division in early spring or fall

Uses: With a long season of bloom, bee balm is used in wild gardens and in beds and borders. The flowers are beloved by hummingbirds and butterflies.

Bergenia, Pigsqueak

Bergenia cordifolia

Zones: USDA 3–8

Bergenias originated in Siberia and Mongolia, so they are perfectly happy in low temperatures when covered with snow. Thick, rounded evergreen leaves, often a foot long, grow crowns and are edged with red in cold weather. Spikes of pink or white waxy flowers bloom in drooping clusters.

How to grow: These plants prefer light shade and good moist soil with plenty of organic matter. They are easy to grow, but foliage is easily damaged.

Propagation: By division or from seed

Uses: Use bergenia for rock gardens, front edges of borders, and plantings on difficult slopes.

Related species: The winter begonia, *Bergenia ciliata*, develops large, rounded leaves that are densely hairy on both sides. *Bergenia purpurascens* has dark greenish-purple leaves.

Bleeding Heart
Dicentra species

Zones: USDA 3–8

Bleeding hearts, so poetically named, have heart-shaped pendant pink or white flowers with spurs at the base and fernlike attractive foliage. *Dicentra spectabilis* is the showiest, but its flowers finish in spring and its foliage disappears in midsummer. Other species continue to bloom all summer.

How to grow: Bleeding hearts need open or partial shade with an evenly moist, slightly acidic soil. Plenty of peat moss must be used when planting. Pine needles or pine bark are good for mulching.

Propagation: By division in early spring or from seed; roots are fleshy and sold by the number of eyes present on plant starts. Transplant self-sown plants.

Uses: This plant is a lovely sight when planted in a shady bed or woodland border.

Related species: *Dicentra eximia*, the fringed bleeding heart, will bloom until frost if given protection from the heat. *Dicentra formosa* is a rose-colored species and is about 18 inches high. *Dicentra spectabilis* is the garden favorite with deep pink or white flowers blooming from May to June on arching 24-inch stems. *Dicentra scandens* is a climber with yellow flowers.

Boltonia
Boltonia asteroides

Zones: USDA 4–8

Boltonias are native American wildflowers found in poor or damp soil as far north as Manitoba, Canada, then south to Florida and west to Texas. Plants resemble asters with sturdy stems, narrow leaves, and dozens of white flowers in clusters. Blooming from late summer into fall, a well-situated boltonia will be covered with bloom.

How to grow: Boltonias prefer average garden soil in full sun. Like many wildflowers, they are easy to grow and will be larger in moist, fertile soil.

Propagation: By division in spring or fall

Uses: Since most boltonias grow five to eight feet high, they are best at the rear of the garden. A line of these plants will become a flowering hedge of great charm. They can be used with ornamental grasses or mixed with fall asters.

Related varieties: 'Snowbank' is an excellent, four-foot selection of the species and now a garden classic. 'Pink Beauty' is not as vigorous but has soft pink flowers.

Brunnera, Siberian Bugloss
Brunnera macrophylla

Zones: USDA 3–7

From western Siberia, these plants are perennial forget-me-nots, named in honor of Swiss botanist Samuel Brunner. Some catalogs still call this species *Anchusa myosotidiflora*, its previous name. Showy blue flowers about ¼-inch across bloom in clusters during spring. The leaves are large and heart-shaped on slightly hairy stems. Plants can reach 2 feet in height but usually grow about 18 inches tall. Where summers are cool, leaves grow larger.

How to grow: Brunneras thrive and spread in deep, moist soil with an abundance of organic matter, in full sun (only in the North) or partial shade. They will, however, do reasonably well in a dry spot if they have shade.

Propagation: By division or from seed

Uses: They are lovely when massed in the front of a border and when naturalized at the verge of a wooded area or in a wild garden along a stream or by a pool. After blooming, the large leaves make an effective ground cover.

Butterfly Weed, Milkweed
Asclepias tuberosa

Zones: USDA 4–9

Butterfly weed is a native American wildflower that is at home in both the wild garden and the perennial border, attracting hummingbirds and butterflies. Blooming from late spring into summer, the sprays of small yellow, orange, or red-orange flowers are striking in their beauty. The plants bear thin leaves and are most attractive when in flower.

How to grow: Butterfly weed grows easily in full sun and tolerates a wide variety of soil types but performs best in average garden soil with good drainage. Once a butterfly weed develops a good root system, it becomes a long-lived, drought-resistant plant.

Propagation: By division in early spring or by seed

Uses: Butterfly weed does well in meadows and in wild gardens. The flowers can be cut for fresh bouquets.

Related species: The swamp milkweed, *Asclepias incarnata*, has pinkish flowers on two- to four-foot stems and will do well in wet environments.

Campanula, Bellflower

Campanula species

Zones: USDA 4–8

The botanical name is from the Latin word for "bell" and refers to the shape of the flowers. Bellflowers vary in size, shape, and plant form but are usually various shades of blue, lavender, and white. They bloom from late spring into early summer.

How to grow: Bellflowers need a good moist (but well-drained) soil with plenty of organic matter mixed in. In the North, plants will tolerate full sun as long as the soil is not dry, but elsewhere a spot in semishade is preferred, with more shade needed farther south. Frequent division and transplanting keep up the vitality of your plants.

Propagation: By division or by seed

Uses: Plants are beautiful in the border, useful in the rock garden, and fine for the shade or wild garden.

Related species: *Campanula carpatica* blooms at a height of ten inches with solitary blue flowers. It is effective as an edging or tumbling over a small rock cliff. *Campanula glomerata*, or the clustered bellflower, usually bears a dozen blossoms in tight clusters at the top of a 14-inch stem. *Campanula persicifolia*, or peach bells, bears white or blue flowers on stems up to three feet high and prefers moist soil. It is an excellent cut flower.

Chrysanthemum

Chrysanthemum species

Zones: USDA 4–9

Chrysanthemums are highly variable members of the daisy clan, numbering more than 200 species of ornamental plants. Leaves are typically divided and aromatic. Stems are strong, and flowers are showy. Many types form dense clusters of new shoots in spring. In the South, some types bloom in spring and fall.

How to grow: Chrysanthemums prefer well-drained, evenly moist soil in full sun. The majority of chrysanthemums are late-blooming, easily grown short-day plants with flowers initiated by decreasing day length. They benefit from pinching main stems and side shoots back several times until midsummer, which promotes bushy growth before the flower buds form. They can be trained into showy forms. Professional growers often keep stems short by chemical means.

Propagation: By cuttings, by division, or from seed

Uses: Garden mums (*Chrysanthemum* x *koreanum*, formerly *Dendrathema* x *grandiflorum*) come in a number of flower styles and colors. Mums can be purchased as rooted cuttings from nursery suppliers to be set out in spring or as pot mums in full bloom in fall.

Related species: *Chrysanthemum* x *superbum*, the Shasta daisy, produces four-inch flowers on one- to three-foot stems.

Cardinal Flower

Lobelia cardinalis

Zones: USDA 2–9

A fiery color glows near a woodland stream at the end of summer. This is a colony of cardinal flowers, growing wild in North America. These deep-red tubular flowers on spikes two or more feet tall bring the same magical drama to the home garden and attract hummingbirds, besides.

How to grow: Cardinal flowers need moist, rich soil. In southern regions they like a lot of shade, but in places where summers are cool they prefer more sun. They can survive occasional dry periods. Protect plants from slugs.

Propagation: By division in spring or fall, also from seed

Uses: Mass cardinal flowers in clumps in moist, partly shaded garden spots. They combine well with ferns.

Related species and hybrids: *Lobelia syphilitica*, blue or white, is similar in form to *L. cardinalis* and has been hybridized with it. *L.* 'Ruby Slippers' has four-foot spikes of ruby-red flowers. *L.* 'Grape Knee-Hi' is a dwarf hybrid with vivid purple flowers for many weeks in fall.

Columbine

Aquilegia species

Zones: USDA 3–8

Columbines, beloved by hummingbirds, are perfect for cut flowers and have a long season of bloom. Midsize spurred flowers with complex form bloom on wiry stems, floating above a rosette of compound leaves. Single, double, and even triple flowers come in red, yellow, blue, white, pink, purple, or a combination.

How to grow: Columbines are easy to grow in fertile, well-drained garden soil, in full sun or partial shade. Many types live for only a few years, so allow a few plants to self-sow for continued stock. For neatness, cut back stalks after plants finish flowering.

Propagation: From seed

Uses: Columbines are excellent in beds and borders. Dwarf forms are good for rock gardens.

Related species: *Aquilegia caerulea*, Colorado columbine, has sky-blue blossoms and white centers on wiry stems growing to two feet. *Aquilegia canadensis* is the wild Eastern columbine, with graceful flowers having long, red spurs and yellow faces on one- to two-foot stems.

Related varieties: The hybrid types vary between one to three feet in height and are available in many varieties and colors. Among the best are the 'Music' hybrids.

Coneflower, Purple

Echinacea purpurea

Zones: USDA 3–8

This heat-tolerant native grows wild from Ohio to Iowa and south to Louisiana and Georgia. Prickly, cone-shaped heads of bronze-brown are surrounded by rose-purple or white petals (ray flowers) on stout stalks from two to four feet high. Leaves are alternate, simple, and coarse.

How to grow: Coneflowers are sturdy and easy to grow in almost any well-drained garden soil in full sun. If soil is too good, the flowers may need staking.

Propagation: By division in spring or from seed

Uses: Coneflowers are excellent for the back of a small garden border and are a welcome addition to a wildflower garden.

Related species: *Echinacea pallida* is a similar wildflower species from the Midwest with thinner, more graceful, pale pink petals.

Related varieties: 'White Lustre' and 'White Swan' are two varieties with white flowers; 'Bright Star' bears maroon flowers; and 'Magnus' has rosy purple petals with a dark disk.

Coralbell, Alumroot

Heuchera hybrids

Zones: USDA 3–8

Coralbells were named for their reddish flowers on trim spikes above small leaves. Then breeders crossed several species. Gardeners now have a diverse group of plants with large, lobed, ornamental leaves combining green, silver, and purple tones. The leaves grow in basal rosettes from thick root-stocks. The flowers are tiny white, green, or red bells clustered on one- to two-foot stems. Some cultivars have very showy flowers, but others are grown mainly for foliage. Most types bloom in spring but a few bloom in summer or fall.

How to grow: In areas with hot summers, heucheras like partial shade, but usually they prefer full sun. Plant them in good, well-drained garden soil with a high humus content, and keep the soil moist in summer. In winter, coralbells resent wet soil and often will die if their "feet" are wet. Every three years they must be divided to prevent crowding.

Propagation: By division in spring or from seed

Uses: Coralbells are lovely in a border or when planted among rocks, rock walls, and in the rock garden.

Related species: *Heuchera americana* is the native type and has been used in many of the hybrids with good leaf color. *H. micrantha* and *H. villosa* have larger, more varied leaves. *H. villosa* requires more shade than other species.

Coreopsis

Coreopsis species

Zones: USDA 4–9

Several coreopsis species are popular in the garden, all of them sporting bright daisylike flowers on wiry stems. Height varies with species and cultivar, ranging between nine inches and three feet. Plants bloom in shades of yellow, orange, and pink, with lance-shaped, oval, or threadlike leaves.

How to grow: Coreopsis species are happy in almost any well-drained garden soil in full sun. They are drought-resistant and an outstanding choice for hot, difficult places. Deadheading and frequent division keep plants going strong.

Propagation: By division in spring or from seed

Uses: Excellent for wild gardens, containers, and in garden beds, these flowers are also popular for cutting. The smaller types look great in hanging baskets and as edging plants.

Related species: *Coreopsis grandiflora* 'Sunray' bears double golden-yellow flowers on two-foot stems. *C. lanceolata* 'Brown Eyes' has big yellow daisies with brown splotches on plants over two feet tall. *C. verticillata* 'Moonbeam' has primrose yellow daisies in low-growing carpet and is a landscaping favorite. *C. rosea* is similar in form to 'Moonbeam' but has pink flowers. It is not as strong a grower.

Daylily

Hemerocallis species

Zones: USDA 3–9

Each showy, six-petaled daylily flower opens, matures, and withers within 24 hours. Orange, yellow, cream, peach, lavender, and wine-red are the main colors. There are over 30,000 named varieties in many heights (one to five feet) and flower sizes. Daylilies have fleshy roots topped with clumps of curving, sword-shaped leaves that can grow up to two feet long. After the foliage develops, the tall, straight, branched stalks appear, bearing numerous flower buds. The flowers on a single stalk open a few at a time for a period of several weeks.

How to grow: Daylilies prefer good, well-drained garden soil in full sun and can grow whether soil is wet or dry. They benefit from partial shade in the South. Fertilize plants when new growth begins. Divide plants and refresh the soil with compost every few years. Protect plants from deer.

Propagation: By division in spring or fall, sometimes from seed

Uses: By mixing varieties, you can have a succession of bloom from spring to late fall. Use daylilies as ground cover on banks and in flower borders. Everbloomers are good container plants.

Related varieties: 'Stella D'Oro' has golden blooms on one-foot stems and is everblooming; 'Catherine Woodberry' has pale, orchid-pink flowers on 30-inch stems; 'Hyperion' is a fragrant yellow lily blooming midseason on 42-inch stems.

Dianthus, Carnation, Pinks
Dianthus species

Zones: USDA 3–10

The old-fashioned name, "pinks," comes from the serrated flower edges, which look as if cut with pinking shears. And the name of the color "pink" is said to come from these flowers, which have been popular in gardens for hundreds of years. The many dianthus species and hybrids come in red, white, orange, purple, cranberry, and of course, many shades of pink. Flower size ranges from less than an inch to several inches wide, and height ranges from just a few inches to several feet tall.

How to grow: Dianthus prefers average to rich well-drained soil in full or nearly full sun. Refresh older plantings by dividing and resetting plants every few years.

Propagation: Named cultivars must be grown from cuttings or divisions, while others can be grown from seed.

Uses: Dianthus grows in beds and in pots equally well. Flowers last a long time in bouquets.

Related species: *Dianthus caryophyllus* is the florist's carnation, which is usually greenhouse grown in conditions that are neither too hot nor too cold; *D. barbatus* is sweet William, a biennial that sometimes lasts for several years; *D. gratianopolitanus* is the gray-green leaved mat-forming type that blooms once a year and is excellent in flower borders and rock gardens.

Ferns
Varied genera and species

Zones: Types for all zones

Ferns are grown for great texture and their ability to thrive in places that are too damp, shady, or compacted for other plants. There are many types with varying preferences and sizes. Some are evergreen and leathery, while others die down to the ground in fall and return in spring.

How to grow: Find the right fern for the soil type and exposure you have, and it will make itself at home. Most types prefer moist shade. Some ferns spread rapidly, so if your space is small, select nonrunning types. Water plants well after planting to help them settle in. Before long they will be totally carefree except for removing last year's fronds from deciduous types.

Related genera: *Athyrium nipponicum* 'Pictum,' the Japanese painted fern, is noninvasive. Its silver foliage brightens shady gardens. *Athyrium felix-femina* is similar with graceful green foliage. *Asparagus densiflorus*, asparagus fern, is not a true fern but looks like one in southern zones where it is hardy. *Dryopteris felix-mas* is over two feet tall with strong green color and waxy texture. *Polystichum polyblepharum* has golden fiddleheads that open to dark, shiny, evergreen fronds. Maidenhair ferns (*Adiantum* species) have lacy, delicate leaves. There are many other ferns, some for every type of climate.

Epimedium, Bishop's Hat, Barrenwort
Epimedium species

Zones: USDA 4–8

These long-lived plants deserve to be used more widely. Low-growing foliage of great distinction and delicate spring flowers make epimediums a good garden choice. Flowers sometimes bloom before plants leaf out, in soft colors of white, yellow, rose, and lavender. The foliage makes a trim ground-cover layer. The leaves, somewhat heart-shaped on wiry stems, may be green, purple, or green with red or purple flushes or veining.

How to grow: Epimediums like good, well-drained, somewhat moist garden soil in open shade, though they like some morning sun. They do well under tree canopies but need water if the soil becomes dry. In spring, remove the previous year's foliage if it is spotty and to show off new flowers.

Propagation: By division or from seed

Uses: Epimediums are good ground covers on slopes, under trees, and in other shady spots. If you have a shaded retaining wall where the flowers can be seen at eye level, they are ideal.

Related species: *Epimedium grandiflorum* grows about a foot high with white flowers tinged with pink at the tips of the spurs. *E. x perralchium* 'Frohnleiten' has handsome purplish leaves and is evergreen in the South.

Foxglove
Digitalis purpurea

Zones: 4a–9a

Columnar plants with large, bell-shaped flowers opening from bottom to top, fox-gloves are garden classics that bloom at about the same time as roses. Size varies with growing conditions and plant species, but many grow four to six feet tall, with flowers two to three inches long. The color range includes white, ivory, peach, pink, deep rose, and purple. Plants are short lived and sometimes die after blooming.

How to grow: Provide moist rich garden soil with good drainage and a touch of shade in the afternoon. In cooler, moister climates, full sun is better. Set plants two or more feet apart to prevent overcrowding. For more blooms on shorter stems, cut the central spike most of the way down before the flowers are fully formed. You'll force growth of many side shoots with flowers on them all. Deadhead plants after they flower, but allow at least a few flowers to ripen fully into tan pods full of brown seeds, and sprinkle the seeds onto cultivated ground where you would like more foxgloves.

Propagation: From seed and also by division in early spring

Uses: Foxgloves make good mass plantings and look best when set against a background such as a fence, wall, or wooded area.

Related species: *Digitalis grandiflora* and *D. lutea* are yellowish flowered forms that are longer lived than *D. purpurea*.

Gaillardia, Blanket Flower
Gaillardia grandiflora

Zones: USDA 2–9

Yellow and red blanket flowers are daisies with serrated tips on the ray petals. The plants are very tough and cheerful with downy green leaves growing in low rosettes and have a hairy texture. The plants naturalize in sunny gardens and even on sand dunes. Most types grow two feet tall with daisies about three inches wide, but others can be one to three feet tall.

How to grow: Gaillardias tolerate drought and grow well without any fuss at all in full sun, in any garden soil that has good drainage. Deadhead plants for renewed bloom and tidy beds.

Propagation: By division in spring or fall, also from seed

Uses: Blanket flowers are good for meadow gardens, garden borders, raised beds, and mass plantings. They make good cut flowers.

Related species and hybrids: 'Goblin' is red with yellow tips, 'Golden Goblin' is pale yellow, 'Burgundy' has wine-red petals, and 'Lollipop' in multiple colors is double and round. *Gaillardia pulchella* is the half hardy type of blanket flower. 'Yellow Plumes' is recommended for use as a summer annual.

Geranium, Crane's-Bill
Geranium species

Zones: USDA 4–7

Hardy geraniums are clump-forming perennials that bloom in a generous flush in late spring or early summer. The five-petaled flowers vary in color and size. The range includes pastel pinks and blues, white, rose, and deep magenta sometimes accented with black centers. The leaves are usually green, somewhat rounded, and lobed. Plants range from a few inches to a few feet tall. A few types climb or scramble onto bushes.

How to grow: Garden geraniums need good well-drained garden soil in full sun or light shade in areas with hot summers. Shear plants back for neatness after the blooms have all opened. You may get regrowth and a second crop of flowers. Thin or divide when plants become crowded.

Propagation: By division for named cultivars or from seed

Uses: In a border or a rock garden, geraniums are lovely plants. They make excellent ground cover and are striking when grown along a wall, with the stems and flowers tumbling over the edge.

Related species: *Geranium cinereum* is a low-growing plant usually reaching about eight inches in height with one-inch pink flowers. *G. macrorrhizum* is a vigorous species with large pink flowers, lots of vigor, and thick roots that are easy to transplant.

Gaura
Gaura lindheimeri

Zones: USDA 5–9

Gaura grows wild from Louisiana to Texas and south to Mexico, which shows that it is tough enough for regions with hot summers. It has delicate pink or white flowers under an inch wide, in big clusters on branched stalks. Stems of the native type are taller, but most hybrids are two to three feet tall.

How to grow: Gauras need full sun in good, deep, well-drained garden soil because the tap root is very long. They are both drought- and heat-resistant. Cut back the stalks if they have mostly finished blooming and look seedy.

Propagation: By division in spring or by seed. Gaura can bloom the first year from seed if it is started in early spring.

Uses: Perfect for both a dry garden and a wild garden, gauras are also very attractive in a formal border. In northern climates, they bloom late in the season and are charming when planted with asters and ornamental grasses.

Globe Thistle
Echinops ritro

Zones: USDA 4–7

Globe thistles are stalwart plants that produce metallic-blue blossoms with perfectly round flower heads atop ribbed stems. Plants grow two to five feet tall and almost as wide. The spiny-edged leaves are white and woolly underneath.

How to grow: Globe thistles require full sun for strong growth but are not fussy about soil. Once established, they are very drought-resistant. Protect plants from aphids, and stake them if necessary.

Propagation: By division in the spring or by seed

Uses: The larger species are impressive when used in background plantings or when grown as specimen plants. The smaller types are attractive in a bed, border, or wild garden.

Related species: *Echinops sphaerocephalus* is a species that is much taller, sometimes reaching seven feet, and is best used where a strong statement is needed.

Related varieties: 'Taplow Blue' has intense blue color in the flowers and, at only two to three feet tall, is well behaved in borders.

Goat's Beard, Wild Spirea

Aruncus dioicus

Zones: USDA 3–7

Goat's beard is an enormous and showy perennial that can grow as high as six feet and look like a bush. The handsome compound leaves are deep green and have serrated edges. In early autumn, the plants come into bloom, producing many dramatic plumes composed of tiny, white flowers. The plants bring color to the garden after the usual spring show has passed.

How to grow: Goat's beard is easy to grow as long as light shade and rich moist soil are provided. It grows well in moist bottomland and should never lack for water during the summer.

Propagation: By division in the spring or from seed

Uses: Plant goat's beard in the rear of the border in the light shade of high trees. It grows well by the waterside. The white plumes show best where the plants have a dark, tree-filled background or are in front of a wall or fence.

Related species: *Aruncus aethusifolius* is a dwarf variety that makes a six- to eight-inch mound of feathery leaves and one-foot spires of white, plumelike blossoms.

Helenium, Sneezeweed

Helenium autumnale

Zones: USDA 4–9

Looking just a bit like sunflowers, heleniums are bright and cheerful in shades of gold, rust, orange, and red. They flower in the fall with huge masses of two-inch blooms on branched stems three to five feet tall. They have a common name, swamp sunflower, which is not surprising. They are more often called sneezeweed because the inconspicuous green leaves were once commonly used to make snuff. Although native to North America, they were not popular in gardens here until European breeders worked with them.

How to grow: Sneezeweeds like moist, very rich soil and a location in full sun. Set the plants two or more feet apart. Stake taller types. To keep tall types neater, cut them back very hard around July 4. They will branch out and bloom on shorter, bushier stems. Deadhead plants after blooms have started to fade.

Propagation: By division in early spring and from seed

Uses: Experiment with dwarf forms in the front of the garden border and in pots, but use the tall, standard types toward the back of perennial borders and in mass plantings. They are longlasting cut flowers.

Grasses, Ornamental

Gramineae family

Zones: USDA 3–10

The foliage and seed heads of showy ornamental grasses help to extend the garden season through winter. The stems, or culms, of true grasses are round and hollow, and stem sections are joined by solid nodes. Roots grow deep into the ground, making the plants drought tolerant. They are used to competition in fields and meadows. Flowers are usually feathery or plumelike and feature an awn, or a barbed appendage, that is often quite long. Moving in the wind, grasses add vitality to the garden scene.

How to grow: Most grasses prefer well-drained soil in full sun. There are exceptions; some tolerate wet soil, and some accept shade. The only chore connected with growing perennial grasses is the annual pruning of the dead stems and leaves before new growth begins to emerge.

Propagation: By division in spring

Uses: Large types make beautiful specimen plants and screens. Some lower-growing varieties make excellent ground covers. Adding interest to the perennial border, the fine textures of grasses help to blend and unify contrasting plantings. Grasses blend nicely with foundation plantings.

Related species: Some of the most popular species of grass are listed here. *Calamagrostis acutiflora stricta*, or feather reed grass, reaches five to seven feet and tolerates wet soils. Reed grass blooms late in spring, showing its seed heads through the following winter. *Helictotrichon sempervirens*, or blue oat grass, is valuable for its blue color and the form of the leaves. It grows to two feet. With its red leaves, *Imperata cylindrica rubra*, or Japanese blood grass, makes a fine ground cover. *Miscanthus sinensis* 'Gracillimus,' or maiden grass, forms a fountain of thin, arching leaves. In the fall, tall seed heads are formed that open into plumes persisting well into winter. *Miscanthus* 'Zebrinus,' or zebra grass, looks like a tropical plant that has adapted to the North. Reaching a height of eight feet, the arching leaves are dashed with horizontal bands of a light and creamy goldenbrown that only appears as the summer heats up. Massive clumps are formed over the years. Other varieties of *Miscanthus* develop into bold specimens with graceful winter plumage. *Pennisetum alopecuroides*, or fountain grass, produces leafy fountains about three feet high and blossoms on arching stalks. Pampas grass (*Cortaderia selloana*, Zones 7 to 10) grows in the South with showy white or pink plumes on 6- to 12-foot stems. There is also a dwarf type of pampas grass only a few feet tall.

Hosta, Plantain Lily

Hosta species

Zones: USDA 3–8

Hostas are popular, because they give color and texture to perennial gardens from mid-spring until mid-fall. Large clumps of basal leaves with pronounced veining and smooth or wavy edges distinguish hostas. Leaves come in various shades of green, often with variegations. Lilylike flowers on tall stems (or scapes) in white and lavender bloom from late spring to late summer. Size and shape vary tremendously, with petite types a few inches tall for rock gardens at one end of the scale and giants with a single plant the size of a half whiskey barrel at the other.

How to grow: Hostas do best in good, well-drained, moist garden soil with plenty of humus. They require some sun to partial shade to deep shade, depending on the species and variety. In the North, they like more sun. They need protection from slugs and deer.

Propagation: By division for named cultivars or from seed

Uses: Hostas are the backbone of the shade garden. The smaller types are excellent in the border or as ground cover. The larger varieties become elegant specimen plants forming gigantic clumps of leaves over the years. They are also excellent in pots.

Lady's Mantle

Alchemilla species

Zones: USDA 3–8

Lady's mantles are attractive plants usually grown for both their round, pleated foliage and their unusual chartreuse flowers. The plants grow between 8 and 14 inches high, with lobed leaves of silvery gray-green that bear silky hairs. The flowers appear in early summer, standing well above the leaves, and last for several weeks.

How to grow: Lady's mantles are easy to grow in average garden soil where summers are cool and moist, preferring some protection from hot sun in midsummer. In warmer parts of the country, they need a moist, fertile soil and light shade. As the summer progresses, the plants become larger and do not look as neat. Divide or thin if plants become too crowded.

Propagation: By division in spring. Plants sometimes self-sow.

Uses: Use lady's mantle in the front of the garden border or along the edge of a low wall where the leaves are easy to see. The flowers can be used for bouquets.

Related species: *Alchemilla alpina,* alpine lady's mantle, grows about eight inches high; *A. erythropoda* grows six inches high. *A. mollis* has taller flowers with a yellowish cast. Pick them for bouquets and wreaths before they are fully opened.

Iris

Iris species

Zones: Types for USDA 3–10

Iris germanica

The diverse iris genus contains more than 200 distinct species and countless cultivars. Iris is the goddess of the rainbow, and you can find iris blooms in pink, blue, lilac, purple to brown, yellow, orange, almost black, and white. There are no true reds. Many types of iris have fine foliage, whether short or tall, which is a good thing, because the flowers have only a brief period of bloom. They return reliably year after year. Irises usually have basal leaves in two ranks—linear to sword-shaped—often resembling a fan, arising from a thick rootstock (or rhizome), from fibrous roots, or, in some species, from a bulb.

How to grow: Most irises need full sun. Except for those like the water flag *(Iris pseudacorus),* which delights in a watery spot, or the Japanese iris *(I. ensata),* which thrives in humus-rich moist soil, most irises also prefer a good well-drained garden soil. If plants are protected from iris borers, they become permanently established in the garden.

Propagation: By division after flowering or in the fall or from seed

Uses: Even though the bloom period is short, a bed of irises is ideal for a flower garden. There are also irises for the poolside and the pool, the wild or woodland garden, the early spring bulb bed, the cutting garden, and the rock garden.

Related species: *Iris germanica* (tall bearded iris), hardy from Zones 4–8, usually comes to mind when people think of irises. The flowers come in a multitude of color combinations and sizes, with hundreds of new varieties introduced every year. This iris is usually spring blooming, but some rebloom in fall. *I. cristata* (crested iris), hardy in Zones 5–8, prefers partial shade and a humus-rich soil and blooms in early spring. It is lavender-blue with a two-inch yellow crest across a six-inch stem. *I. ensata* (Japanese iris) is hardy in Zones 6–8. Richly colored blossoms are often more than six inches wide on stiff, tall stems, blooming in June. The blue flag, *I. versicolor,* is a lovely three-foot wildflower from the Northeast that appears in ditches and boggy areas along country roads. It is a great pond plant. *I. pseudacorus* (yellow flag) is also a beautiful plant for a bog or at the edge of a pond or pool. The flowers, blooming from May to June, are yellow on 40-inch stems. It is beautiful but can be invasive. *I. sibirica* (Siberian iris), hardy in Zones 4–8, has large flat lovely 3- to 4-inch flowers on 30-inch stems and great foliage—the swordlike leaves stand erect and eventually form a large clump.

Lavender

Lavandula angustifolia

Zones: USDA 5–10

Lavender is an aromatic herb originally hailing from the Mediterranean. The genus name, meaning "to wash," alludes to the ancient custom of scenting bathwater with oil of lavender or a few lavender flowers. Plants tend to be shrubby, usually with square stems and narrow evergreen leaves that are white and woolly when young. Flower spikes are terminal clusters of lavender or dark purple flowers, blooming in late June and bearing a pleasing scent.

How to grow: Lavender plants want full sun and well-drained, sandy soil—preferably nonacidic. In areas where there is no snow cover, the plants should be mulched. In colder areas, prune back the dead wood in the spring.

Propagation: By soft cuttings in spring or from seed

Uses: Lavender is perfect as a low hedge and in clumps next to rocks. It is also suitable in front of stone walls that face away from the wind.

Related species: *Lavandula stoechas* is the classic lavender of Greece and Rome. It has bolder flowers of red-purple. It is not hardy north of Zone 7.

Liatris, Blazingstar, Gayfeather

Liatris species

Zones: USDA 3–9

Blazingstars are good garden plants native to North America. They have linear leaves and very stout stems three to six feet tall, growing in clumps from thick rootstocks. The small fluffy florets are set along tall spikes, flowering from the top down, which is very unusual.

How to grow: Blazingstars need good, well-drained soil in full sun to succeed. Wet winter soil will usually kill the plants. The taller varieties sometimes require staking. They are especially valuable as cut flowers.

Propagation: By division of older plants in spring or from seed

Uses: Use blazingstars in large clumps in beds and borders. They are popular and long-lasting cut flowers.

Related species: *Liatris spicata*, with purple or white flowers on spikes three to five feet tall, is the most popular type for gardens. *L. pycnostachya*, the cattail or Kansas gayfeather, grows up to five feet and bears spikes of purple flowers. *L. scariosa*, or the button snake-root, bears purple or white fluffy disk flowers on spikes from three to six feet tall.

Ligularia

Ligularia species

Zones: USDA 5–8

This is a bold plant for garden use. Its name comes from the Latin word *ligula*, which means "little tongue," referring to the tonguelike shape of the large petal on each of the ray flowers. The plump, large leaves in rosettes are either round or kidney-shaped and are sometimes toothed. The plants bear tall sprays or spires of yellow or orange flowers in summer, on strong stems.

How to grow: Ligularias do best in partial shade and good, humus-rich garden soil that is kept evenly moist. Since the roots form large clumps, plenty of space should be allowed between plants.

Propagation: By division in spring or from seed

Uses: Ligularias are great in the back of shady beds, along borders, in bogs, or planted at the edge of water gardens. The plants prefer afternoon shade.

Related species: *Ligularia dentata* 'Desdemona' has green leaves up to a foot wide and yellow flowers. *L. stenocephala* is similar with yellow spikes of flowers, not wide sprays.

Peony

Paeonia species

Zones: USDA 3–7

A collection of peonies in bloom presents a view of exquisite, huge flowers in white, pink to rose, red, lavender, and yellow. Those four to six inch flowers, double or single, are the norm. Even when bloom has finished for the summer, peony foliage is attractive. Herbaceous peonies, usually *Paeonia lactiflora*, include many excellent cultivars and hybrids, old and new. Most peonies are shrubby plants with thick roots and large, compound, glossy green leaves on reddish stems. They bear large, many petaled, showy flowers.

How to grow: Autumn planting is best; the peony prefers full sun and good, well-drained, moisture-retentive soil rich with humus. Plant with the "eyes" or growing points to the top about 1½ inches below the soil surface. Mulch the first year to protect from severe cold. Stake before blooms open. Deadhead after flowering.

Propagation: By division of the roots

Uses: As specimen plants, in beds or borders, and in the cutting garden, peonies can be an important part of any garden.

Related species: *Paeonia mlokosewitschii*, or the Caucasian peony, bears yellow flowers about five inches across. *P. suffruticosa*, the Japanese tree peony, is actually a woody shrub, usually reaching a height of five feet and a spread of six feet. *P. japonica* has exquisite single white flowers on trim plants and prefers shade.

Garden Phlox
Phlox paniculata

Zones: USDA 3–9

Phlox is easy to grow, great for garden color, and marvelous for cutting. Plants grow in clumps with strong stems that bear simple lance-shaped leaves. These stems are topped with clusters of fragrant, showy, five-petaled flowers, each blossom rising from a narrow tube. The color range includes white, rose, pink, purple, lavender, and magenta. Some flowers are bicolored.

How to grow: Provide rich, well-drained soil in full sun or light shade and plenty of water during the summer. Plants are susceptible to powdery mildew, so space them 18 inches apart to promote air circulation. Divide plants every three years to keep them vigorous.

Propagation: By division or from seed

Uses: Phlox can be grouped by color or mixed. The taller types work best at the rear of the border.

Related varieties: The Symons-Jeune strain of *Phlox paniculata* was developed for strength of stems and resistance to mildew. *P. stolonifera* has white or purple flowers in spring on ground-cover plants under a foot tall. *P. drummondii* is an annual and is biennial in the South. *P. carolina* is similar to *P. paniculata* but blooms earlier and has more resistance to mildew.

Physostegia, Obedient Plant
Physostegia virginiana

Zones: USDA 3–9

In bouquets, the flower spikes can be positioned the way the arranger likes and they will hold that shape, hence the name obedient plant. This spreading perennial grows one to three feet tall, with attractive white, purple, or pink blooms on spires. The whites are a little shorter than the colors and have a refreshing look on a hot day. These popular plants fill in the border in late summer, which can be an in-between time for perennials. Leaves and flowers are arranged on distinctly square stems.

How to grow: Phystostegias are easily grown in average garden soil in a sunny location. In hot climates, they appreciate a little shade in the afternoon. They tend to spread aggressively, so if this is a problem, confine them to weatherproof containers or plant something else.

Propagation: By division in spring or from seed

Uses: Extra divisions can be grown as pot plants. The main uses of physostegia are as cut flowers and in perennial flower borders.

Related varieties: 'Crown of Snow' and 'Rose Crown' can be grown from seed. 'Bouquet Rose' is three to four feet tall with plentiful flowers of deep pink. 'Summer Snow' is under three feet and has showy white flowers.

Poppy
Papaver orientale

Zone: USDA 3–8

Moving with the breeze, poppy flowers with crinkly, silky petals on graceful stalks four feet tall are a focal point in any garden. The blooming period, though brief, is an important garden event, for each flower measures four inches across. Oriental poppies come in standard orange as well as scarlet, watermelon-pink, pale pink, and white. The foliage stays low and is covered with fine hairs. It disappears for part of the summer and returns in fall and spring.

How to grow: Poppies are undemanding, wanting only good, well-drained soil in full sun. Drainage is especially important in the winter, for roots will rot if they stay wet. Place the crown three inches below the soil surface and mulch plants, especially during the first winter, to prevent heaving.

Propagation: By division in the fall or from seed

Uses: Use poppies in beds or borders in combination with other perennials or by themselves.

Related species: *Papaver nudicaule*, the Iceland poppy, is shorter-lived and smaller than oriental poppies, with a color range including cream, oranges, and yellows. 'Champagne Bubbles' is a good cultivar. It grows in winter and spring in the South.

Primrose
Primula species

Zones: USDA 5–7

Primroses come from climates ranging from mild to extreme, in a range of sizes from a few inches to a few feet tall. Although there are many species, only a few are widely available. Find rare types through plant societies and catalogs. The colors are beautiful, sometimes improbable, shades of lipstick pink, deep blue, gold, yellow, red, and purple, and many more. Not all species come in all colors.

How to grow: Most primroses prefer moist but well-drained soil, cool but not freezing temperatures, and average fertility. Garden primroses can be divided in fall and immediately replanted at improved spacing, taking care not to harm the taproots. Partial shade is best for most types but this varies.

Propagation: By division and from seed

Uses: Use primroses in pots, in garden beds, and naturalized in streamside gardens.

Related species: *Primula veris* is the wild type, primrose yellow, which has been used in many hybrids. *P. denticulata*, the drumstick primrose, has globes of flowers atop straight stems. *P. heladoxa* is a candelabra type with narrow whorls of flowers at intervals on the tall stems. *P. japonica* likes boggy soil. It is another candelabra with showy flower sprays or whorls two feet tall. *P. viallii* is pink and pointed, with flowers opening from the bottom up; and *P. bulleyana* has rusty orange flowers.

Pulmonaria, Lungwort

Pulmonaria officinalis

Zones: USDA 4–7

Pulmonarias bloom very early in spring and have interesting foliage from spring through fall. The leaves grow in basal rosettes and in some types are marked with silver-white splotches. The flowers may be blue or pink and in some cases start out pink and fade to blue, so both colors appear at once on the same plant.

How to grow: While the plants will persist in poor soil, they do best when planted in rich, moist garden soil in partial to full shade. They need very little care once established. Remove damaged leaves and transplant if they become too crowded.

Propagation: By division in fall or from seed

Uses: Lungworts are excellent plants for the shade garden, the wild garden, and as ground covers. They can be used on sloping ground shaded by trees—a difficult site for growing most other plants.

Related species: *Pulmonaria angustifolia* 'Azurea' is a European plant with green leaves that bears brilliant blue flowers. *P. saccharata* and *P. longifolia* have silver splotches on their leaves. *P. saccharata* 'Berries and Cream' has showy silver foliage veined and edged with forest green.

Salvia, Meadow Sage

Salvia species

Zones: USDA 4–9

Many perennial salvias of varying hardiness and appearance are available to the gardener. *Salvia officinalis*, culinary sage, usually about two feet tall, has gray-green leaves and white or lavender flowers. *Salvia x superba* ('Blue Queen' is good) is a sterile hybrid. It has gray-green, paired leaves covered with tiny hairs underneath on square stems growing up to three feet high. They bear dense spikes of showy, violet-purple flowers.

How to grow: Salvias need full sun and good garden soil with excellent drainage. Do not crowd the plants. After flowers have finished blooming, trim them off for neatness and a second showing.

Propagation: By division or from cuttings for named cultivars, and from cuttings or seed for culinary types and species.

Uses: Uses vary with the type of salvia, but all can be massed and used in flowerbeds and borders.

Related species: *Salvia azurea*, or the blue salvia, is a native American plant reaching five feet in height and bearing deep blue flowers. 'Grandiflora' is a variety that has larger flowers. *Salvia involucrata* has hot cherry-red flowers. *Salvia leucantha* has shrubby, tall growth and multitudes of purple and white velvety flowers.

Veronica, Speedwell

Veronica spicata

Zones: USDA 3–7

Speedwell is a plant of the roadside with masses of pretty flowers that "speed you well." In Ireland, a bit of the plant was pinned onto clothes to keep travelers from accidents. Plants have simple, oblong, two-inch leaves on strong stems. There are many types, ranging from prostrate to several feet tall. The tall forms bear slim, densely branched spikes of small white, blue, pink, or purple flowers in summer.

How to grow: Speedwells will succeed in any good, well-drained garden soil in full sun or partial shade. Plants rarely survive in overly wet soils in winter.

Propagation: By division or from seed

Uses: The taller varieties are beautiful in both bed and border, as well as in the rock garden. They are good cut flowers.

Related species: *Veronica latifolia* 'Crater Lake Blue' bears flowers of deep blue on 18-inch stems. *Veronica prostrata* is a mat-forming type with deep blue flowers on four-inch stems. *V. longifolia* is similar to *V. spicata*.

Yarrow

Achillea species

Zones: USDA 3–7

The botanical name refers to the Greek hero, Achilles, who is said to have used yarrow to heal wounds. Yarrows grow between one and three feet high, blooming from June until frost. Flowers are small and arranged in flat heads on top of stout stems. The foliage is finely cut and resembles a fern.

How to grow: Yarrows tolerate drought and are suitable for any garden soil that has good drainage. Plants perform best in full sun, though they will put up with a bit of shade.

Propagation: By division in spring or fall, also from seed

Uses: Yarrow are excellent in garden borders and mass plantings. Fresh or dry, they make good cut flowers.

Related species: The wildflower *Achillea millefolium* is suited for the meadow or wild garden; the cultivar Achillea, 'Crimson Beauty,' bears rose-red flowers on two-foot stems. *Achillea filipendulina* and its hybrids are sturdy plants with golden flowers that are particularly long-lasting, whether in the garden, freshly cut, or dried. 'Coronation Gold' was developed to commemorate the coronation of Queen Elizabeth II and has been a garden standard since 1953.

Frequently Asked Questions

Q: I planted a peony in a sunny location with well-drained soil a few years ago, but it never bloomed. What's wrong?

A: Assuming that deer didn't eat the flowers, you probably planted the peony too deeply. Dig up the plant in early fall and inspect the roots for any unusual damage. Adjust the pH of the soil to between 5.5 and 6.5. Replant so that the crown—the part where the buds form—is one to two inches below the soil surface. Water deeply and apply mulch so the plant can reestablish itself.

Q: When do I divide clumping perennials such as coralbells and Japanese iris?

A: Both coralbells and Japanese iris can be divided in the earlier part of fall or very early in spring. In fall, there should be time for the roots to establish themselves for a few weeks before the ground freezes. In spring, make sure there is enough rain or irrigation to encourage regrowth and establishment of the roots. Flowering will be reduced while the plants adjust to their new places, but in another year or two they will be exceptional.

Q: Why do some of my "full sun" perennials burn up in my southern garden?

A: Garden books describe the light requirements of perennials according to the average intensity of light in North American gardens. However, the same plants that need full sun in New England may need protection from the hot afternoon sun in Georgia. Look for regional growing guides and experiment with different species under various amounts of sun and shade. Also, use mulch to help keep the soil temperature lower.

Q: I hear a lot of botanical lingo at my garden club meetings these days, and I'm confused. What is a genus and what is a species?

A: In books and on plant tags, plants are identified with two names, the genus followed by the species, for instance *Crocus tomassinianus*. *Crocus* is the genus name, or major subgroup; *tomassinianus* is the species, or particular type of crocus. *Crocus sativus*, the saffron crocus, has the same genus name but is a different species. The word *genera* is the plural of genus. Related genera are grouped into the same family.

Q: Most of the perennials have finished blooming, and I'd like to clean up the garden. How far down can I cut the plants?

A: It's important to leave the crown of the plant undisturbed so the basal leaves can continue to grow and produce food for the plant's winter survival. Cut flowering stalks down to about four inches. The remaining stubble will mark the plants' locations so that you won't disturb them during bulb planting or winter gardening.

Q: It's midwinter and my bulbs and some perennials are beginning to emerge. Should I cover the plants to protect them from the elements?

A: Bulbs and perennials usually begin their growth at the right time and are prepared for additional cold weather. Remove a bit of mulch from around the plant. This will cool the soil and slow some of the growth. Just allow the plants to grow naturally, and they'll bloom when the time is right. Cold snaps will not hurt emerging leaves or closed buds.

Q: I put some tulips from my garden into a bouquet but they drooped. Did I do something wrong?

A: Tulips need to drink a lot of water to keep their firmness in arrangements. After you cut them, bring them inside and recut the stems with a very sharp knife. Rest them, up to their heads, in a bucket of water containing floral preservative according to directions or in plain cool water. A few hours later, use them in a bouquet. They may still move or droop a little, because tulips keep growing and changing even after they have been cut.

Q: Which perennials are easiest to grow from seed? I have a big garden and a tiny budget.

A: The answer depends on your conditions and whether you want to sow the seeds indoors or out. You probably would like to grow perennials that will bloom in summer from an indoor planting in

winter or at least bloom the following year. Seed size is often an indication of easiness to grow, because a large seed is easier to handle and has more food stored for the emerging plant. Some of the quickest and easiest perennials to sow are rudbeckia, columbine, butterfly weed, purple coneflower, chives, coreopsis, Shasta daisies, foxglove, yarrow, hollyhock, and sage. Daylilies, hosta, and iris also grow easily from seed but take a few years to reach flowering size.

Q: I'm growing some oregano, and it is doing really well. When should I harvest it?

A: Harvest oregano and other perennial herbs when they have grown large enough to pick and especially when they are starting to form flower buds. The flavorful oils are at their peak at this time. Continue as needed for the next few weeks. In cold climates, hardy herbs need a break from heavy harvesting beginning 45 days before the first frost, so they can prepare for winter.

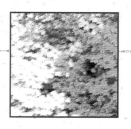

CHAPTER 7

Trees, Shrubs, and Vines

A landscape with no trees can look new and bare, lacking in distinction, but a landscape with too many trees can seem spookily dark and crowded. Overgrown shrubs make a house look old and neglected before its time. But when the trees and shrubs are right for the site and coordinate with the other plantings, everything falls into place in such an inviting manner. Trees and shrubs are relatively permanent landscape features that need little care, and they provide shade, privacy, and beauty with their flowers, berries, form, and foliage.

This chapter gives basic information on designing with woody plants: trees, shrubs, vines, and canes. It will help you select the right plant for the right location, from among the wide array of available choices. It may take discipline to narrow down to just the right few!

Designing with Woodies

If you've been thinking about a landscape plan for your yard, it's time to get it onto paper. Make a scale plan on graph paper (see Chapter 4, page 83), and assess woody plant options for various landscape functions. Consider their size and shape and whether they are evergreen or deciduous. Do they offer flowers and fruit or berries? In what season are they most colorful? Is fruit drop going to be a problem? Do the leaves change color in fall? Sketch in your choices, or make cutouts from garden catalog pictures, and test them in different locations on the plan.

Creeping shrubs, like junipers, can serve as evergreen ground covers. Low, bushy shrubs, such as Japanese spirea and potentilla, blend nicely into flower gardens or the front of a planting around the house. Larger, rounded shrubs can be grouped into clusters to define space or create privacy. More compact cultivars that mature when around four feet high, for example 'Newport' viburnum, can be used

> ## EVERGREENS FOR COLOR
>
> Plant a coniferous shrub garden for winter color. Use evergreens with a variety of different shapes and leaf colors—gold, blue, gray, and green. In northern climates where winter is long, this kind of garden brightens the yard.
>
> Suitable shrubs include dwarf firs, pines, hemlocks, spruces, heathers, junipers, arborvitaes, and false cypress. Specialty nurseries and catalogs offer other, less common conifers as well. Interplant cone-shaped and vertical evergreens with low and mounded forms. Add some spectacular weeping conifers for excitement, and contrast blue and gray foliage against green and gold. In summer, interplant annuals, perennials, and ornamental grasses for variety.

around a house without much pruning. Taller, denser shrubs and trees are best kept at some distance from the house, where they won't block the view. They make good screens for the property perimeter.

Certain trees, like locusts, have small leaves and are not very dense, so they help create little glens of bright partial shade. Vines on an arbor or trellis can have the same effect. Deciduous trees lose their leaves in winter, letting in sunlight until mid-spring. The appearance of the branches and the color and texture of the bark become important features after the leaves drop.

Vertical shrubs or trees that are shaped like an upright cone or pillar, such as

Mature trees at regular intervals along a road or driveway provide distinction and drama as well as shade.

Evergreens of different sizes, shapes, colors, and textures ensure yearlong seasonal interest, especially in climates where winter is long.

SIZE AND GROWTH

Woody plants, unlike herbaceous perennials, retain the previous years' growth and build on it, becoming much larger with time. A tree may take 30 years to reach its full height. A shrub will never become as tall as a tree, but it will develop and grow larger over the years. Growth becomes moderate once a woody plant reaches its full size.

'Skyrocket' juniper, create formality or emphasis in the yard. They can be striking when placed on either side of a doorway or garden gate.

Using a medley of shapes offers design interest that goes much deeper than the leaves and flowers. Repeating a particular kind of shrub at intervals can help to unify the design. A shrubbery hedge or a line of trees helps to create a dignified or formal appearance. Massing many specimens of the same type of shrub or tree can also contribute to a coherent, attractive design.

If you already have large trees on your property, the new plantings should blend with them, not be dwarfed by them. It may take larger masses or larger specimens to do the job. If you have large existing trees that are in the way, they can sometimes be retained by having an arborist remove the lower branches (limb them up), to let in more light and allow space for garden plants and furnishings below them.

This little stream spills prettily along its rocky bed under the trees. Mosses, lichens, and ferns thrive in the shade and moisture. If given a scene of such perfection, take care not to disturb it with inappropriate plantings.

The full size of a woody plant depends on its environment. A tree growing in ideal conditions will grow larger than the same type of tree in a spot to which it is poorly adapted. In general, trees and shrubs growing in full sun will be larger and fuller but perhaps not as tall. If the same species has to compete with other trees and shrubs, as it would in a forest, it will grow taller than its usual height but with fewer, narrower branches. Root space is a factor, too. A shrub in a container with limited space for roots may reach only a fraction of its natural size.

Some trees and shrubs grow fast, putting on several feet of new growth a year. Fast growers are ideal when quick results are desired. Most fast-growing plants, however, tend to be short-lived. In a new landscape, you may have to blend fast-growing trees with slower-growing, longer-lived ones that will eventually form the backbone of your landscape.

SHADE TREES

Shade trees need to be carefully placed, or they will quickly crowd each other out. Check their eventual width, and plant them so they will barely touch at maturity. Try planting shade trees about 20 feet from the house on the southwest or west side. They make convenient air conditioners, lowering the indoor temperature by as much as 20 degrees Fahrenheit. Deciduous shade trees have the advantage of blocking excess summer sun but letting in light when it is needed in winter, after their leaves have fallen.

FLOWERING TREES

Most flowering trees are smaller than shade trees and are not likely to overpower the landscape. They make excellent accents when planted alone; this is a good use for them on small lots. For larger areas, you can mass them or repeat them to define a straight or curved line. Many

Magnolia trees in spring bloom provide the perfect accent to this entryway.

🌿 *Gloriously clothed with color every spring, this mature border of shrubs leads to a sense of anticipation that is almost as good as the reality. Included are cutleaf Japanese maple, azalea, and pink-flowered dogwood.*

SHRUBS

Shrubs are easy to incorporate into the landscape (see pages 182 to 187). Keeping in mind their eventual height, shape, and width, you can plant them singly as accent plants or together in borders. When used as hedges, they should be planted closer together than

flowering trees, such as flowering crabapple *Malus sargentii*, offer all-season interest, with showy spring flowers, green or purple-bronze leaves in summer, colorful leaves in fall, and bright fruit or attractive bark in fall or winter.

🌿 *Planting tulips, hyacinths, and daffodils under this spring-flowering magnolia tree creates a beautiful and dramatic point of impact.*

they would normally be. Shrubs can serve as a living fence and should be planted equally distant from one another, in a straight or smooth line. Shrub borders and hedges can stand alone or serve as backgrounds to perennial and annual plantings.

Foundation plantings of shrubs and ground covers help to integrate the house with its surrounding landscape. Plant shrubs and vines, and sometimes small trees, in proximity to the walls of the building, but not too close. Find out their full diameter at maturity and space them appropriately.

Low-growing and spreading shrubs are ideal subjects for foundation plantings. Taller shrubs, especially conical or columnar ones, can be planted at the corners of the building or between windows. Do not plant tall shrubs in front of windows.

Decorative vines, like this purple clematis, can be trained to climb fences and trellises, creating living walls of bright color.

SHRUBS FOR SEASONAL BLOOMS

Spring
Azalea
Cotoneaster
Forsythia
Fothergilla
Lilac
Ornamental quince
Rhododendron
Viburnum

Summer
Blue spirea
Butterfly bush
Hydrangea
Potentilla
Rose-of-Sharon
St. John's wort
Scotch heather
Spirea
Summersweet

Fall
Butterfly bush
Rose-of-Sharon
Witch hazel

VINES

Climbing plants are ideal for landscaping, because you can effectively plan for and limit their size. Their eventual height and width are determined by the structures on which they grow. The structures themselves fill the space before the vines or climbers have reached full growth. Be careful not to let them escape their bounds by climbing into nearby trees. Clinging vines such as ivy can damage the house structure by working their roots into the mortar, if it is weak. (You can test it by scraping the mortar with a key: If it resists, there is no danger of damage.) It's better to train vines up trellises set about a foot away from the house.

There are many kinds of vines, and they climb in different ways. Twining vines need something to twist around. The new growth twists onto supports as it grows. Sturdy poles and pergolas make good supports. Examples are kiwi (*Actinidia* species), bougainvillea, bittersweet, morning glory, honeysuckle, wisteria, and black-eyed Susan vine *(Thunbergia*

Honeysuckle makes both a good ground cover and climbing vine for trellises, pergolas, and fences.

alata). All of these can grow prodigiously in a single season.

Vines with tendrils need slender strings, wires, or narrow supports to grasp onto. Examples are clematis, passion flower, and grape. They are easy to train, but do not let them start climbing into trees. They can be used to beautify chain-link fences but need additional wires or trellising to grow on wooden fences.

Clinging vines stick to solid objects. These vines work their aerial roots into the smallest of crevices in solid walls. They can damage some kinds of walls, especially brick walls with old mortar that is beginning to weaken, but are safe to grow if the wall is sound. Do not grow them on surfaces that need to be painted from time to time. They are fine on other kinds of walls and sturdy supports. These vines include ivy, climbing hydrangea *(Hydrangea petiolaris),* trumpet creeper *(Campsis radicans),* winter-creeper, and Virginia creeper. English ivy grows in one form as a ground cover, but once it reaches the top of a tall tree or similar support, it branches out and flowers.

CANES

Raspberries and blackberries grow on thorny canes, which are elongated, semiwoody flowering stems about five or six feet tall. They spread with underground runners, called *stolons,* and can be invasive unless severely checked. But they are worth the trouble for the absolutely delicious berries, which can be eaten, sunwarmed, right off the plants in summer. You may have to cover the ripening berries with netting to protect your crop from the birds.

Cut the canes on blackberries and raspberries when first setting out new plants. The canes are the elongated flowering stems. Leave just a few of the leafy buds at the base of the stems. This eliminates any cane diseases that may have hitchhiked to your garden on the plant. It also discourages spring flowering, letting the plant become well established before moving on to berry production.

Don't pay a professional to have that old tree stump ground out—cover it with a colorful vine like clematis to create a dramatic garden centerpiece.

Trees, Shrubs, and Vines 🌿 169

Thin out one-third of all blackberry and raspberry canes each year to keep them productive. If you've ever tried to walk through an abandoned farm field bristling with blackberry thickets, you know what a thorny tangle these plants can grow into.

Not only does crowded growth make blackberries and raspberries hard to work around, but it forces canes to compete for sun, nutrients, moisture, and fresh air. The result can be smaller berries and more diseases.

As soon as canes have borne their fruit, cut them off at the base to provide more space for new canes. Remove any sick, weak, or scrawny canes. Then selectively remove additional canes from areas that are crowded or creeping into other parts of the garden.

Pruning is easier if you wear thick, thorn-proof gloves and use long-handled pruning loppers. A pair of sunglasses to protect your eyes won't hurt either.

Fruit breeders have given us types of raspberries that are everbearing or repeat bearing,

 Cover ripening blackberries with netting to protect your crop from birds.

instead of bearing fruit just once a summer. Most raspberries grow in USDA Zones 4–8.

Blackberries, too, have been worked on by the breeders, and you can purchase thornless types that are delicious and have very large berries. Some of these prefer to have their canes staked to poles or other supports. They are self-pollinating and easy to grow, performing best in well-drained soil in Zones 5–8.

CARE AND PRUNING

Once planted and established, a woody plant needs little care—much less than most other plants. It has a few continuing needs to attend to, including mulching, feeding, watering, pest control, and pruning. See Chapters 2 and 3 for basic information on these topics.

Even the neatest trees drop leaves, needles, and small branches. It is a waste of organic matter to throw them into the trash. Shred them and use them in the compost pile or as mulch under trees and around shrubs and perennials. However, if they have been affected by disease or carry some kind of pest, they should be discarded.

SKIP STAKING

Unless you are planting young trees in areas prone to strong winds, staking can actually do more harm than good. If staked improperly, with rubbing or tight wires, the bark and trunk can become damaged, sometimes irreparably. Staking also interferes with the natural movement of a tree swaying in the wind. Research has shown that swaying helps trees develop stronger, tapered trunks that will serve them well and keep them sturdy for decades.

Where staking is unavoidable, use flexible stakes and ties that have a couple inches of slack so the tree can continue to move. Pad the trunk or slip a section of rubber hose over the supporting wire so it won't damage the tree. Remove the stakes as soon as the tree has rooted enough to become self-supporting.

This wooden arbor is covered with grape vines, creating a cool and inviting shaded retreat.

CLIMATE ZONES AND WOODY PLANTS

Like perennials, trees and other woody plants have multiple factors that affect their hardiness in a particular site. Cold tolerance is a primary determinant. You can't grow an orange tree in Minnesota unless you grow it in a greenhouse to protect it from freezing temperatures. Other trees and shrubs tolerate varying degrees of cold, as measured by the USDA Hardiness Zone Map (see pages 10–11). They are assigned to a zone range where they are most likely to succeed. But hardiness zones are indications only. Good snow cover, protection from wind, and excellent growing conditions may mean that you can stretch the zone somewhat. Within a species, certain plants may be hardier than average and are often used to breed hardier varieties. Plant explorers help here, bringing genetic material from colder climates for crossing with strains of the same species growing in a warmer climate. For instance, explorers brought rhododendron and camellia seed from colder climates in China and Korea and cross-pollinated the plants to get tougher, more cold-tolerant varieties.

The ability to tolerate hot, dry summers; soggy, gray winters; or a particular amount of winter chilling also comes to bear on what grows where. For instance, many supposedly hardy trees and shrubs from the Pacific Northwest will not thrive in the Midwest or Northeast. This is not because of cold but because of hot, dry summers. Plants that are adapted to cold conditions, like apple trees, often will not grow well in the South. These plants need cold temperatures to signal a time of dormancy or a time to flower.

Local nurseries and botanical gardens are good sources for information concerning cold hardiness as well as whether a given plant will do well under local conditions. Always ask before you buy. A good nursery will sell those varieties that are just right for the region's climate. Woody plants are far more susceptible to temperature change because they don't die back to the ground

Sun-warmed berries are a tasty summer treat.

in winter. Instead, their buds and branches are exposed to winter's coldest temperatures and can even be tricked into premature growth by unseasonably warm temperatures, only to be damaged when cold weather returns. But a plant that is not at the edge of its USDA hardiness zone will probably be able to endure the variability of a normal winter without any damage.

Trees

Trees, shrubs, and some vines are woody plants, but the boundaries among the groups are not always clear. Woody plants come in all shapes and sizes, from tall and upright to low and creeping. Aside from producing wood, these plants have one thing in common: persistent stems. This means that the stems survive from one year to the next, unlike perennials. Many woody plants lose their leaves in the winter or during the dry season, but the stems survive and produce new leaves the following year.

🍂 *Shrubs and trees lend form and texture to an otherwise barren winter landscape.*

A tree is sometimes defined as a perennial plant that bears only one single woody stem, the trunk, at ground level. Shrubs often but not always have multiple stems or trunks. Size is not the determining factor here. Pruning can change that. A tree trained as a bonsai, under two feet tall in its elegant small pot, is still a tree, not a bush. The fact remains, though, that landscape trees are usually dramatic, shaping the garden space with their presence and large form, and becoming ever more valuable with age.

🍂 *People are not the only beings who like trees and shrubs. During the summer, the leaves of this shrub effectively hide and shelter birds and their eggs, but in winter the nest is revealed.*

 Clusters of hydrangea flowers start blooming at the end of spring, deepen in color in midsummer, and fade to tan as fall frost brings down the foliage.

Design and hardiness are not the only factors to consider when selecting a tree for your landscape. Choose trees that have wide crotch angles to avoid weak branches and wind or ice damage. The crotch (or branch) angle measures the distance between the trunk and the base of the branch. An upright branch has a narrow crotch angle of less than 45 degrees. A sturdy, wide-angled branch has a 45- to 60-degree crotch angle.

The problem with branches that have narrow crotch angles, a common occurrence on trees like Bradford pears and plums, is that they are not well supported on the trunk. If coated with ice in a winter storm, they may split off. The narrow branching angle can also catch moisture and encourage diseases.

Another problem arises when upright branches with narrow crotch angles near the top of a young tree begin to grow as fast as the main trunk. You must prune the branches back to keep the trunk taller and dominant. Otherwise, the tree develops a split leader, two trunks

SLOW- AND FAST-GROWING TREES

Fast growers can fill the yard quickly, but they may not be as sturdy and long-lived as slower growers.

Fast-Growing Trees

Ash
Catalpa
Cork tree
Arizona cypress
Eucalyptus
Hackberry
Honey locust
Japanese pagoda tree
Poplar
Red mulberry
Tulip tree
Willow

Slow-Growing Trees

Ginkgo
Linden
Red maple
Sugar maple
Bur oak
English oak
Pin oak
White oak
Pine
Sourwood
Spruce
Sycamore

growing side by side. In severe weather, the trunks can crack apart, and the tree may be finished for good.

PREVENT PROBLEMS

Choose pest- or disease-resistant species or varieties instead of problem-plagued trees. When you take the time to select a tree ideally suited for your site, your chances of long-term success are great. But they're even better when you check the track record of the tree you have in mind. If it's prone to insect or disease attack, continue your studies to find alternative, untroubled species or varieties. Because large shade trees can live for decades, even centuries, spending an extra hour or two determining the best tree to plant will pay off for a long, long time.

Instead of European white birch, try disease-resistant river 'Monarch' or 'Avalanche' birches. A substitute for a silver maple tree is 'Celebration' maple. Try substituting 'Crusader' hawthorn for rust-susceptible hawthorns and 'Metroshade' plane trees for disease-susceptible London plane trees.

PEACOCK TREES

Add spice to the landscape by growing "peacocks," which are trees with uniquely colored foliage held all season long. Some of the choices you might consider are red-leaved Japanese maples, golden-leaved box elders and tulip trees, or purple-leaved Norway maples and beech trees. Some trees with colorful foliage are commonly available at garden centers and nurseries. Others can be found at specialty nurseries.

From subtle shades of green to dazzling purples, yellows, or reds, a remarkable variety of woody plants are available to satisfy nearly any need.

🍂 *Once established, woody plants need surprisingly little maintenance to keep them healthy and beautiful.*

AUTUMN COLOR

Include some shade trees with bold fall color for an exciting finish to the growing season. As autumn approaches, trees begin breaking down green chlorophyll and storing the components away for winter. This reveals underlying leaf coloration, which was there all along but hidden beneath the green pigments.

The best trees for fall color include maple, birch, sourwood, ginkgo, tulip tree, red oak, linden, and white ash (such as 'Autumn Applause'), all of which are outstanding when nights are cool and days are sunny.

Choose younger and smaller trees to plant over larger ones. The motto "bigger is better" is not true in this case. Although you can have nearly full-size trees planted in your yard (at a whopping price), smaller trees transplant more easily and grow more quickly than larger trees. They also cost less and are easier to handle without hiring landscapers.

TIPS FOR PLANTING A TREE

🍃

- Select a site with good drainage and plenty of room for top and root growth.
- Water the tree well before planting. If it is bare-root, soak the roots in a bucket of water for an hour or two. Plant in the afternoon or evening or on a cloudy day.
- The hole for a tree should be wide and relatively shallow. Loosen and improve the soil in the site, especially if it is exceptionally poor, but dig the hole for the tree just as deep as the root ball. Make sure the roots are supported, with no air pockets. For a bare-root tree, you may need to make a cone of soil at the bottom of the hole and spread the roots across and down. After planting, the top of the soil should be at just the place where the roots and trunk come together, known as the *root collar*.
- Fill the hole with soil and lightly pack it around the roots.
- After planting, water well but do not overwater. Continue watering as needed, and do not let the soil dry out completely until the plant is well established, which can take months to a year, even if it is a drought-tolerant species.

Directory of Landscape Trees

*I*n this directory you will find some of the best landscape trees, hardy in most but not all parts of the country. For each type of tree listed, you will find names, hardiness zones (with an *a* for the colder portion of the zone, and a *b* for the warmer portion of the zone), appearance and features, best uses, and related species or varieties. Use this directory to locate trees that interest you and that are well suited to your needs, and then find living examples of them. Any popular type of tree that thrives in your climate may be growing in your neighborhood, a nearby park, or an arboretum or college campus with conditions similar to yours. Take the opportunity to see how it looks once established—and how large it can become. Or go the other way around, and find a beautiful, suitable tree growing in your community, find out what it is and what it needs, and plant one like it.

Beech, American
Fagus grandifolia

Zones: USDA 4a–9a

This majestic species is one of the most remarkable trees of eastern North America, where it forms dense groves in deciduous forests. A tall, massive tree, the American beech can grow to more than 80 feet tall, providing dense shade. It has a beautiful silvery gray bark, the nicest coloration of all the beeches. The deciduous leaves are oval and pointed, toothed on the edges. They are dark green in summer, turn golden-bronze in fall, and often persist much of the winter. The small, edible nuts are protected by a prickly outer coating.

How to grow: The American beech does best in full sun but tolerates partial shade. It likes relatively moist, yet well-drained, soils.

Uses: The size of this tree limits its use to large properties, where it quickly becomes the focal point. It is a huge and domineering tree, and its dense shade and shallow roots eliminate all competition.

Related species: The European beech *(Fagus sylvatica)* has smaller leaves and darker gray bark and is less hardy. The deeply purple-leaved beech is called *F. s.* 'Atropunicea' or 'Purpurea.' The copper-leaved beech is *F. s.* 'Cuprea' and has leaves of a lighter shade of purple.

Sargent Cherry
Prunus sargentii

Zones: USDA 5a–9a

The Sargent cherry is the hardiest of the ornamental cherries and one of the largest and most beautiful as well. The abundant spring flowers are deep pink and appear a week or so before most double-flowering cherries. Black fruits, beloved by birds, appear in summer. The trees have polished, chestnut-brown bark and dark green deciduous leaves that turn red in fall.

How to grow: Plant Sargent (and other cherries) in full sun in well-drained soil. It is not difficult to transplant and is somewhat longer lived than other cherries, sometimes attaining 50 years.

Uses: Trees can be used as specimens and shade trees on larger properties. They can also be used as street trees, if their large size is taken into account.

Related species: *Prunus serrulata*, the Japanese flowering cherry, has double pink flowers of remarkable beauty and usually grows in Zones 6a to 9.

Related varieties: *Prunus sargentii* 'Columnaris' has a narrow form and is better adapted to city conditions.

Crape Myrtle
Lagerstroemia indica

Zones: USDA 7a–9a

This is a flowering tree with multiple large, showy flower panicles in electric colors that sizzle across the branches—pink, purple, red-violet, and white. Crape myrtle is a broad-crowned deciduous tree that is variable in size, averaging about 20 to 25 feet, but potentially taller. Dwarf forms are also available.

Often multistemmed, it has smooth, sculptured gray bark that gently exfoliates, showing multishaded underbark. Dappled shade allows for the growth of complementary ground covers beneath its leaf canopy. The petals are crinkled, like crepe paper, and appear recurrently July through September.

How to grow: Transplant container-grown or balled-and-burlapped plants into slightly acidic, well-drained soil. The crape myrtle will not flower well in the shade, where it is subject to powdery mildew. It can get tip blight if planted too far north. Encourage recurrent blooms by tip pruning spent flowers.

Uses: Used as a tree or shrub, crape myrtle is a good choice as a specimen plant, for borders, or to plant near a corner of the house.

Dogwood
Cornus florida

Zones: USDA 5b–8b

This native of the eastern United States is one of the most popular flowering trees. A deciduous tree of medium size (20 feet in most areas) with a spreading habit, it has large white or pink blooms, which appear all over the tree before the leaves emerge. The actual flowers are yellowish and small, but each cluster is surrounded by four large, showy bracts, making a spectacular display. The leaves turn bright scarlet in the fall, and the red berries are a good food source for birds.

How to grow: The flowering dogwood grows best in a rich, acidic, but well-drained soil in partial shade or full sun. It will not tolerate prolonged drought.

Uses: The flowering dogwood's year-round beauty makes it a perfect accent plant. Because of its modest size, it suits the smaller lots of modern homes.

Related species: *Cornus kousa* is later flowering but just as showy. Bracts are more pointed. 'Summer Stars' has flowers that last nearly two months in late summer. *C. mas* is the cornelian cherry, with earlier but less showy blooms than *C. florida*. Its red or yellow fruits are edible.

Related varieties: There are many varieties of flowering dogwood. *C. f.* 'New Hampshire' is the hardiest form, often flourishing in colder zones where other flowering dogwoods have failed.

Douglas Fir

Pseudotsuga menziesii

Zones: USDA 4b–6a

Douglas fir, a cone-bearing member of the pine family, is native to western North America. It is favored as a cut Christmas tree in some areas of the country. This pyramid-shaped ornamental tree has winglike branches and a unique, youthful habit in which the upper branches are ascending, while the lower branches descend. It is distinguished from other narrow-leaved evergreens by its scaly, long, pointed terminal buds and curious cones. No other cones of native conifers have persistent scales with conspicuous, protruding, three-pointed, forked bracts. The Douglas fir has flat, blunt needles with two white lines on the underside of the leaf, which are variable in color.

How to grow: This tree needs humid conditions and moist, well-drained acidic to neutral soil. It will not survive arid, thin, infertile soil and dry atmospheric conditions.

Uses: The Douglas fir makes a fine specimen tree and can be used as a screen. It holds its short needles when used as a Christmas tree.

Ginkgo, Maidenhair Tree

Ginkgo biloba

Zones: USDA 4b–8b

This ancient oriental, single-species genus is believed to be the oldest flowering plant in existence, though it is now apparently extinct in the wild. It can grow from 40 to 80 feet tall. The ginkgo's foliage has the unusual habit of hugging spur branches instead of forming a broad crown. This results in branches that grow in every direction. The exotic, parallel-veined green leaves are fan-shaped but often deeply notched at the center tip. They turn butter-yellow in autumn. Male and female flowers are on separate trees. Naked seeds, produced in late summer and fall, are plum-shaped with a fleshy outer coat that smells like rancid butter when decomposing. Curiously, the seeds are considered gourmet fare and are highly touted in the Orient, where they are also used in herbal tonics.

How to grow: This survivor is tough enough to tolerate differing soil pH, many soil types, moisture variations, and light exposures. The ginkgo needs little pruning and is virtually free of pests and diseases.

Uses: To avoid fetid fruit, plant only male trees as specimens or shade trees. Ginkgo is a good city street tree. In autumn, the yellow leaves tend to fall all at once and can look most decorative near a gray stone walk, until they go brown.

Gum

Nyssa sylvatica

Zones: USDA 5a–9a

The sour gum is a beautiful shade tree with fire-engine red fall foliage. Native to the eastern United States, it is a favorite plant of bees. This water-loving plant is also known as tupelo, pepperidge, and black gum. Sour gum grows pyramidally in youth but with maturity forms an irregularly rounded crown. With cultivation, it grows to about 25 feet by age 30. One of the first trees to show color in fall, sour gum's glossy green leaves turn scarlet. Its bitter, fleshy, blue-black fruit is favored by bears and birds and follows pollination of female trees. Older trees have dark, blocky-textured bark.

How to grow: Moist, acidic soil is required. This tree needs protection from the wind, and light shade will decrease its spectacular show of autumn leaves. For best performance, transplant in spring, using local stock. Tap-rooted sour gum transplants poorly unless balled-and-burlapped or container-grown plants are used.

Uses: Sour gum is used as a specimen, shade, or street tree and is also naturalized or used in mass plantings.

Hornbeam

Carpinus betulus

Zones: USDA 5a–7a

This is a good landscape tree, usually growing to about 40 feet tall. It has a pyramidal form while young but spreads out more at maturity. It is often heavily pruned for hedging and topiary effects. Oval, deciduous green leaves have toothed edges. The bark is a handsome gray, and the foliage turns yellow in fall.

How to grow: A tree that manages to grow well in difficult conditions, the hornbeam can be planted in practically any well-drained soil, moderately acidic to moderately alkaline, in full sun to light shade.

Uses: This species can be used as a small shade tree or kept small for screens, hedges, and patio containers.

Related species: The American hornbeam (*C. caroliniana*) is native to eastern North America and has bright yellow to orange-red fall color. It would be used more frequently, but it is hard to transplant.

Related varieties: *Carpinus betulus* 'Columnaris' and 'Fastigiata' have a tight, narrow form. There are also weeping and purple-leaved forms of hornbeam.

Juneberry
Amelanchier arborea

Zones: USDA 3b–8a

The juneberry is native to eastern North America but has abundant and similar relatives in other parts of the continent. This small, often multistemmed, deciduous tree or tall shrub grows to 25 feet in height. It offers color in all seasons: in winter, with smooth gray bark delicately streaked with longitudinal fissures; in spring, with its delicate white flowers, appearing just as the leaves start to burst out; in summer, with its red berries that gradually turn black; and finally, in fall, with its beautiful orange-red oval leaves.

How to grow: Juneberry is tolerant of various soils and exposures, though it blooms most heavily in full sun.

Uses: It can be trained as a small tree or encouraged to develop multiple trunks by pruning. Juneberry is often planted in naturalistic landscapes, not only for its appearance but because it attracts birds.

Related species: There are several similar *Amelanchier* species, some more shrublike than the species mentioned. They are all interesting landscape plants.

American Linden
Tilia americana

Zones: USDA 3a–8a

This is the native eastern North American species of linden, also known as basswood. The American linden is a tall, stately tree, growing to more than 100 feet. Pyramidal in youth, the tree develops a more rounded crown at maturity. It has gray to brown bark and large, toothed, heart-shaped, deciduous leaves. They are dark green above and pale beneath, turning yellow or yellow-green in the fall. The yellow flowers would not be particularly noticeable without their pervading fragrance.

How to grow: This tree transplants readily and does best in deep, rich, moist, well-drained soils with full sun or partial shade. Never plant the American linden over a parking area, such as a driveway; the sticky nectar that drips from the flowers can damage car paint.

Uses: American linden is a good choice for a specimen tree or for naturalizing large lots and parks.

Related species: A smaller-leaved linden, the European linden *(Tilia cordata)*, is the most widely planted ornamental species and offers many varieties.

Honey Locust
Gleditsia triacanthos var. *Inermis*

Zones: USDA 4b–9a

Honey locust is a tall, pod-bearing, deciduous shade tree with a short trunk. Its ornamental foliage is lacy and medium to fine in texture. The tree's mature size is variable, growing in the 30- to 70-foot range, taller in the wild. Honey locust is a rapid-growing tree whose fall foliage is yellow to yellow-green. Its fruit is a long, reddish-brown, straplike, curved pod produced in late summer. Its shade is dappled and permits plant growth beneath the canopy.

How to grow: Plant honey locust in full sun and limey soil. It's adaptable to a range of conditions, including drought and high pH, and is tolerant to road salt spray.

Uses: To avoid thorns and litter problems, use an unarmed, podless selection as a shade tree. Webworm is this plant's worst enemy. Leaflets are small and break down quickly.

Related varieties: 'Shademaster,' a superior podless cultivar with a vaselike form, is fairly resistant to webworms. 'Skyline' is noted for its golden fall color and upright form. 'Summergold' has gold-green leaves in summer.

Southern Magnolia
Magnolia grandiflora

Zones: USDA 6b–9b

This is a splendid, broad-leaved evergreen tree, native to the southeastern United States. The standout qualities of the magnolia include its large, flamboyant flowers and attractive, waxy, tropical-looking leaves, both of which add distinction to the garden landscape. It is a handsome, low-branching tree, reaching heights of 60 to 80 feet. It displays wooly young buds and eight-inch-long, thick, shiny leaves. The huge, solitary blooms are white and exude a lovely fragrance. Its fruit is three to four inches long and conelike, revealing red seeds when opened.

How to grow: Plant container-grown or balled-and-burlapped plants in spring. The soil should be fertile, deep, well-drained, and slightly acidic. This tree tolerates high soil moisture but should be protected from wind. Avoid transplanting once it is situated. It can be pruned after flowering, if needed. Pests are not a particular problem.

Uses: Southern magnolia is used in the South as a specimen tree, but it does have a good deal of leaf litter. It is best used where it has ample room to develop without having to cut off the lower limbs.

Sugar Maple
Acer saccharum

Zones: USDA 3b–7b

Sugar maple (also called hard or rock maple) is a popular choice for its razzle-dazzle red, orange, and yellow fall colors. Native to the northeastern United States, the sugar maple is well known as the source of maple syrup and maple lumber for furniture. It is a short-trunked, large, spreading tree that can reach heights of 50 to 70 feet or more. The pointed leaves are four to six inches across, with five lobes. Nonshowy chartreuse flowers appear in early spring, preceding the leaves.

How to grow: The sugar maple requires a well-drained, fertile soil and plenty of room to grow. Do not plant it in dry, compacted soil or too close to streets where road salt is used.

Uses: This plant is best used as a shade or specimen tree. It is resistant to storm damage.

Related species: Among the larger-growing maples, the Norway maple *(Acer platanoides)* is particularly popular. This species offers many varieties, including some with deep purple, red, or variegated leaves. *Acer palmatum,* the Japanese maple, has pointed, star-shaped leaves of varying narrowness and is found in many sizes and colors.

White Oak
Quercus alba

Zones: USDA 4b–9a

Not only does this tree grow to a massive size—up to 150 feet with an 80-foot spread—but it can also reach a great age: 800-year-old trees have been known to exist. The white oak has a pyramidal form when young but becomes broadly rounded in maturity. The oak leaves, narrow at the base, have five to nine rounded lobes. They are dark green in summer and turn red before falling.

How to grow: The white oak is slow growing and must be planted as a small tree, because its deep taproot makes transplantation difficult. It prefers full sun and a deep, moist, well-drained soil that is slightly acidic. Its leaves tend to acidify the soil over time.

Uses: The white oak makes a splendid specimen tree for parks and spacious properties.

Related species: A good substitute for the white oak in moist soils, the swamp white oak *(Quercus bicolor)* has leaves that are broad and undulated on the edges rather than lobed.

Eastern White Pine
Pinus strobus

Zones: USDA 3a–9a

This was once among the tallest trees of eastern North American forests. Unfortunately, it is now rare to see one any taller than 100 feet. Young white pines are pyramidal in shape but lose their lower branches as they age and take on a wind-beaten look. The tree is attractive at both stages. Its persistent needles, soft for a pine, are grouped by fives and are bluish-green in color. The cones are large and decorative.

How to grow: This pine is easily transplanted. It grows best in fertile, moist, well-drained soils, and, though it prefers full sun, it can tolerate some shade. It can be pruned into an attractive evergreen hedge.

Uses: The eastern white pine is an exceedingly handsome landscape tree; some rate it as the best ornamental conifer. Given lots of room, it makes an unforgettable impression as a landscape plant. The eastern white pine is not a good city tree because of its susceptibility to pollution and salt damage. It is prone to damage in winter from ice storms.

Related species: The Japanese white pine *(Pinus parviflora)* is a slow-growing, smaller pine.

Redbud
Cercis canadensis

Zones: USDA 4a–9a

The redbud is native to eastern North America and is striking in wooded areas where its reddish-purple flowers grow, closely and tightly aligned on slender stems, before the leaves unfold in spring. The distinctly heart-shaped green leaves are six inches across. The tree is small and graceful, with spreading, slightly drooping branches. Height at maturity is approximately 20 to 30 feet.

How to grow: Plant young trees in the spring in well-drained soil in sun or partial shade. Thin upper branches if lower ones are struggling from lack of light under a dense canopy.

Uses: An easy and attractive choice as a single specimen or in groups. Select plants from your own region because the hardiness varies with trees originating in more northern or more southern locations.

Related species: *Cercis chinensis* is similar in form but is smaller (ten feet) and a little showier in flower. It grows with less cold tolerance in Zones 6 to 9.

Norway Spruce
Picea abies

Zones: USDA 3a–7b

With its perfect, pyramidal shape, the Norway spruce makes a fine live Christmas tree for the yard. It is rather stiffly formal in its youth, but older branches produce pendulous branchlets, giving it more charm as it ages. Its needles are dark green year-round. The cones, borne sporadically, are particularly large for a spruce. It can reach more than 100 feet in height, even under cultivation.

How to grow: Grow in full sun in just about any soil, though moist, sandy, well-drained soil is preferred. The Norway spruce does best in cool climates. Give this tree plenty of space, because it will lose its lower branches—and much of its charm—if crowded or shaded at its base.

Uses: This tree makes a striking specimen plant or an excellent windbreak.

Related species: The Colorado blue spruce *(Picea pungens glauca)* is renowned for its blue needles.

Sycamore
Platanus occidentalis

Zones: USDA 5a–9a

The sycamore is a very tall native tree from eastern North American forests. Specimens well over 150 feet tall are not uncommon. Its bark is strikingly white and flakes off in patches to reveal green, gray, and brown bark below. The wide, lobed, deciduous leaves resemble sugar maple leaves. The massive trunk and branches give it a noble appearance.

How to grow: Plant sycamores in full sun or bright partial shade, in deep, moist soil. They will grow in dryer soil. In some places, the sycamore is no longer recommended because of its susceptibility to blight.

Uses: Requiring a great deal of space to grow well, the sycamore is suited to planting in open, rather moist places where there is plenty of space. It does not get diseased under these conditions.

Related species: The London plane tree *(Platanus* x *acerifolia)* is a cross between the sycamore and the European plane tree. Its bark is not as colorful, but it does not get the blight that has brought down sycamores in some places.

Weeping Willow
Salix species

Zones: USDA 3a–9a

Weeping willows are wide, tall trees with curtains of drooping branches that sweep the ground. Their small, narrow leaves appear in very late winter, giving the trees a golden look. They become green as they mature and turn yellow in autumn. The fast-growing trees have great beauty, but they also have the unfortunate attribute of dropping many small and large branches quite frequently.

How to grow: Plant weeping willows only in moist locations, well away from houses or other structures and underground pipes and wires. The roots can block pipes and drainage tiles in their search for water. New plants grow very easily from cuttings or even from relatively large branches that are stuck into boggy soil and kept moist for several months in spring.

Uses: Suitable only for open spaces with a lot of moisture in the soil, the best use of weeping willow is in low places where you need something to help drain the soil or next to a pond or lake where the full beauty of the weeping willow can be appreciated.

Related species. Willows *(Salix* species) are extremely diverse, with shrubs and trees of many shapes for diverse climates.

Yellowwood
Cladrastis kentuckea

Zones: USDA 4b–8a

The yellowwood is native to North Carolina and Kentucky but is used in a wider area. The color of its wood gives it its name. It is a slow-growing, low-branching tree, 30 to 50 feet tall and even wider in spread. It forms a rounded crown. In winter, the zigzag pattern of branching makes it interesting. In late spring it produces pealike white flowers that resemble wisteria.

How to grow: Plant in full sun in ordinary, well-drained, slightly acidic soil. It dislikes alkaline soils. This tree is drought-tolerant and cold-resistant when well established.

Uses: An excellent landscape tree for both flowers and foliage, yellowwood is also a good shade tree.

Directory of Popular Landscape Shrubs

Shrubs are upright woody plants that differ from trees because they have multiple main stems. They are usually, but not always, smaller than trees. In ordinary speech, shrubs are bushes, and there are people who don't make much distinction among the many kinds. They prune them, one and all, into shapes that horticulturists have been known to snidely call "meatballs." If a shrub has been trimmed and trained out of all semblance of its natural form, it can look tortured instead of beautiful. On the other hand, if left totally untrimmed, some kinds of shrubs start spreading and growing in all directions, just begging for control at the hand of a gardener. The best way to select and grow shrubs is to learn about their similarities and differences and use the information to plant the right choices in places where they fit the scene and stay healthy without major reconfiguration of the soil or butchering of the branches. In this directory, you will find some of the most suitable and popular kinds of garden shrubs, in all their diversity: flowering, nonflowering, low-growing, tall, evergreen, and deciduous. Each entry contains essential information: the zone range, description, instructions for growing and pruning, uses, and related species and varieties.

Azalea
Rhododendron species

Zones: USDA 3a–10

The name *azalea*, which is not a technical term, refers to those popular shrubs that are part of the enormous *Rhododendron* genus. They generally have smaller, less leathery leaves than other rhododendron and have flowers spread evenly all over the bush, rather than in trusses. Sizes range from under a foot to six or more feet tall. Flowers bloom in spring in jewel colors of pink, red, rose, purple, magenta, and white. Some types are deciduous, some evergreen.

How to grow: Plant azaleas in rich, well-drained, highly acidic soil in full sun or partial shade. Blooming will be more generous in sun. Prune for shape after flowers have finished blooming. Remove seedpods to direct energy back to the plant and away from seed formation.

Uses: Used mainly in shrub borders and as foundation plantings, azaleas are also good as potted plants.

Related varieties: Azaleas come in a great diversity of size, shape, and hardiness. Check local suppliers for types that do well in your region.

Bridal-Wreath
Spiraea x *vanhouttei*

Zones: USDA 3b–8b

Most spireas are spring-bloomers with numerous tiny white or pink flowers. The Vanhoutt spirea grows 6 to 8 feet in height, spreading 10 to 12 feet in diameter. It has a distinctly fountainlike growth habit, with a round top and arching branches recurving to the ground, covered with tufts of little white flowers all the way. Its leaves are greenish-blue, turning plum-colored in the fall.

How to grow: Although the shrub will grow well in medium shade, full sun produces more flowers. The bridal-wreath adapts well to most soils. To keep the shrub in top shape, prune back one-third of the old flowering wood annually after it finishes blooming.

Uses: An excellent accent plant, the bridal-wreath is also good for informal hedges or screens and is well suited to mixed shrub borders.

Related species: The garland spirea (*Spiraea* x *arguta*) is similar to the bridal-wreath but has less pendulous branches and a better covering of flowers in spring. The bumald spireas (*Spiraea* x *bumalda*) are summer-flowering spireas with pink to whitish flowers.

Blueberry
Vaccinium species

Zones: USDA 4a–7b

Midsized shrubs, blueberries have clusters of white, somewhat bell-like flowers in spring and edible blueberries in summer. Leaves are pointed ovals, green and a bit leathery, that turn crimson in the fall. Depending on the variety, the dense shrubs are two to five feet tall and almost as wide. A mature bush can produce ten quarts of berries or more per year.

How to grow: Order the named varieties for best-tasting fruit. Plant in well-drained, very acidic soil in full sun or bright partial shade. Little or no pruning is needed. Plant several types together for good pollination.

Uses: Blueberries are easy to include in the landscape the same way you would use azaleas. They can be part of shrub borders and also grow well in bright partial shade at the edge of wooded areas.

Related varieties: Highbush or rabbiteye blueberries grow farther south than other types. 'Bluecrop,' 'Herbert,' and 'Early Bluejay' are good producers. 'Elliott S. H.' is self-pollinating.

Butterfly Bush
Buddleia species

Zones: USDA 4b–9

Butterfly bushes have pointed clusters of small flowers at the ends of their many branches, making a rounded bush of flowers. Blooms are usually purple, rose, magenta, or white. Heights range from two to six feet. The foliage is deciduous and fairly ordinary looking, but when in bloom the bushes are alive with butterflies and hummingbirds.

How to grow: Plant butterfly bushes in full sun in rich, well-drained soil. In cold winters, bushes usually die back to the ground and should be totally cut away at the end of winter. In southern zones, the canes can be cut back to a few feet in height. Butterfly bushes grow readily from cuttings and layering.

Related species and varieties: 'Honeycomb' is a yellow-flowering type for Zones 6 to 9. *B. davidii* can reach eight feet, in Zones 5 to 9. *B. alternifolia* is hardy in Zones 4b to 7.

Camellia

Camellia japonica

Zones: USDA 7a–9a

Camellias come mainly from China and Japan. They have pink, red, or white single or double flowers of great beauty, often three to five inches across. Blooms appear in fall, winter, or spring. The leaves are very shiny and deep green, two to four inches long, and are evergreen. When mature, long-lived camellias can take the form of small trees about 20 feet tall but usually are more shrublike at heights of 5 to 10 feet.

How to grow: Plant camellias in partial shade in moist, acidic, rich, well-drained soil. Protect the plants from wind and sunscald in winter. Mulch to keep the roots moist. Prune after flowering is finished if necessary to improve the form.

Uses: Camellias make striking accent plants. They can be used as foundation plantings where they are hardy if the soil is suffi-ciently acidic. Where hardy, they are excellent in wooded areas.

Enkianthus

Enkianthus campanulatus

Zones: USDA 4a–7b

A dome-shaped shrub or small tree, the enkianthus has a bushy to umbrella form and small reddish-beige, veined, bell-shaped flowers in dan-gling clusters. There are also types with white or pink flowers. Plants may reach heights of 15 to 20 feet when mature, if allowed to grow in tree form. Leaves turn pumpkin-colored in fall before dropping.

How to grow: Plant in full sun to bright partial shade in acidic, well-drained, average soil. Prune for shape in late spring after flowering, removing sucker growth.

Uses: Use as an accent plant or in foundation plantings and shrub borders. This plant looks wonderful when seen from below, with the viewer looking up into the flowers.

Euonymus, Burning Bush

Euonymus alata

Zones: USDA 4a–8a

With ridged stems and vaselike upright form, burn-ing bush, also known as winged euonymus, is an attractive deciduous shrub. The leaves are small pointed ovals and are remarkable for the fiery pinkish-red foliage color that appears in autumn and remains a bright spot for several weeks. The shrubs become more spreading as they mature at a height of 10 to 15 feet. Insignifi-cant yellow flowers are followed by attractive red berries.

How to grow: Plant in full sun or bright partial shade in any soil as long as it is well drained. Prune for shape, thinning branches as necessary while the bushes are young. Prune to limit size if you wish.

Uses: An adaptable plant, it can be used for many landscape purposes, including shrubbery borders, hedges, accent plantings, foundation planting, screening, and even large containers.

Fothergilla

Fothergilla species

Zones: USDA 5b–9a

The dwarf fothergilla *(Fothergilla gardenii)*, native to the southeastern United States, is a low-growing shrub, while the large fothergilla *(Fothergilla major)*, which is similar, can attain heights of up to ten feet. The tip of each of the spreading branches is decorated in early spring with an erect cluster of white, very fragrant, petalless flowers, creating the typical bottlebrush appearance of the shrub. Its leaves, rounded but somewhat irregular, don't appear until later. They are dark green, turning bright shades of yellow, red, and orange before dropping in the fall.

How to grow: This shrub requires an acidic, peaty, sandy loam with adequate moisture but good drainage. Although it does well in partial shade, it blooms and colors best in full sun.

Uses: The dwarf fothergilla is a choice plant for borders, founda-tion plantings, and mass plantings. No pruning is required.

Heather

Erica carnea

Zones: USDA 3–7

With small white or pink flowers in winter and early spring, heather is an appealing low, bushy shrub. It usually stays well below two feet tall but becomes wide with age, loaded with flowers in long, showy clusters. The tiny leaves stay on all winter.

How to grow: Plant in moist, acidic soil in partly shaded areas. Trim for neatness after flowers fade. Tip cuttings root in late summer, but naturally layered branches can usually be found if you scratch around under established plants. Clip off a portion with good roots attached and reset it elsewhere to start a new colony.

Uses: Good for winter color, heather can be used to clothe difficult slopes in shady areas and also makes a good ground cover and understory plant below trees.

Michigan Holly

Ilex verticillata

Zones: USDA 4a–9a

This shrub, with its deciduous, soft, spineless leaves, is a rather unhollylike holly. Its long-lasting red berries aligned along slender branches make it a winter feature after the leaves drop. The foliage is dense, and shrubs grow with an oval form and numerous branchlets. The leaves, 1½ to 3 inches long, are dark green and turn yellow in the fall. The flowers are insignificant, but the red berries last right through the winter if they're not eaten by the birds.

How to grow: Michigan holly does well in full sun or partial shade and moist, rich soils. This is an acid-loving plant that will do poorly in neutral or alkaline soils.

Uses: The shrub makes a good accent plant for spots where its winter color will be appreciated. It is a fine choice for mass plantings and wildlife gardens. At least one male must be planted among several females for fruiting to occur.

Related varieties: 'Sparkleberry' is one of the more spectacular selections, with numerous, long-lasting crimson berries.

Hydrangea

Hydrangea species

Zones: USDA 5a–9b

Hydrangeas are diverse shrubs noted for flowers in large clusters, which may be mounded, globular, flat, or spiked. Stems branch somewhat. Each flower head has both sterile and fertile florets. The sterile flowers are the showy ones, with a papery look. They are 1 to 1½ inches in diameter and can be white, pink, purple, or blue, depending on both the variety of hydrangea and the acidity of the soil.

How to grow: Hydrangeas need plenty of water and rich soil and will grow in full sun or bright partial shade. Mulch to maintain cool, moist conditions for the roots. Remove faded flowers and cut out deadwood.

Uses: Hydrangeas can be used in shrub and perennial borders and as foundation plantings. They are often used in containers, sometimes as seasonal or holiday potted plants. Oakleaf hydrangea is a good shrub for planting in wooded areas and in shrub borders.

Related species: *Hydrangea quercifolia*, the oakleaf hydrangea, has long-lasting white flowers in spikes and, unlike other hydrangeas, grows well in wooded areas in partial shade, preferring moist, well-drained, somewhat acidic soil. *Hydrangea* 'Annabelle' with white, globular flower heads, also grows in these conditions. Lacecap hydrangeas such as 'Blue Wave' have flowers in flat, showy heads with a lacy appearance.

Hypericum

Hypericum prolificum

Zones: USDA 3–8

A medium-size bush with bright yellow flowers, hypericum is also known as St. John's wort. Plants grow one to four feet tall and wide, with many clustered, upright branches with dark green, shiny, somewhat pointed leaves. Flowers appear in summer and can be an inch wide. The fruits are greenish-red and have become popular in flower arrangements.

How to grow: Plant in well-drained, somewhat dry soil in full sun. Plants adapt to different soil types. Prune for shape if necessary.

Uses: Herb gardens, dry areas, and flower borders.

Leucothoe

Leucothoe fontanesiana

Zones: USDA 5b–9a

This southeastern United States native is a low-growing evergreen shrub with attractive flowers resembling lily-of-the-valley in spring. It usually reaches three to six feet in height and width. Its spreading, arching branches droop with the weight of the pendulous fragrant clusters of creamy white flowers. The leaves are leathery and dark green, three to six inches long. They often take on a bronzy to purplish color in fall and winter. Tight, low, dwarf forms are available.

How to grow: This shrub is a good choice for partial to full shade, though it will tolerate sun if mulched and protected from drying winds. It prefers moist, well-drained, organic soils and acidic growing conditions. If it gets too leggy, it can be cut back to the ground.

Uses: Leucothoe is a good ground cover and is excellent for mass plantings. It nicely hides the base of other shrubs that become leggy over time, especially rhododendrons. Both flowers and leaves are used in bouquets.

Related varieties: There are numerous cultivars around with varying leaf colors and sizes. Some of the best have variegated green and white leaves or dark purple ones.

Lilac

Syringa vulgaris

Zones: USDA 3–7

Lilacs have what it takes to come through some very cold winters unharmed and gladden many hearts in spring. They are tall, upright shrubs laden with broad but pointed clusters of highly perfumed, lavender flowers amid green, heart-shaped leaves. There are white-flowered types, too. Plants may be 12 feet wide and 15 feet high.

How to grow: Full sun is best, though lilacs will grow in partial shade. They prefer neutral soils with good drainage. Remove old trunks and unwanted suckers occasionally.

Uses: Lilacs are good accent plants but have no special features after their mid-spring bloom. They can also be planted in a line as an informal, blooming hedge.

Related species: There are many other species of lilac, some earlier or later bloomers and many with equally interesting perfumes. They are often used to extend the common lilac's all-too-short flowering season.

Related varieties: The so-called French hybrids are improved forms of *Syringa vulgaris*.

Mock Orange

Philadelphus coronarius

Zones: USDA 4a–7b

With long branches loaded with pure white, fragrant flowers, mock orange is a popular garden shrub wherever it is hardy. It blooms once each spring. Flowers are about an inch wide. Most types are single but doubles are available. Leaves are pointed ovals and drop in fall. Mature bushes can be 12 feet tall and wide.

How to grow: Plant shrubs with ample spacing between them, in any soil. They do best in rich soil with good drainage, slightly acidic to neutral. If necessary, prune after flowers finish for overall plant shape and to keep the bushes from getting too thick or the canes too old.

Uses: This is a large deciduous shrub, best used in a shrubbery border or as an informal hedge.

Pieris

Pieris japonica

Zones: USDA 6a–8a

There is something attractive about this shrub in every season, which explains its general popularity. It is usually about six feet tall but can be taller when mature. Its evergreen, narrow, pointed leaves are shiny all winter. New growth in spring may have distinctly red tones. The flowers are small and white to pink but occur in very showy, drooping clusters about five inches wide, early in spring. Flower buds are in evidence all fall and winter.

How to grow: Plant in well-drained, rich, somewhat acidic soil in bright partial shade. Prune after flowering and remove seed heads. Protect from high winds in winter.

Uses: A mainstay for foundation planting, pieris has almost every landscape use in borders and as a background plant. It combines well with spring bulbs.

Rhododendron
Rhododendron species

Zones: USDA 3–8, mainly

Rhododendrons come in many diverse species, but most people use the word to refer to *Rhododendron catawbiense* and its hybrids. These shrubs have large, leathery, shiny leaves and bright trumpet-shaped flowers in large trusses that bloom in late spring or summer. They have a lot of landscape impact with their colorful red, lavender, white, yellow, and pink globes of flowers, about seven inches wide. The plants vary from dwarf types to rangy natives 15 to 20 feet tall. The leaves are evergreen.

How to grow: Plant rhododendrons where they have room to grow to their large mature size. Plants prefer partial shade and rich, moist, acidic soil that is well drained. Remove seed heads carefully, so as not to disturb emerging shoots. Prune for shape after flowers bloom, only if necessary.

Uses: Woodland gardens, shrubbery borders, and foundation plantings.

Rosemary
Rosmarinus officinalis

Zones: USDA 6–10, indoors elsewhere

Rosemary is a shrub that comes in all sizes; not only is it rooted easily, it is also grown from seed and sold while small. The somewhat pine-scented leaves are flat but needle-shaped. Lightly touching the leaves releases the scent. The stems are woody, and small blue or, rarely, white flowers appear along the stems. Rosemary may be upright or prostrate and, where it is hardy, grows as high as six or seven feet. More often, it is grown in pots and kept to smaller sizes. It takes well to pruning and is sometimes seen in cone-shaped or ball-shaped topiaries.

How to grow: Plant rosemary in containers or in the garden, in any light, well-drained soil of average fertility. Prune for shape, and protect from wind and bitter cold below 10°F.

Uses: Best known as a culinary plant, rosemary leaves are used to season lamb, fish, soup, and other foods. In the garden, it makes a good shrub or hedge where it is hardy. The prostrate form can be used as a ground cover. Rosemary is elegant and easy in containers.

Smoke Tree
Cotinus coggygria

Zones: USDA 5a–7b

This tall shrub from Europe and Asia is multistemmed and deciduous with an open, spreading form. The smooth, satiny leaves are nearly round and are blue-green in color in the species, purple in some varieties. The flowers are borne in large, long-lasting, fawn-colored, feathery inflorescences, appearing in summer and lasting through fall. Purple-leaved forms have purple inflorescences. It can grow 15 or more feet tall but is easily pruned to a smaller size.

How to grow: Full sun is best, especially for the purple-leaved varieties. The smoke tree tolerates just about any soil. Pruning this shrub is a compromise between two goals: obtaining dense foliage growth (with heavy annual pruning) or stimulating abundant flowering (since blooms only appear on wood three years old).

Uses: The smoke tree is good for shrub borders and mass plantings. The varieties with colorful foliage make nice accent plants.

Related varieties: Many purple-leaved varieties exist. 'Royal Purple' is a particularly choice specimen.

Witch Hazel
Hamamelis virginiana

Zones: USDA 4a–9a

Common witch hazel is a small ornamental shrub or tree that grows up to 20 feet in height and spread. It is remarkable for its fall flowers, usually being the last shrub of the year to bloom. The flowers are yellow and fragrant, bearing four straplike petals. They are borne in loose clusters, and the display can last from two to four weeks in late autumn. The leaves are irregular in shape—nearly rounded but with toothed margins. They are medium green in summer, turning golden before dropping in the fall.

How to grow: Witch hazel does best in full sun to light shade and adapts to most soils. In the wild, it prefers moist situations.

Uses: The common witch hazel is used as an ornamental woodland tree or as the back of a shrub border.

Related species: The vernal witch hazel *(Hamamelis vernalis)* is similar to the common but blooms in late winter, often while the ground is still covered with snow. Its flowers are yellow to red. 'Arnold Promise' is a very good choice.

Frequently Asked Questions

Q: What makes some hollies produce berries when others don't?
A: Hollies have either male or female flowers, not both, on each plant. Only the females produce berries. To have berries, you need both a female holly and a pollen-producing male of the same type in the same vicinity. Other reasons for lack of fruit include a shortage of sunlight where the female is planted and severe drought while berries are forming.

Q: I have several hydrangeas, all of which are the same kind. Why are some blue flowering while others are pink?
A: The availability of aluminum in the soil and the soil's pH determine the color of your type of hydrangea. If the pH is high, or alkaline (7.0 or above), the flowers will be pink. Blue flowers develop when the soil is acidic (4.5 to 5.5). In between, flowers are purplish. To ensure blue flowers, lower the pH with a sulfur-based product. Raise the pH with lime for pink blossoms.

Q: Why doesn't my wisteria bloom? It looks healthy and grows so well that it must be pruned often.
A: You may be pruning off next year's flower buds. Encourage short side shoots for flower buds by partially pruning the longest side branches. To limit excessive growth, do not fertilize wisteria. Wisteria blooms best with ample exposure to the sun. Root pruning may shock the plant into flowering. In June, use a spade to cut a six-inch deep circle about two feet from the base of the plant. In addition, some wisterias take more maturity than others before they start to bloom.

Q: Is a rhododendron an evergreen? Mine has leaves that are turning yellow.
A: Some rhododendrons are evergreen, keeping their green leaves through the winter, and other types are deciduous and lose all their leaves. But all evergreens, whether they have leaves, like rhododendrons and magnolias, or needles, like pines and spruces, drop some of them every year in a regular cycle. Usually the two-year-old leaves and needles turn yellow and drop, but the younger ones stay green, unless the tree is sick. Then in spring, new leaves or needles form and mature, and the cycle begins again.

Q: We recently moved to a four-year-old house. I don't like the landscape design used by the former owner, but some of the shrubs and trees are nice. Can we move them?
A: As a rule, the bigger the plants, the harder it is to move them. Azaleas and rhododendrons are exceptions, because their roots are fairly shallow. Pines and other trees with deep taproots are the most difficult to move. In most regions, this is best done on cool, moist days in spring or fall. You need to figure out what you can move and where you will move it. Dig the planting holes before digging up and moving the shrubs, to minimize the length of time they will be out of the ground. Prune lightly, especially bushes. Dig up the shrubs. A general guideline is to allow a foot in diameter of root mass for every inch of trunk diameter, but if it is a shallow-rooted shrub, allow more. Mark a circle all the way around the trunk or main stems where you will dig, and then make shovel cuts, angled slightly inward, on that line. Go around a few times, until the root

ball rocks a bit with a little push. Then lift it up onto a tarp or wheelbarrow, and plant immediately. Firm the soil, and water the plant in its new location. Keep the soil moist but not soggy for several months or longer.

Q: We have cold, windy, changeable winters, and I've had some winter burn on my boxwoods. How can I protect them?
A: Wrap boxwood and other evergreen shrubs with burlap to prevent winter burn. When the soil is frozen, the sun is bright, and the wind is strong, evergreens lose moisture from their exposed leaves and cannot replace it through frozen roots. The foliage scorches to brown and the stems may die back—or even worse, the whole shrub may die. Burlap, though far from elegant, makes a good "coat" for the shrub and ensures that you will have a nice-looking plant when spring arrives. This also works for coniferous evergreens like arborvitae. Be sure to water these shrubs well in the fall so they'll have plenty of moisture stored.

If you prefer, you can build a temporary wire frame around small shrubs that are likely to suffer winter damage in your area and fill it with straw or leaves for winter protection. This provides insulation from winter's worst cold.

Q: I read about people using spreaders to help shape their fruit trees. What are spreaders, and would they help me train some young pear and apple trees?
A: Use spreaders on young fruit trees to correct narrow branch angles. Fruit trees are particularly prone to developing upright branches that are weak and subject to splitting off during ice storms. They just grow tall instead of slowing down to flower and fruit. Shifting them into a more productive mode begins with creating a wider branch angle. When the tree is young and flexible, place short wooden struts (spreaders) in the gap between a shoot and the trunk to force the branch down into a wider angle. Slightly older branches can be tied to a stake or weight to pull them down into position. Once the branches mature enough to become firm and woody, you can remove the spreaders, and the branches will stay in place.

Q: I bought a small balled-and-burlapped shade tree from a nursery and am about to plant it. My neighbor says I can just leave the burlap on. Is this correct?
A: You should remove the burlap and any strings or wires just before planting the tree. These days, some burlap is nonbiodegradable, made from synthetics. Even if it is natural burlap and will eventually rot, its presence may discourage feeder roots from growing outward and getting established in the new site.

Q: I see a lot of gorgeous flowering trees in my neighborhood, and I'd like to have some, too. When should I get them?
A: Buy flowering trees and shrubs in the spring and pick them out while they are in bloom. That way, you see the exact flower type, size, and color you will get. You will probably be buying fresh stock that has just arrived at the nursery for the season. Trees purchased in the fall may have been in the nursery lot all summer, which is stressful for them. To save money, you can sometimes find places where the price of flowering trees has been reduced because they have just finished flowering.

Index